The Dynamite Kid

The Dynamite Kid

Brian Blessed

LONDON   NEW YORK   SYDNEY   TORONTO

To Mum and Dad,
Hilda and William

This edition published 1992
by BCA
by arrangement with Bloomsbury Publishing Ltd.
Copyright © 1992 by Brian Blessed

The moral right of the author
has been asserted

PICTURE SOURCES

George Blessed: pages 12 *top*, 13 *top*; Gill Blessed: page 13 *bottom*;
Rosalind Blessed: pages 3 *bottom*, 5 *bottom*, 6 *top*, 8 *top right*, 16 *bottom*,
18 *top right & bottom left*, 21 *middle*, 22 *top*, 23 *top*;
Eric Broadbent: page 20 *top*; Harry Dobson: page 24; K. J. C. Jackson: page 6 *bottom*;
National Portait Gallery, London: page 14 *top*; Colin Picton: page 8 *top left*;
Colin Picton & Cedric Webster: page 10 *top*; Sheffield City Council: page 14 *bottom*;
South Yorkshire Times: page 17 *bottom*; *The Star*, Sheffield: page 15 *bottom*;
Michael Taylor: page 2 *bottom*; United States Air Force: page 23 *bottom*;
Simon Warner: page 22 *bottom*; Simon Warner/Brontë Society,
Haworth: page 19; Cedric Webster: pages 2 *top*, 7, 8 *bottom*,
10 *bottom*, 21 *top left*; *Yorkshire Post*: page 5 *top*

Sonnet V from *Lollingdon Downs* on
page 155 reproduced by permission
of the Society of Authors as the
literary representative of the
Estate of John Masefield

CN 6717

Printed and bound in Germany
by Graphischer Großbetrieb Pößneck GmbH
A member of the Mohndruck printing group

Contents

Acknowledgements

Writing this book has rekindled wonderful memories of people, places and events from my childhood and teens, and my enjoyment has been all the greater for the renewal of acquaintance with old chums. The book has been a tremendous team effort. For entrusting treasured photographs to me I owe an immense debt of gratitude to Fred Lawson, Trevor Parks, Colin Picton, David Dunbar, Susan Windle, James A. Longden, Michael Taylor, Arthur Thompson, Thelma Cooper, Rudi Shelley, the late Ruth Wynn Owen, Jack Eades and Rhoda Brierley and her son Giles. Cedric Webster melted my heart with his photographs of the Yorkshire countryside. Adrian Rigelsford displayed great ingenuity in unearthing, with the generous assistance of the *Daily Mail*, a vast array of photographs of Bruce Woodcock. Similarly fine efforts were made by members of the management and staff of Sheffield City Hall, and by Martin Olive of Sheffield's Libraries and Information Service and Peter Meads of PMC Communications, Sheffield.

Hearty thanks must go to Gilbert C. Higson, who conveyed to me with appropriate drama the story of Barnburgh's 'Cat and Man' church, to Peter Johnson for allowing me to draw on his stunning account of the Barnburgh pit disaster and to Mr Bellamy for making my dream of seeing the *Flying Scotsman* come true. As a result of our meeting I obtained marvellous photographs of the *Scotsman* from the kindly K. J. C. Jackson of Crewe. The redoubtable Elizabeth Oldfield of the *South Yorkshire Times* bent over backwards to help me, and a big hug and a kiss will be in order when I next see her. The Yorkshire influence is also much in evidence in the masterly photographs by Simon Warner, who greeted with a whoop of delight my shy request on the phone to use his pictures.

On the family side, my brother Alan and his wife Anne worked their socks off for me. Mum and Dad laughed heartily as I prodded their memories and my daughter Rosalind smiled with loving patience at my earnest requests for photographs. Without the inspiration of my wife Hildegard I would never have written the book. She has been a tower of strength, and I cannot thank her enough. My gratitude also to my mother-in-law Josephine Zimmerman, who in the early stages helped with the grammar.

In a short space of time I have developed with my literary agent Rod Hall a close and creative relationship that has proved inspirational. I am similarly grateful to Bloomsbury, my admirable publishers, not least for bringing me into contact with the talented editor Richard Dawes, who has delighted me with his subtlety, scholarship and humour.

Most of all I should like to thank that fine actress Daryl Back, who worked so painstakingly on the manuscript. Her amused tolerance of my appalling spelling amazed me as, with love, dedication and a keen professional eye, she encouraged and stimulated me until the book finally took shape. Without her monumental energy and ability I would have been in desperate trouble. Miss Back is an angel.

1

The Toad

'Oh my God! 'E looks like a toad!' said my mother as she cast her eyes on me for the first time.

'And 'is body looks like a rabbit . . . a cooked one at that! I've never seen anything like it. What's the matter with 'is face? It's all bashed about – 'e looks as if 'e's been in the ring with Joe Louis!'

It was five a.m. on 9 October 1936, at the Mexborough Montague Hospital in South Yorkshire.

To allay my mother's fears Nurse Kilner, the midwife, explained that the marks and swellings on my misshapen head would soon disappear. She insisted that these were usual and only to be expected when tongs had been used to pull the baby out. Needless to say, none of this kind reassurance calmed my mother down, and she poured out her misgivings:

'I don't know, I've been lying 'ere for two weeks, in agony with swollen legs, waiting for 'im to make up 'is mind to come and, when 'e does, 'e looks like this! No wonder 'e's overcooked – 'e's ages overdue. Now they've 'ad to drag 'im out. Why was 'e so stubborn? Oh dear, I don't know what my 'usband Billy's going to say when 'e sees 'im.'

In total despair, my mother burst into tears, as the nurses did all in their power to cheer her up.

'Wait, Mrs Blessed, till his eyes open. That'll make a big difference to the way he looks,' Nurse Kilner whispered, as she rocked my mother back and forth in her arms.

'I don't mind the way 'e looks,' said a voice from the next bed. 'I'd love 'im whatever 'e looked like. Would yer mind, Mrs Blessed, if I 'eld 'im for a bit?'

'Not at all,' said my mother, wiping away the tears, as she suddenly remembered that the lady making the request had just lost her own baby.

'Oh please, Mrs Brindley, I'd be very 'appy for you to hold 'im anytime. Just feel free to reach out and take 'im.'

Within seconds I was in the poor woman's arms as she cooed over me, repeating to my mother:

'Oh, 'e's lovely . . . lovely . . . what a sweet boy 'e is. Your 'usband will be that proud.'

It was about four miles from our home in Goldthorpe to the hospital, and dad arrived, by bus, at four o'clock that afternoon. He was a coalminer and, like most men in the area, worked at the Hickleton Main Colliery, one of the largest pits in South Yorkshire. His shift started at six in the morning, which meant he had to rise at four-thirty, and didn't finish until one-thirty in the afternoon. His response, on seeing me, was not unlike my mother's:

'Good God, Hilda, couldn't you 'ave done better than that?'

Fortunately, my mother had cheered up a bit by now, and she was capable of sharing a laugh with him. But when Uncle George, my father's brother, added that when his son, Gary, was born, he too looked like a monkey, she could only sigh:

'I'm gettin' a lot of comfort from you two!'

The days passed, and my reptilian appearance continued to inspire a great deal of comment. All the same, the nurses maintained that ugly babies frequently became the prettiest later on and that the eyes could make a difference. So when my eyes finally opened they choroused:

'What did we tell you? His eyes are lovely. Oh, Mrs Blessed, we've never seen such pretty eyes.'

'Aye, 'e'll break lots of girls' 'earts,' added Mrs Brindley.

My mother was slightly reassured:

'Aye, 'is eyes dun't 'alf make a difference . . . but 'e still looks like a toad!'

On the day of departure, on the 105 bus with Dad, my mother

2

kept me well covered up in case people tried to steal a look at me. On arriving home they both employed a great deal of cunning to avoid contact with all the friendly neighbours. They would have succeeded but for big fat, all-embracing Mrs Dancy, who lived next door. She was enormous, about twenty-four stone, and cooked bread for everybody in the street. Greatly loved, and devoted to my mother, she gently barred the way to the front door with her impressive bulk.

'Yer not goin' in, you two, till I've seen that baby of yours.'

'Oh, Mrs Dancy,' Mother choked out. ''E's nothing special, and 'e's very overcooked . . . in fact, 'e's downright ugly.'

'I'll be the judge of that! Stop frettin' yerself. I've seen hundreds of babies – there's nowt to worry about.'

Mother reluctantly pulled back the lace to reveal my weird features.

'Oh, 'e's right grand, Hilda! What a lovely lad. Yes, 'e's a bit overcooked and pulled about, but 'e will be champion. His face will soon smooth out. But, I'll tell you this: I've never seen such nice eyes. Is 'e on the breast?'

'Aye,' said my mother. 'But 'e doesn't get much satisfaction, so 'e's supplemented by Ostermilk.'

'Couldn't be better. It means 'e's got the best of both worlds,' smiled Mrs Dancy. 'Now, I've 'eld you up enough. Off inside, and let me know the minute you need any 'elp.'

Home was 30 Probert Avenue, Goldthorpe. It comprised a sitting-room, large kitchen and bathroom downstairs, three bedrooms upstairs, with a nice little garden at the front and a much larger one at the back. The avenue curved round like a horseshoe, embracing in total about a hundred standard, brick-built, council houses. Most of the people living there at the time were in the process of having families; a new generation was being born. From house to house the noise of babies filled the air, and my father said that the place was like a giant incubator.

All the men in the avenue appeared to be coalminers and so were either on a night or a day shift. With military punctuality they would don their working clothes, give their wives the customary wave and march, in straight lines, to their respective pits.

Times were hard, and as a coal hewer my father could expect to earn only one shilling and threepence for each ton of coal he dug out. The amount varied between thirteen and fourteen tons a day, bringing his take-home pay to between five and six pounds a week. With rent of eleven shillings a week, plus the usual outgoings on food and clothes, there was not much left.

The great fear was being injured in the mines; even a small, niggling injury, let alone a fatal one. If a miner was injured he was put on the dreaded sick pay and it was very hard to make ends meet. The longer he was off work the harder it became for his family to live properly.

All the people of Goldthorpe and the surrounding villages lived with the constant threat of a major catastrophe. The forlorn siren sent shivers down everyone's spines. Because of this shared sense of danger, and the struggle to earn a living, they developed a keen sense of loyalty and brotherhood.

The young mothers found every minute of their day taken up with cooking, washing, darning and other chores. On Mondays, wash day, each mum could be seen bending over the wash tub, armed with a large stick, thicker at one end, and a big yellow bar of soap. They would lift the stick and thump it down through the soapy water as hard as they could, at the same time twisting and turning the washing. The next stage was to wring it out with the heavy mangle and then, weather permitting, to hang it up to dry. If the weather was bad they spread the washing out on the wooden clothes-horse in front of the fire, since it had to get dry one way or another.

It was a matter of pride that each family should possess as fine a pram as possible in which to show off their baby. After careful thought my parents chose a handsome shiny black model – black was considered very smart and helped to highlight the white lace of the interior beautifully. Even so, my mother still spent a great deal of time dodging down alleys to avoid inquisitive neighbours.

'I'm sorry, I can't stop,' she would cry out. 'I'm in such a hurry. See you tomorrow.'

Years later Mrs Dancy told me that I really did look like the back end of a bus!

Then, quite suddenly, I developed an aversion to Ostermilk and started to lose weight rapidly. Dr Mills didn't know what to do and my parents were at their wits' end until a schoolteacher friend of the family, Dolly Mann, recommended that they try me on Nestlé's condensed milk. This worked wonders and quickly restored my health and weight. To this day I find it irresistible, and can polish off a whole tin in a flash.

When I was about four months old my unpromising looks started to improve: my straight, black hair began to lighten and curl; my flat nose and strange facial markings disappeared; even my wide, toady mouth started to look almost human. By six months, my hair was thick, with golden curls, and my now more developed features were highlighted by much-admired dark-brown eyes. My mother's customary trot with the pram had now slowed down and indeed shopping took much longer to complete than was necessary. Requests to have a look at me were granted to every passer-by and compliments echoed from one end of Goldthorpe to the other.

'Oh, Mrs Blessed, what a lovely baby!'

'Oh, what eyes . . . oh, what hair!'

'Oh . . . Ooh . . . oh . . . '

The cooing and lovey-dovey chatter seemed endless, and my mother loved every moment of it. No longer was she the denizen of the side streets and alleyways – the high street was her domain!

One of my earliest memories is of speaking clearly for the first time. I was about eighteen months old, and the usual 'Mama' and 'Dada' had been pouring from my lips for some time. There then came an experience that is still vivid in my mind. Mrs Dancy, who was my constant companion, started a tug-of-war with my rattle. She pulled one way, I pulled the other. The effort was exhausting and was making me red in the face. The injustice of it all! After all, the rattle was mine! Try as I could, it was impossible to wrest it from her grasp. Finally, as she pulled it free, purple with rage I blurted out:

'Bugger!'

Mrs Dancy roared with laughter and rushed inside to call my bemused parents. She repeated the game, and I obliged with further

'Buggers'. Needless to say, it was not a word I was encouraged to use as the months passed – but where had it come from?

My recollections of those early days are of complete calm and happiness. The love my parents had for me was self-evident. I remember rocking in my pram in the front garden for hours, just looking at the dandelions and daisies, and my mother would open the sitting-room window, coyly bend her head, and gently coo to me:

'Hi-dee.'

This immediately made me respond in the same way as I, too, bent my head.

'Oh, Billy,' she would say to my dad. ''E's so good, 'e's no trouble at all, 'e's so quiet . . . Oh, look, there 'e goes again.'

'Hi-dee.'

On one occasion, when I was two years old, I proved to be not quite so angelic. Mother had taken ages to knit me a lovely white woollen jumper. She had left the room for a moment, to empty the bath she had been washing me in, when I spied the garment. I distinctly remember that the fire was low and obviously needed 'mending'. Picking up the jumper, I threw it on the fire and it went up in flames – so quickly that my mother was unable to rescue it.

Although she never smacked me, her tears of anger and frustration haunt me to this day. Poor Mother! It had taken her so long to make that jumper and wool was not easy to come by.

At night I would have my little brown lion, Leo, beside me on my pillow. His friendly, dark eyes would look at me as I sucked at the end of his flat nose. I would then be aware of my parents watching me.

'Hi-dee,' I would say, making them giggle with pleasure.

Sitting on a mat in the garden and watching all the cats that came to call was a favourite occupation of mine. Probert Avenue was full of cats of all sizes and colours. Our next door neighbours were Mr and Mrs Burns and their daughter Betty, who had a beautiful golden retriever called Wendy. This dog had a very gentle nature and the most endearing face, and I spent long summer days in the garden with it. (Perhaps the cats and dogs

6

of that sweet time explain why nowadays my home is like a menagerie.)

Between the ages of four and five I became aware of the war. It was great fun to be taken, in my pyjamas, to the air-raid shelter which my father had built in the back garden. Sitting in the corner, in my little wooden chair with a tray attached, in front of a single-bar electric heater, I would eat my fish and chips and thoroughly enjoy all the comings and goings: people carrying candles and lanterns appearing from time to time to give my parents the latest news.

The excitement of the war was manifest everywhere. The Germans were the focal point of every conversation. How strong were they? How big were their army, navy and air force? One thing was for certain: everybody felt fully confident that we would defeat them in the end.

Just as I had soon grown to the impressive age of five, so had the other children in the avenue. Now the street was full of scores of us, invading every nook and cranny in our tireless personal quests.

We were known as the Probert Avenue Gang: lads dressed like myself, with grey short trousers, grey socks, Balaclava helmets and hobnailed boots. Games of every description were the order of the day, and soccer matches, with twenty kids a side, raged up and down the street, with a pig's bladder or tin can for a football.

Our parents would roar advice and support from their sitting-room windows as, red-faced and pouring with perspiration, we proudly displayed our cuts and grazes.

Mrs Dancy and I were as thick as thieves. Bread-baking day was an event not to be missed and usually took place on Wednesday or Thursday so that everyone in the street had plenty of bread for the weekend. Sitting on top of a pile of pillows on the large, faded leather sofa, with my legs swinging rhythmically with delight, I would observe the ritual. In would come Mrs Dancy, her gargantuan body possessed of surprising speed, carrying an enormous clay bowl full of flour. She would carefully transfer the flour to the scrubbed surface of the broad wooden table until there was a mountain of it. She would then add water from old, dented, white enamel jugs, as well as large slabs of her homemade butter and the vital yeast.

Then, rolling up the sleeves of her black rustic blouse, revealing her massive forearms, she would pound away.

Clouds of flour would float into the air, whitening her grey hair and sticking to her horn-rimmed glasses. Her concentration, as the folds of fat on her face and neck shook with the effort, was absolute.

Thump, bang, bash, wallop – she would beat hell out of the mounds of dough. Then she would ease herself across the room, poke the fire and apply more coal, and big red and blue flames would shoot up the blackened chimney.

'Lovely, Mrs Dancy,' I would cheer. 'Put more on and make it spark!'

Opening the black-leaded oven doors, she would check that the temperature was just right before taking out the black trays. The work of forming different-sized loaves would then begin. Long, short, fat, thin, big, small – the shapes were endless. Amid them all would be scores of gingerbread men for the children; each with raisins for eyes, nose and mouth. All these fine creations would then be quickly placed back in the oven, and the heavy black doors shut again. While the bread cooked, Mrs Dancy would give herself a good wash down, clean her spectacles and, for the umpteenth time, put a humbug in my mouth. We would then sit by the fireside and she would read me stories from the *Beano*.

When at last the bread was taken from the oven, the good lady would cut me a large piece of crust and cover it with butter. Oh, my! The smell of the still-warm bread, combined with the taste of the melting butter, made me trill with contentment:

'Oh, thank you Mrs Dancy.'

'Yer welcome, lad. And don't forget yer gingerbread man.'

'I won't. I'll bring me *Dandy* tomorrow.'

'OK, lad. Goodnight. God bless.'

We all adored our comics. It was always exciting to run down the stairs and pull the *Daily Herald* through the letter-box and find your comic enveloped inside it. On Tuesdays I would receive the *Beano*, with its lovely rich colours and Biffo the Bear on the cover, and on Fridays the *Dandy*, with Korky the Kat. One of my favourite characters was Desperate Dan, who lived on cow pies!

We were at the age when our mums were busy stitching, mending shirts and pullovers, and making extra clothes, for we were soon to start school. The whole idea of school was a mystery to me. I didn't know what to expect.

The great day arrived and our mums gathered together in the street to escort us half a mile to Highgate Junior Mixed School, which was situated exactly halfway between Doncaster and Barnsley.

The outlook from the school was very pleasant, with fields surrounding it and two good playgrounds set near the communal air-raid shelters. The whole place, built of red bricks with bright, white windows, had a cheerful look.

Standing there in a large group, we nodded our pleasure and satisfaction.

'In you go then. . . ,' our mums urged, and we immediately felt a surge of panic.

'Don't worry,' they reassured us. 'We'll pick you up at four o'clock.'

In we went, holding each other's hands. The teachers quietly ushered us into the assembly hall to be addressed by the head-mistress, Mrs Jarman, who was rather a heavy woman with black hair and dark eyes. She wore a dark-red cotton suit, with a white shirt and a dark tie, and appeared kind but firm as she slowly and clearly explained the school rules.

I didn't like the sound of it at all and was wishing that I was on my railway embankment when my thoughts were interrupted by a kindly voice:

'Hello, lad, my name is Mrs Gommersell and I'm your teacher. As you're at the end of the line, would you mind following me and leading your friends to the classroom?'

'Yes, Miss,' I replied.

Down a long corridor we trouped, passing walls half covered in prettily designed tiles, and entered the classroom.

'Please take your time and try to find your desks. Your names are on them and the older children will help you to find them.

Please ask me any questions you like. I want you to be happy and at home here.'

We each found our desk and, on opening the lid, were pleasantly surprised to find a picture book and an apple and an orange sitting there. We spent the rest of the morning trying to draw and paint the fruit and were then given lunch in the assembly hall.

There, we were given our pink gas masks to try on, which to us was great fun. When all the straps had been adjusted to ensure a reasonable fit, we took part in our first war drill in the air-raid shelters. Sitting in rows, on wooden planks, receiving instructions from a Home Guard sergeant, we giggled mercilessly. I was particularly raucous, as I'd caught the gaze of the lovely Sheila Bennett, who lived on the farm across the road.

The sergeant and teachers explained that sometimes we might have to sit there for a long time, and suggested that to keep our spirits up we learn a few ditties such as:

The Germans came in four by four,
Big fat Goering, stuck in the door,
Singing Oo-la-la-la,
Oo-la-la-la,
Oo-la-la,
Wee, wee, wee!

At the end of the song's many verses we howled hysterically.

Afterwards we were led back to the assembly hall to bed down on mattresses for our afternoon nap. This was then the usual procedure for four and five-year-olds.

When the bell sounded for the end of the day we were conducted in an orderly fashion to the loving arms of our mums.

'Look, Mam! Look!' I puffed up with pride as I displayed my drawing of an apple. 'I did it all myself!'

'It's lovely, lad . . . lovely,' enthused my mother.

'I've drawn it for you, Mam. For keeps.'

The next few days of school followed the same pattern, and by the end of the week I had learnt 'o' for orange and 'a' for apple. School was proving to be fun, but not nearly as much fun as the delights of Saturdays. For then, as soon as the sun was up, the street would start to reverberate with the shouts of children at play.

I would inspect my dad's air-raid shelter to see if any frogs or toads had fallen in, before joining in the usual two-hour football match. After this I would rush up Goldthorpe Road to marvel at all the goodies in the window of Booth's shop. My wildest dreams would be fulfilled by the occasional appearance of a Red Indian on a lead horse. I simply adored these, but they cost sixpence each – a lot of money. Also, the chance to buy one occurred only every six months or so, and then you had to be very lucky as there were usually only two for sale at a time.

My passion for these Indians was shared by one of my chums, Geoffrey Green, a serious, mature, well-built lad with dark hair and chubby cheeks, who was a year older than me and lived close by. We each owned an Indian, but during the previous six months we had played with them so much that the paint had almost worn away. The horses, which had been shining black, were now faded and dull.

One Saturday, with our noses pressed flat against the window, our eyes were riveted on the new arrivals. What mouth-watering ecstasy: the brilliant, multicoloured head-dress of the Indian chief ran down his body to touch the black saddle and point at the wonderful white horse he sat on. Only two inches high and four inches long, this magical artefact was nevertheless the essence of grace and speed.

'Oh, crikey!' I whispered. 'Do you see that horse?'

'Aye,' moaned my companion. 'And look in that corner – there's one that's black and white like Zorro's.'

Sparks flew from our hobnailed boots as we sped into the shop. Tall, angular Mr Booth smiled quietly as we each poured out our requests and dug deep into our pockets to produce the long-saved-up twenty-four farthings that made up the price of sixpence.

Nearly swooning with excitement, we raced out of the shop and down the road to show all the lads our purchases. Later, my white horse would stand proudly in my bedroom, casting disdainful eyes on the faded black one.

11

'It looks just like Hopalong Cassidy's horse, dunnit?' I asked my mother excitedly.

'Well, lad, I think it's even prettier.'

At the time, my league table of cowboy heroes was as follows. Hopalong Cassidy was first, followed by Johnny Mack Brown. Then came Zorro, the Phantom, Tex Ritter, Roy Rogers, Bob Steele, Gene Autry, the Lone Ranger and Tonto.

That day, my eagerness to get to the Saturday matinée at the local cinema was quashed by dad, who calmly explained:

'It's all right, lad. Yer've got plenty of time to get there, so sit down nicely and eat some snap.'

The cloth was laid out and mother was bent over the fire, toasting bread. When lunch was ready I impatiently stuffed my face.

'Don't gobble your food,' my mother insisted. 'Or you'll get a tummy upset. And here's your twopence: a penny for your ice-lollipop and a penny to get into the cinema. And don't lose it. Just a minute, Hopalong Cassidy! Put this in your mouth.'

It was a large tablespoon of cod-liver oil, followed by the same amount of concentrated orange juice. Most lads found it nauseating, but I quite enjoyed it. It was allotted to us by the government as we were war babies.

At last, sitting in the front row of the penny seats at the Saturday matinée, staring with admiration and incredulity at William Boyd as Hopalong Cassidy, I was filled with happiness. There he was, sitting on a fence in his jet-black outfit, with his dark eyes, silver hair, perfect smile and infectious laugh. In his heroic voice he said to Gabby Hayes:

'Gabby, I can't understand a word you're saying!'

The whole audience swayed from side to side, sighing with complete satisfaction.

Later that afternoon we returned to our beloved Probert Avenue. The street was lined with trees and high hedges, which hid an intricate labyrinth of dens and secret pathways. The avenue was festooned with old-fashioned gas lamps, casting their mysterious shadows in the gathering dusk. On opposite sides of the horseshoe of houses ran two railway lines: one rusty and disused, the other part of the London and North Eastern Railway, which boasted such engines as the *Mallard* and the legendary *Flying Scotsman*.

The whole landscape was the perfect setting for our million escapades. Spanning the rusty, broken-down railway line was a large iron bridge and this magnificent structure was the focal point of our frenzied activity. Attached to the girders under the railway bridge were dozens of ropes swaying in all directions, and there were also rails underneath, although no one had ever seen a train pass through.

The gang of lads I belonged to was second to none. Our leader, Caldeon Williams, with his open face, blue eyes, curly blond hair and graceful bearing, was, to us, all that was heroic and noble. His sense of fair play inspired us to feats of great courage, as we embarked on our daily 'dasties' – the Yorkshire word for dares. These included jumping off the bridge at various heights, somersaulting over fences and hedges, getting as close as possible to the wild dogs that guarded Earnshaw's orchard, holding your breath till you were blue in the face and, perhaps worst of all, placing yourself within range of the dreaded, sinister dwarf Lennie and his big white stick. Blows from this strange Rumpelstiltskin were fast and furious and to avoid them required speed and agility, not to mention a degree of madness in the first place.

We created a fantasy land full of fire-breathing dragons, swamps seething with ferocious crocodiles, man-eating sharks and flesh-hungry piranhas. There were bloodthirsty vampires, rotting zombies, invaders from another planet, and armies of green Treen warriors from the Dan Dare strip in the *Eagle*. There were fortress-like castles and knights in shining armour, majestic kings and invisible entities; and the bold Professor Challenger from Sir Arthur Conan Doyle's *The Lost World*. For me, that magical time is best conjured up by the words I used in my previous book, *The Turquoise Mountain*:

> We would crawl up the embankment, all choking, dying of thirst in the sweltering heat of the Sahara, or gasp, exhaling our last breath, frozen in the snows as Scott of the Antarctic. Our games were as unending as they were inventive. We had no

toys – we simply shaped our hands into what we were pretending to play with. We could only dream of having a six-shooter like Hopalong Cassidy.

Gradually, like war-torn warriors with energies totally spent, we would make our way home and relax in the back garden of my friend Geoffrey Green. He possessed numerous scrapbooks: a veritable treasure-house of photographs, football programmes and articles from the *Daily Herald* and *Reynolds' News*.

Our whole gang of fifteen or more would sit agog as Geoffrey flashed through the pages with pride or pointed to some unique autograph. Mouth-watering stuff, it would make me swoon with longing. By contrast, my scrapbook, with two pieces of cardboard on the outside, was held together with coarse string.

Though none of us could measure up to Geoffrey, we could each, on occasion, produce some original surprise that would fill even his eyes with envy. On one such afternoon I proudly presented a matchbox in good condition, with a few matches in it, and the Channel swimmer, Captain Webb, on its front. The effect was instantaneous, and each lad related his admiration for the noble captain.

'Imagine swimming all them miles!' remarked Colin Picton, his small, wiry frame tense with awe and concentration.

'I can't even swim a yard,' said another lad.

There was no doubt at all that Captain Webb was a great favourite, and this was substantiated by the fact that I received three good clay marbles for the matchbox. The conversation did not stop there, for everyone started to sound forth on the subject of heroes. Emphasis fell on Scott of the Antarctic, as Gerald Athey painstakingly took us through every mile of that famous expedition.

Surprisingly, Gerald was fifteen years old, twice our age, but somehow he fitted in perfectly with the gang and acted as mediator with our parents whenever they questioned our way-out activities. By nature, he was calm and tolerant, with a wisdom beyond his years that everyone respected. We christened him the 'Wise Owl'.

Gerald's sensitive voice conveyed dramatically all the characters and events from that ill-fated expedition, and when he finally finished with Scott's own words: 'I do not regret the journey; we took risks, we knew we took them, things have come against us, therefore we have no cause for complaint . . . ', we sat quietly with tears in our eyes.

In an instant the rapt mood had evaporated, and we pressed on further in our quest for the great ones. I must have seemed rather like Toad of Toad Hall as I took centre stage, expounding passionately on the amazing strengths of Hercules and Samson. I raged up and down the garden, uninhibitedly acting out scenes from their lives, forcing rounds of applause from the appreciative lads.

Gerald himself applauded and laughed at my exaggerations. It was only when I insisted that Strang the Terrible, the giant with a club who was in the *Beano* every week, was a friend of mine and lived in a cave beneath my house, that he kindly steadied me.

About this time my dad gave me the welcome news that I could have the air-raid shelter to play in.

'You can 'ave it, lad. It's no use – it lets water in.'

'But what if we get bombed, Dad?'

He shrugged.

'Don't worry, Brian, lad. This house is solid, and they'll probably only bomb Sheffield and places like that. The most we're going to get is a bit of shrapnel.'

Certainly, the shelter did ship water, but it proved to be only a few inches deep and soon soaked away. It was the perfect place to hide in and to keep my old pots, pans and makeshift aquarium. In fact, the terrible creatures that I kept in my aquarium – natterjacks, common toads, frogs, smooth newts and great crested newts – earned me the nickname of Baron Frankenstein. Many adults couldn't understand this preoccupation of mine, and said that I was unnatural, but my parents were sympathetic and encouraged my hobby. However, my mother did berate me once, for allowing a large toad to walk across the living-room floor, causing Mrs Burns to scream and run out.

From the time that I first learned of their existence, I felt a deep yearning for the age of dinosaurs; it was heart-breaking to hear that they no longer roamed the earth. Any talks on the radio about these creatures would command all my attention and lift my spirits. I would listen to explorers, on the cherished BBC Home Service, describing how the earth must have been millions of years ago: the air much thicker and syrupy, as a result of the luxuriance of the gigantic trees and plants. Afterwards I would pester my dad with questions until I fell asleep in his arms.

The job I hated most at this time was having to go to my grandmother's (on my mother's side of the family) to beg for soap, sugar, butter and tea. My mother was a perfectionist when it came to keeping our house in order, but despite all her sacrifices to make ends meet, at times she found the task almost impossible. Rationing was severe, and once you had used your quota of coupons for the week, that was that. Everyone felt the pinch. People would barter, swapping clothing coupons for food ones, for example. The permutations were endless, but everyone helped everyone else, and somehow survived.

I noticed that my mother wore the same clothes almost all the time, whereas I always had a plentiful supply. She pledged that I would never wear clogs as long as she lived and in this she was helped by my father, who repaired all our footwear, hammering a generous supply of nailed studs into the leather soles.

But when the situation became desperate I would have to trot over the bridge to the back streets of Goldthorpe to knock on my grandmother's door for help. The black market was thriving, and she always had a reserve supply of groceries and washing materials, as her sons and daughters worked in the appropriate factories. However, if neighbours were visiting her at the time I knocked, she would vehemently denounce my requests as ridiculous, insisting she had nothing and asking what I thought I was up to. She would then sit me down in the kitchen and tell me to wait.

Once the neighbours had gone her face would soften and she would give me the goods. Alas, this was all too complicated for a six-year-old like me, and her first reaction on seeing me was always the one I remembered.

When, after six months of these unhappy journeys, my mother asked me to go yet again, I nearly burst a blood vessel:

'Oh no, Mam! No . . . I won't go!' I groaned.

'Please, Brian. Please,' she pleaded. 'I don't know which way to turn . . . I've got nothing at all – no tea, sugar, soap – nothing. Your dad will have no tea and no butter on his bread, and you know how hard he works.'

My mother's pleas made me beside myself with unhappiness but still I insisted:

'I'm not goin' to go. I can't stand my grandmother's face. As soon as she sees me she says, "Oh, no! Not him again!" '

'But, Brian,' my mother explained, 'she's only pretending, so as to fool the neighbours!'

'I don't know what you're talking about!' I cried, and started banging my head on the wooden table. My mother's reaction to this was to completely ignore me, after quietly saying:

'You'll stop doin' that when it 'urts.'

Of course, I did, and at the same moment she sat down by me and burst into tears. To see my lovely mother so distraught devastated me, and I hurriedly put my arms about her, saying:

'Don't worry, Mam. I'll go . . . '

When I arrived at my grandmother's house, she did exactly as I have described. In fact, this time the expression on her face was worse than ever. She performed a right song and dance: her eyes disappeared into her head and her cheeks and jowls shook like some giant blancmange.

'Oh, no!' she groaned. 'It's him again!'

This time I'd had quite enough.

'Aye, it's me,' I shouted. 'It's that "Tommy Handley is here".' (This was a reference to *ITMA*, a BBC radio programme of the time.) 'And I don't want yer bloody tea, or yer bloody soap, or any bloody thing else. I'm goin' to see me Aunty Saran and see if she'll gee me something . . . so take all yer groceries and stick 'em up the pig's arse on the second shelf!'

17

With that I left and headed towards my nearby aunt's, not having a cat in hell's chance of achieving anything.

Arriving on Aunt Saran's doorstep, exhausted with worry, I poured out my story through floods of tears. Her eyes never flickered as she took me by the hand and led me to the fireplace. With her lace handkerchief, she wiped my face and, still not saying a word, placed one of her four black and white cats in my lap.

The flames of the fire sent shadows dancing around the room, and the dark, heavy curtains added to the feeling of warmth. A welcome mug of sweet tea, laced with a generous portion of Nestlé's milk, relaxed my entire body.

Time stood still as I half dozed. And when, as if in a trance, I was politely escorted to the door, I scarcely noticed the large carrier bag that had been placed in my hand. It was full to the brim with goodies, the sight of which took my breath away.

'Oh, Aunty,' I gasped, as I pulled out a long, dark-green slab comprising five large soap cakes, each one many times bigger than any I'd seen before. There was a two-pound bag of sugar. Two pounds, mind you. Normally the most I could beg for was four ounces. The miracle continued as I spied three pounds of salted butter, a large packet of tea and a generous number of cakes. Aladdin himself could not have beheld such riches!

'Thank you so much, Aunty,' I blurted out. 'Mam will be so happy.'

The silent benefactor rained kisses on my cheeks and gently ushered me into the night.

On arriving home, I hid the booty outside the front door and went in. Mother was horrified to see me empty-handed as I told her of my hopeless mission. At once she burst into tears and cried out:

'Oh, my God! I'm at my wits' end!'

'No, Mam, no!' I shouted. 'It's all right, I'm only kidding.'

As I hurriedly displayed my collection, her eyes grew ever wider.

'By gum,' she said, almost swooning. 'I've never seen anything like it. It'll last us for months.'

THE TOAD

With that, she gave me the biggest hug and kiss ever recorded in the history of the universe.

My father had four brothers and two sisters, who all had impressive, dark-brown eyes and shared strong emotions and a cast-iron determination. Three of my uncles – Albert, Tom and Alan – like my father, worked in the pits.

Their favourite magazine was *The Art and Science of Coal Mining*, which used to cause a great deal of discussion in our sitting-room. Six-foot tall, powerfully built and flamboyant, Uncle Alan would make the room shake with his vivid demonstrations of how miners coped in certain emergencies. His multiple contortions would include lying face-down and making himself ten inches high, and then propelling himself forward, like a lizard, to show how miners sometimes had to crawl through incredibly narrow tunnels.

On Friday 24 April 1942 there was a violent underground upheaval at nearby Barnburgh colliery, where my Uncle Alan worked. Thirteen miners were buried alive and four others were killed in the crush. It was an horrific incident – the shock waves were felt on the surface for miles around – the like of which had never before been recorded in South Yorkshire. The agony of the disaster was felt in every village. I remember sitting there listening, with horror and wonder, as my uncles quietly discussed the tragedy. People wept and prayed but throughout it all displayed great courage and dignity – the hallmark of the working class.

Rescue teams set out with no great hopes of finding any survivors. For their part, the trapped men had no means of indicating that they were still alive. A suggestion that there would be no survivors and that the pit should be sealed was rejected by the miners and their leaders. The plight of the trapped men was accelerated by the lack of food, then water (with only their own urine to drink), and then light.

A human chain of rescuers, forty men lying on their stomachs passing excavated material back out of the pit hand to hand, made slow progress through the solid ground. These were the most difficult circumstances imaginable – moving past the dead bodies of luckless workmates – but they kept on. On the surface, sisters, wives, mother, sweethearts and friends kept up a vigil.

Goldthorpe was as silent as the grave as people went about their daily affairs in a solemn manner, hardly daring to ask how the rescue was going. The days passed and it seemed that the poor miners were doomed. We children sat under the gas lamps and whispered with disbelief that the miners were hundreds of feet below where we were sitting. I begged my dad not to go to work as I was so frightened it would happen to him.

Down below, the trapped miners finally gave up. It is a tradition that when there is no hope left men take off their boots and lie down to die. Like a father singing a lullaby to his baby son, the oldest miner of the group had to do the same to a young lad of seventeen, but this was not to sleep.

Then suddenly there came the tap-tap of the rescue party and at once they realized they were saved.

The relief felt by everybody was unimaginable. What an amazing rescue! What marvellous people! God, I was proud to live in South Yorkshire.

What was also amazing at that time was our magical Bush radio, in its wooden case. It was the centre of the universe, entertaining us with marvellous shows on the BBC Home Service and Light Programme, such as *Captain Blood, Journey to the Other Side of the Sun, Paul Temple* and *Dick Barton: Special Agent*. There, in the sitting-room, transfixed by the tension, we would hear Noel Johnson, as Dick Barton, exclaim at the end of an episode:

'It's no use chaps, we're overpowered!'

'How's he going to get out of this one?' I would groan.

'With one gigantic leap, he was free,' my father would shoot back, prompting great amusement.

Happiness abounded in our home from morning till night, particularly when we were listening to *ITMA*, starring Tommy Handley, and *Happydrome*, with the celebrated Ramsbottom and Enoch and Me.

One day my father told me that we were going to go on a week's holiday to my Uncle George and Aunt Florrie's house.

THE TOAD

They lived in a far-away fabled land: Newbiggin-by-the-Sea, near Newcastle-upon-Tyne. The magic seaside!

They had two children: Gary, eight, and Gill, five, and although I rarely saw them more than twice a year, they were like brother and sister to me.

That summer of 1942 proved to be one of the happiest of my life. My memories of the journey were of smoke, wheels and pistons, the sound of the guard's whistle, and the reassuring rhythm of the train and the carriages. Mum and Dad smiled with contentment as we powered past fields and meadows, villages and towns, until we finally stopped at York to change trains.

There was standing room only in the next train, except for a narrow seat for my mother, and Dad started conversations with all and sundry. Tired now but happy, I found relief by sitting on a suitcase until, suddenly, Dad pointed out the mighty Tyne bridge, which we were about to cross.

Oh, my God! We're so high, I thought. What if the bridge collapses?

Finally, the station sign – Newcastle-upon-Tyne – came into view. It seemed we had come millions of miles!

We mounted the steps of a lovely little yellow and white bus, so different from our red ones in Yorkshire, and my blissful state continued as I marvelled at the music of the Geordie accent. My head was continually patted by these friendly folk as their voices sang in my ears:

'Oh, ye'll love Newbiggin, and doan't forget to catch me a crab!'

Twenty-five miles to go . . . twelve . . . ten . . . five. Dad's hands enveloped me as he pressed his grinning face close to mine.

'Look to yer right, lad. To the dark blue below the light blue of the sky.'

My heart rose, and the intensity of the rapture forced me to hold on to my parents with all my might.

'The blue, Dad. The dark blue . . . Is it . . . ?'

'Aye, lad. It is. It's the sea, Brian lad . . . the seaside, for miles and miles.'

That was my first glimpse of Newbiggin.

On our arrival at the house, Aunt Florrie, Uncle George and Gill gave us a grand greeting. Gary stood slightly behind them, nervously fiddling with his striped tie. We observed one another in perfect stillness, until he broke the atmosphere with a wink. Our embrace was clumsy and shy, provoking a great deal of laughter from all present.

'Come in quickly,' said Aunt Florrie, 'or your tea will spoil.'

The feast laid out in the smart, cheerful living-room consisted of salmon and salad, sandwiches of many kinds and masses of cake and other sweet things.

Uncle George, my father's eldest brother, had begun work in the mines but had left the job to attain a top position at the Royal Liver Society. We were all very proud of Uncle George: a robust, strong man of medium height, with penetrating eyes and a powerful personality. His strength of character displayed all the marks of a self-made man, but his determination was coloured with a tremendous sense of humour.

Uncle George dominated the proceedings by telling funny stories, and as he completed his tales Gary's knowing gaze said it all: it was time for us two to race off to the beach with a bucket and spade.

Oh, the heavenly smell of the sea – so fresh and salty! Paddling, running, racing, walking.

'Oh, Gary!' I shouted. 'It's right grand. I've never seen anything like it!'

Later that night, lying on our makeshift bed in the dining-room, admiring the luminosity of Gary's watch, we only just managed to fall asleep.

The sun was scarcely up when we tiptoed out of the house into the fresh morning air. We had no thoughts for breakfast – our objective was to explore the low-lying rocks while the tide was out.

The sea was so far out that you could barely see it.

'Perfect,' said Gary. 'Now follow me.'

Throughout the night, he had described to me how, when the tide went out, the rocks captured masses of different forms of sea life, and as we hopped from rock to rock he excitedly pointed to sudden movements in the rock pools.

THE TOAD

'See that, Brian? That's a rockling. That fish must weigh at least seven pounds!'

As I glanced at it, the silver-coloured specimen shot down to the safe depths of the pool.

'Watch yer step,' Gary warned.

Suddenly we were transfixed, for the pale-green lagoon in front of us seethed with multicoloured shore crabs.

'By, gum,' I whispered. 'They're all the colours of the rainbow.'

'Yes,' nodded Gary. 'But you can't eat them. They're poisonous – mainly used by fishermen for bait.'

'What a shame . . . they're so pretty.'

My hands enclosed dozens of the creatures as I put them in my large bucket for closer examination. Their colour combinations were endless, ranging from black with yellow spots to iridescent blue with red stripes. Held aloft, against the bright morning sun, they took my breath away.

As we progressed, each small pool revealed its own forms of life. The ripples from the sea ebbed and flowed through small, connecting waterways, forcing the dark red and green seaweed to reveal subtly camouflaged fish, hermit crabs and black eels.

Our earlier excitement had become a shared stillness as the mystery of the seashore engulfed us. When at last my guide judged the time to be right, he motioned me on.

'See those big, rusty metal structures ahead, Brian? They're boilers from the bowels of a ship which was wrecked here ages ago. Sometimes I've seen large grey seals and sea otters swimming around them.'

'My God,' I gasped. 'I hope I see some!'

'Anything is possible where the sea is concerned,' added Gary.

My mentor explained that you were not allowed to take crabs (at least, the red variety) away from the rocks, unless they were over four and a half inches long; that was the law. He then took me by the hand and guided me to the fringes of the sea itself. Suddenly, all around us, were easily accessible, seven-foot-deep gullies. Climbing down into them Gary pointed out scores of long, dark recesses, populated by hundreds of crabs.

'The big eating crabs are right at the back, see Brian?'

He was absolutely right. Once my eyes got used to the dim light, I could see countless eyes watching me, and heard the strange ticking noise that crabs emit as their jaws open and close. Gary's face was close to mine as the sea spray from above gently soaked our hair and he warned me that we needed to keep a careful watch on the tide, as it would soon rush in where we were standing.

'You need proper fisherman's hooks to get those crabs out,' said Gary. 'As you can see, some of them are about ten inches wide across their backs ... Anyway, we must be going – people have been taken by surprise by the speed of the tide. They got stranded and cut off.'

Within seconds we had ascended the gully and were heading back towards the shore, where a fair-sized crowd had gathered, in front of the lifeboat station, to see the fishermen's catch of the day.

Fresh fish of various kinds were laid out in neat rows to tempt the would-be buyer. We were fascinated by these creatures of the deep, and Gary described each specimen with the expert's ease – an achievement that did not escape the fishermen. In response to my repeated gasps of wonder, they invited me to stand bare-foot on a huge red crab. With a back about two feet wide, it had the strength to bear my weight and to walk.

After this first golden morning, each day proved to be magical. During adventurous walks, Gary would point to the church at the far end of the bay that was gradually falling into the sea or, passing the bowling green, would point to Uncle George advising my father not to be short with his first two woods. The flat surface was not something that Dad was used to, crown green bowling being his natural game. Further along the cliffs, we would spend hours by the estuary of the strangely sinister tidal river called the Wansbeck, watching the powerful undertow tear sand off the sides of the embankment.

The hours and days passed by sublimely in visits to the beach, song, stories and smiles. When the holiday ended we felt that there would be many more like it. The efforts of my Aunt Florrie and

Top: Six months old and no longer a toad, with Mum and Dad outside our house in Probert Avenue, Goldthorpe.
Bottom: With Mum and Dad on holiday with neighbours in Newbiggin-by-the-Sea, Northumberland.

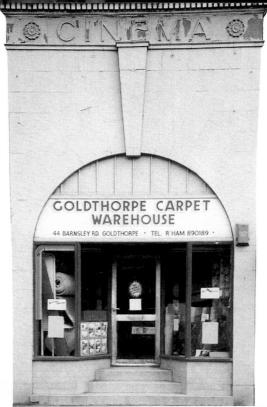

Left: The centre of my universe, the Picture House — now, alas, a carpet warehouse.
Below: A Highgate Junior Mixed School production of *The Men of Gotham*. I'm the lad on the right-hand end of the back row, my face screwed up with embarrassment. I much preferred boxing!

The tomb of Sir Percival Cresacre at St Peter's Church, Barnburgh. He was the knight in the 'Cat and Man' legend which gave me such nightmares.

St Wilfrid's Church, Hickleton. The entrance harbours the skull, with the inscription 'Today for me – tomorrow for thee'.

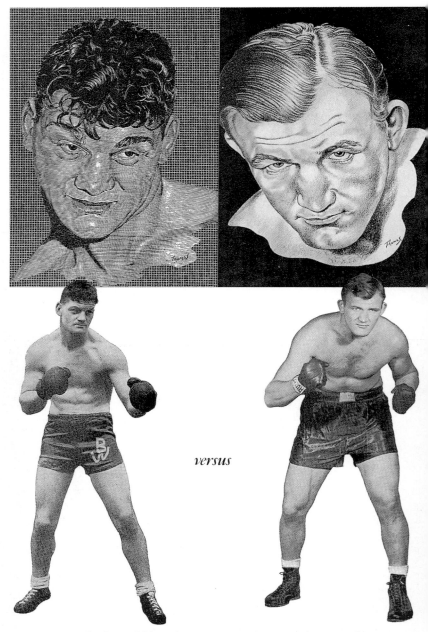

Left: Bruce Woodcock, my lifelong hero. Hector at the gates of Troy could not compare with him. *Right:* The awesome giant American heavyweight boxer Joe Baksi. Some people in London still ask for 'a Joe Baksi' meaning 'a taxi'.

DAILY—ONE PENNY

~~RIL 27, 1942~~

~~the~~ Desert Railway

~~ng~~ tanks being taken to the base to be made fighting fit in a ~~s~~ plays a great part in tank recovery and New Zealanders and ~~orpe~~ are beating all records in laying miles of track.

EIGHT MEN SAVED FROM YORKSHIRE PIT TRAP

Contact Made With Five More, All Safe and Unhurt

AN EPIC OF RESCUE WORK

From Our Own Correspondent

MEXBOROUGH, Sunday Night

EIGHT of the 17 miners who were trapped in Barnborough Main Colliery, near here, at 6 p.m. last Friday, were rescued to-day, alive and unhurt, apart from cuts and bruises. They had spent 44 hours in the trap.

Shortly before ten o'clock to-night it became known that five more men were safe and unhurt, contact having been made with them. A sixth man was dead.

These five men could not be released immediately owing to the difficult position in which they were found. Water and food have been passed to them. They have given their names and said they are unhurt.

The rescue workers, who part in one of the organised of

All that remains of the Hickleton Main Colliery. Its winding wheel is still; its history will live for ever.

The London and North Eastern Railway line, seen from Mrs Parkin's house where we waited for the *Flying Scotsman*.

The earth-trembler itself, great smoking dragon of our dreams, the *Flying Scotsman*.

At last, after forty-eight years, I get to see the *Flying Scotsman*, in a warehouse in Hounslow.

Above: 8 May 1945 – VE Day. Victory in Europe is celebrated in Probert Avenue.
Right: Now middle-aged, standing outside 30 Probert Avenue, my childhood home.
Below: Probert Avenue today. Apart from the cars, little has changed since the 1940s.

Uncle George, Gary and Gill, had instilled a permanent glow in our hearts.

Weeks later, back at school, I was reminded vividly that there was a war on. Mrs Jarman gathered fifty or more of us together in groups, each one of us wearing our gas masks, to watch Sergeant Hardcastle douse a small incendiary device.

'You see, children,' she explained, 'if the sergeant should make the slightest mistake he would be killed instantly.'

Needless to say, the stocky Home Guard sergeant, lying flat out on the ground and directing the nozzle of his fire extinguisher at the centre of the flames, won the day.

'Thank you, Sergeant, for your expertise and for your fine bravery . . . Now, children . . . three cheers for the sergeant . . . Hip, hip . . . '

'Hooray.'

I loved every minute of infant school, and my teachers, who used all manner of interesting activities to develop and hold our attention. In addition, I was fascinated by every pond in the neighbourhood and during lunchtime one day I sped to the nearest. My intention was to fill my jam jar with smooth newts and pondweed, and then to surprise Mrs Jarman by presenting it to her.

My pride at catching several fine specimens knew no bounds, and I rushed back and knocked on her door and handed her the jam jar. Never have I seen anyone so repulsed – her face contorted with disgust as she thrust it back.

'Take the filthy creatures away . . . They make me feel positively sick, you horrible boy!'

It was my first experience of being profoundly hurt. Her words paralysed me.

'B-b-b-b-but . . . ,' I stuttered.

'Never mind the "buts",' she ranted. 'Just look at the state of the corridor . . . caused by your filthy boots!'

So keen had I been to show her the contents of my jam jar, that I had forgotten to wipe my boots. Immediately, I was dragged by my ear to my classroom, to the amazement of the kindly Mrs Gommersell. In front of all the class, I was given a severe caning and a hard slapping on the inside of my upper legs.

The whole experience shattered me. For days I brooded, eventually deciding on a campaign of retaliation. I wasn't prepared to take this lying down. After all, I was one of the best fighters in the school!

The weapon I chose to carry out my plan, from my varied arsenal, was my strongest catapult, which I had made myself. It consisted of a steel handle with prongs, strong black rubber from the inner tube of a car tyre, and a leather pouch capable of holding several good-sized pebbles. My aim was deadly accurate over a considerable range.

For days, with tireless patience, I spied on the horrible 'witch' as she took her customary route home on her bicycle.

Then, one day, hidden in the long grass in a roadside ditch, I released the first thunderbolt right into the middle of her backside, as she conveniently lifted herself off the saddle to pedal uphill.

The roar she let out as she fell off her bike, landing on a grass verge, could be heard in Pontefract!

'Oh, my God!' she screamed, as she hopped about trying to soothe the painful area.

'Whoever you are . . . I'll get the police onto you! Just you wait!'

With the stealth that only a child possesses, I slipped back through the thicket and melted into the adjacent woodland.

During the following month the Phantom struck several times. A special assembly was called at school and, with Sergeant Gruber in attendance, Mrs Jarman called for any information that would lead to the arrest of her assailant. All the children present nodded obediently to the plea, and shouted in hollow tones:

'Yes, Mrs Jarman.'

'Right then . . . ,' she continued. 'Find the culprit!'

Never have children laughed so much at, or taken so little heed of, the orders of a headmistress.

My diligent attempts to track down the offender impressed everyone. Periodically, I would knock on Mrs Jarman's door to announce that we were not having any luck in finding the individual but we would continue searching. This she appreciated, adding:

'Keep up the good work, Blessed.'

Needless to say, the Phantom was never found.

This was my final year at infant school and my parents informed me that they were going to give a party to celebrate my seventh birthday. It was a terrific occasion, with all my chums there and lots of homemade crackers. Dad made me a smashing wooden tommy-gun, just like the ones that the British soldiers had, complete with a wooden wheel with jagged edges that could be spun round, rubbing against a thin strip of plywood to produce a wonderfully loud noise.

Another nice surprise was the arrival of all the teachers, including Mrs Jarman, who dug into the food and appeared to have a good time.

After Musical Chairs and Pass the Parcel my parents announced that, while they washed up, we could romp around as we pleased. We all poured out into the garden and our activities got more and more boisterous as we wrestled, boxed and played with our home-made bows and arrows. Then the lads produced their catapults, me included. Pulling back the rubber thongs, we pretended to fire at one another. My steel weapon attracted everyone's attention, including Mrs Jarman, whose face was pressed against the window of our sitting-room.

'By gum!' marvelled David Dunbar. 'That's a right grand catapult!'

'Aye,' I roared. 'I can hit anythin', anywhere!'

At that moment I caught Mrs Jarman's gaze and broke into a broad, friendly grin. Funnily enough, my smile was not returned, and her eyes reflected an unquiet mind.

2

Mr Dynamite

'Woodcock! What a funny name!'

'Well, that's what they call him, Brian,' Geoff Green explained, and we both burst into hysterical laughter. Woodcock. Wooden Cock. It was one of the least inspiring names I'd ever heard.

'Me Dad says he's a right good heavyweight,' Geoff continued. 'He's over six feet tall, with broad shoulders, a thin waist and he's got a terrific straight left and a bloody marvellous right hand. Everyone says he's going to win the British, the European and then the World championships.'

'Don't be daft. Nobody can beat Joe Louis, the World Champion,' I told him. 'He'd make mincemeat out of Woodcock!'

My room was full of photographs of Louis: pictures cut out of *Reynolds' News*, the *News Chronicle*, the *Daily Herald*; in fact, any newspaper or magazine that had a picture of him in it. You name it – I had it.

The 'Brown Bomber' was a boxing legend, with his light-brown skin and impeccable guard – he could hit from any angle: straight lefts, straight rights, left hooks, right hooks, body punches and upper cuts. It was truly majestic to watch him fighting. Sitting in the 'fourpennies' at the Picture House in Goldthorpe, we'd all look up at the enormous screen with our mouths open. Louis had beaten Billy Conn, the giant Primo Carnera, Two-Ton Tony Gallento, Tami Mauriello. He was invincible. What was Woodcock compared to him?

'What's his full name then, Geoff?'

'Bruce Woodcock.'

That sounds a bit better, I thought to myself.

Geoff started to shout across the street as more lads joined us: Caldeon Williams, Cedric Webster, Colin Picton, all pouring with sweat after a hard game of football.

'What's up, Geoff? What's all the fuss?'

'I've just been telling Brian about Bruce Woodcock.'

Colin Picton couldn't contain himself:

'He's bloody marvellous, Brian. The newspapers call him "Mr Dynamite". Some men went over to the Plough Inn in Doncaster to see him train. He made the whole room shake! He hits faster than a speeding bullet; tha can't see his fists, his punches are so fast. He looks like a film star. He's won every one of his fights inside the distance and he's had about twenty. One day he'll fight Jack London for the British Heavyweight title. We think he'll murder London!'

This made me very excited and I grabbed one of my spinning tops. I had lots of home-made tops. The wood was carved into shape with a jackknife, a nail was driven into the bottom and then, with chalk and crayons, wonderful patterns and pictures could be drawn on them: reds, greens, sometimes blue and yellow, or simply white with a red centre. Fat tops, thin tops, small tops, large tops, and they could be any colour you wanted. You would get your whip (mine was bright blue with a thin strip of leather tied to it and knotted three times for added strength) and wrap it firmly around the top. Then, with just one flick of the wrist, you would release it and crack it with the whip once more. It would spin and spin and spin; weaving, skimming, dancing across the ground: twenty, forty, sixty yards, taking off high into the air, and then down it would come, still spinning wildly.

Running like lightning to catch mine before it died on me, I thumped it with all my might and drove it across the railway bridge.

'Watch out!' a woman's voice shouted.

I'd crossed the path of skinny Mrs Keen, who was rather posh and always telling me off.

'You'll blind someone with that thing!'

'I know what I'm doing. Don't worry, I can send it wherever I want.'

By this time my energy had subsided a little, so I teased the top with gentle strokes through Sankey Square, right past the house where Sergeant Gruber, the policeman, lived: another reason for slowing down!

I stared into the top; the whirling colours seemed to open up the very heart of the universe. I spat on the top and wiped it clean on my trousers. Time to give it some new colours: blue with a yellow rim perhaps?

Bashing the top back towards Probert Avenue, I noticed the whole Probert Avenue Gang had arrived, including Tank Guest, the boy who thought he was a railway engine.

'Chuff, chuff, chuff,' he would go as he chugged along the street. The inevitable shrill blast of his whistle would follow: 'Woooaaa-wooo.'

Strangely enough, the gang were still admiring a large photograph of Bruce Woodcock which Colin Picton held possessively.

'Crikey!' I said. 'He looks great! He's like a great big Jimmy Cagney. What's tha want for that picture?'

'I'm not swapping this!'

'Don't be so bloody stingy. I'll give thee six marbles for it.'

'What! Clay ones?' Colin gave me a look of total disgust. 'I don't want no clay ones.'

'No, no. Glass alleys. Straight out of the bottles.'

'Done.'

I was now the proud owner of a Bruce Woodcock photograph!

Up our front path I ran, and straight through our living-room, tapping my makeshift aquarium as I went past, trying to find my mum. There she was, in the kitchen, bent over a tub, scrubbing away, sweat dripping from every pore, washing piles of clothes. The air was hot and steamy. God, how she worked.

'Look, look Mam. Look Mam, look. I've swapped some marbles for this photograph of Bruce Woodcock. He's going to be World Champion one day, and I'll be just like him. He's Mr Dynamite, and I'll be the Dynamite Kid!'

'Yes, indeed. Big, stupid and daft. You'll 'ave your face knocked about, your nose broken and you'll get cauliflower ears! It's a dangerous and silly game and I don't want you fighting with anybody.'

'But I'm "Cock" of my class.'

'That's nowt to brag about. You'd be better off using your brains. And 'ow many times do I 'ave to keep telling you? Stop wiping that top of yours down your trousers!'

All this failed to dampen my spirits. I ran straight upstairs and started pounding my pillows with all my might, winning an imaginary World title.

The hours passed and then tempting aromas began to drift through the air, reaching every part of the house: Yorkshire pudding, green veg, potatoes and thick brown gravy. Downstairs, flames would be flickering, dancing and jumping around in the huge, black-leaded fireplace.

Outside, darkness was beginning to fall. The rusty gas lamps that lined the street spluttered into life, casting curling shadows across the pavement. Soon, through the ghostly darkness, a noise could be heard: nails and steel scraping along the ground; hobnail boots setting off sparks in the dust, heralding the return of my father.

He was an amazing sight and it always thrilled me to see him. Attached to the front of his mining helmet, a small light beamed through the darkness, occasionally catching the whites of his eyes and making him look like some awesome Greek god. His face was stained black as pitch by the ingrained coal dust. It was a daily ritual to greet him and pour out my news. He stooped down and picked me up.

'Hello lad, what's tha got there?'

'It's Bruce Woodcock, Dad. He's going to beat Joe Louis.'

'I know all about 'im, lad. 'E's not in the same class as Louis. They must give 'im time. They mustn't rush 'im.'

Dad had to bang his boots against the brickwork of the house; it was the only way to get rid of the coal dust. Then, in a flash, he was seated at the dinner table. The light glowing from the fire heightened the blackness of his eyes and the whiteness of his teeth as he smiled. Afterwards, I pulled his jacket off for him, hung it up, and joined him at the table.

'Show me your muscles, Dad. Go on, flex 'em once. Go on, Dad.'

He did so.

'My God, tha feels like a rock! Will I ever have muscles like that, eh Dad?'

'Only if you eat up all of your dinner, and don't forget the green stuff,' Mother reminded me as the entered the room. 'And don't pester your Dad. Let him get on with his snap.'

Ignoring her advice, I poured out the news of my day:

'I've been reading the *Beano*, Dad. There's a man in there called Daddy Longlegs, who's ten foot tall. If I ate a million dinners could I be ten foot tall, Dad?'

'You can try, lad,' he replied. 'Nothing's impossible.'

'There were two eight-foot-tall men in the *Dandy*, but the Amazing Mister X crushed them both. By gum, he must be strong. None of them are as strong as Strang the Terrible, though. He beats up dinosaurs! Will you read me a story when you've had your bath, Dad?'

'I will, lad. But you must learn to read them yourself.'

'But I can't read the big words.'

While we talked, I imitated his every move as he ate, mouthful by mouthful, until only the remainder of the gravy was left on the plate. This we slurped down together. Mother stormed in:

'Billy! You've got to teach our Brian better manners. If you drink out of the plate, so will 'e.'

'Your mother's quite right.'

'Are you going to have your bath now, Dad?' I gently asked. 'Otherwise you'll fall asleep.'

Sure enough, the warmth in his stomach and the soothing, relaxing heat of the fire soon sent him into a deep sleep. He was utterly exhausted from his day's work. Holding his shoulders, I balanced him carefully and whispered into his ear:

'You must go and have your bath, Dad.'

Sitting in the chipped enamel bath, eroded by years of constant use, he let me wash his back for him. His skin was hard and covered with lumps, bumps, cuts and bruises and, where dirt had got inside, looked like some vast purple landscape. Hard scrubbing was the only way that I could get him clean.

It's easy for a sun-tanned body to look good, even a poor body. Yet Dad stood there like white marble, chiselled and muscular; he was very impressive.

I was so proud of both my mother and my father. They laboured so hard to make a living and yet they would devote any amount of time to me, encouraging all my efforts and helping to develop my imagination.

It was Friday night, time to sit by the fire and drink hot Ovaltine. The BBC Light Programme gave us an evening of entertainment and as the hours slowly ticked by I plucked up courage, and eventually asked:

'Eh . . . Dad. Can I stay up tonight and listen to the ghost story?'

'No,' Mother objected. 'It'll frighten you to death and you'll get bags under your eyes.'

My father was my only hope.

'Oh, please Dad. After all, I don't have to go to school tomorrow.'

'All right then, lad.'

'You spoil that boy,' Mother commented.

In a short while the BBC announcer said:

'This is the BBC Light Programme. The time is nine-thirty p.m. We present Valentine Dyall as "The Man in Black" in *An Appointment with Fear*. Tonight's story is entitled "Whistle, And I'll Come to Ye, My Lad".'

'I hope you don't have nightmares tonight,' said my mother.

Ten minutes after the programme had finished, my voice echoed down the stairs from my bedroom:

'Dad . . . can I have the light on in my room tonight?'

Saturday morning was by far the grandest day of the week. I leaped out of bed, full of joy and anticipation of the magic that I knew lay ahead. The big thrill was timed for midday, when the Picture House would screen the next episode of *Flash*

Gordon, starring Buster Crabbe. All morning I charged around like a blue-arsed fly.

'Ah tha comin' out to play, Brian?' chimed the voices of the kids in my street.

My technique for joining them from my garden involved leaping over an enormous hedge. Being small and light, it was easy for me to dive over with a somersault and land on my feet. A round of applause always greeted my landing. Waddling down the street, Mrs Dancy shook with laughter.

'I wish I could do that. You'll break your neck one of these days!' she warned me.

'No I won't,' I shouted. 'Because I'm Vultan, King of the Hawkmen from *Flash Gordon*.'

Little did I realize that, thirty years later, I would actually play the part in a film!

'I'm Flash,' Caldeon Williams chipped in.

Of course, Caldeon was ideal as Flash, being the leader of our gang.

The exodus from Goldthorpe was on. The sun was high, and midday was beckoning us on. Run, run, run, down Probert Avenue and up the Doncaster road. There was the centre of the galaxy, our place of worship, the temple itself: the wondrous Picture House.

We virtually flattened the chip shop, our orders flying thick and fast:

'Two-penny worth.'

'One-penny worth.'

'Three-penny worth.'

'But I've only got a farthing!' pleaded little Gary Simmonds.

'Gee 'im a penny somebody, and shut his gob!'

The next moment we were in the queue for the Picture House, shouting, screaming, kicking, stamping, punching and fighting.

'Somebody lift up little Gary, or he'll get squashed.'

It seemed to take years to get into the cinema, but at last there we all were, gazing up at the enormous screen, waiting with bated breath for the projector to whirr into life.

Then the lights went out and the screen lit up as the curtains were pulled back. Mickey Mouse walked on to the screen to thunderous applause. But, after all too brief a time, the cartoons were over: 'That's All, Folks!'

Next, heralded by the trumpeting of a crowing cockerel, it was the Pathé Newsreel. This was put together with a younger audience in mind; no politics here. Instead, football: Manchester United, Wolverhampton Wanderers, the England goalkeepeer with huge hands, Frank Swift, England 10 – Portugal 0. All great stuff, ending with a few brief shots of the King and Queen. It was then we knew that the moment we'd been waiting for was only minutes away.

The curtains remained closed while the projectionist changed reels – time to stuff our fingers into bags of lemon powder. Thoughts raced through our minds: how could Flash have possibly survived? Surely not this time? He was doomed – or was he? Everyone was on the edge of their seat as the curtains parted to reveal space rockets zooming across the screen.

A replay: Flash falling down a cavernous pit. What's going to happen? A button is pressed and a net swings out, catching him just in time, and saving him from certain death.

'I told you that would happen,' proclaimed Geoff Green. We all nodded in deep respect; Geoff could always predict what would happen with unnerving accuracy.

The episode reached its thrilling climax: a gigantic lizard-like monster had Flash in a deadly grip. All the life was slowly being crushed out of him. Death was inevitable.

Oh, God, how we wanted the film to keep going. But red lights flashed around us – it was time to go till next week. We trudged out, filled with dejection yet eagerly discussing the nerve-tingling scenes we had just witnessed.

'Well, Geoff. What's going to happen, then?' someone asked.

'Prince Barin will shoot the monster with his ray gun,' Geoff stated with great confidence. We all knew that he'd be right.

Our initial depression turned into bliss as we charged towards our beloved railway bridge, intent on re-enacting the events of the latest episode. But despite my efforts to join in, my mind was elsewhere. A single idea gripped me so strongly that it made me shake inside: what if I could actually see Bruce Woodcock train?

The Plough Inn in Doncaster – could I get there? Would I be able to watch?

I must go and see 'im. I must try. I must, I kept saying to myself.

I knew that his evening workouts took place on a Saturday, so the time was certainly right.

'Come on, Vultan,' the others coaxed.

'No, I'm going home to have a cup of tea. I'm thirsty.'

'Can't you wait?' Caldeon pleaded. 'You're a Hawkman. Hawkmen don't need tea.'

'This one does. I'll lose all the strength in my wings if I don't go.'

'Well, hurry back then,' Caldeon finally said. 'The Clay Men are coming and you're the only one who can talk backwards. They won't understand us.'

After scrambling up the railway embankment, I hurdled the fence into Mrs Green's garden and crossed the street to our house. In seconds I was in the kitchen, where Mother was ironing.

'Was it a good picture then, Brian?'

'Oh yes, Mam. But it's a long time to have to wait till next week.'

She was watching me closely. She couldn't have known what I was thinking, could she?

'I thought you'd still be playing with the lads.'

'No, Mam. Oh, no . . . I'm just goin' off for a ride on my bike. I won't be long.'

There was no need for her to warn me about being careful on the roads: you rarely saw a car – one every six months if you were lucky.

My Mickey Mouse tricycle was slightly bigger than was normal for my age. A picture of Mickey's face, painted on the frame, was always there staring up at me with a broad smile. Pedalling as fast as I could, I would get up some terrific speeds.

Excitement now raced through me: I knew it was totally wrong to set out on the adventure that beckoned me, but I was helpless. I pedalled on. Doncaster was seven miles away, and the entire landscape would be unknown territory. Hickleton was the furthest

I'd ever ventured, and that was only two miles away. My quest had begun!

Nobody noticed as I left Probert Avenue – it was just young Brian, out on his bike. Nothing unusual about that.

On and on I pedalled, up the Doncaster road.

By gum! I thought to myself. I've really gone and done it now!

Up, up and over the huge railway bridge, past Booth's shop on the left, then into Goldthorpe itself. At last, I was sailing downhill, and there was the Picture House, straight ahead.

'Hello, Brian.'

It was lads from school. They'd recognized me.

'Where's tha goin'?'

'Just for a ride.'

Keep calm, I thought.

'See you.'

'Bye then, Brian.'

Nothing suspected. Good.

Sweat started pouring from my skin, for there was the police station. No other way: I had to go past it. Sergeant Gruber and PC Hawksworth were there talking. I sped straight past. Did they notice me? No. Too many shoppers wandering around and, besides, they were too engrossed in conversation.

There was Mickey Mouse, still smiling and encouraging me to go on:

'Go on, Brian. Keep going. Don't stop now!'

I was safe. Phew, that's that crisis over and done with, I thought.

Uphill again, past the other temple to the silver screen, the Empire, and past Brown's bakery – rushing, heaving, straining, fit to burst, until the road levelled off again. But before long I was climbing yet another hill. Oh, the agony of it. God, it hurt! Crikey! I must rest for a bit. It was far too steep, I realized.

Pushing my tricycle, I trudged past the Italian POW camp in the woodlands, and suddenly there was Hickleton. It's a lovely village with pale-brown houses and pretty windows, but the friendliness of the place evaporated as I spotted an old door in a high stone wall. Through the open door I could see a skull, under which was the inscription: 'Today for me – Tomorrow for thee'. The thought of it made me shudder and redouble my efforts, and in a short time I was through the village. Now there was a signpost in front of me: Brodsworth to the left, Barnburgh to my right.

Again I had the shakes, for Barnburgh was famous for its 'Cat and Man' church. Mrs Dancy had told me the story of the church and I'd had nightmares about it ever since. Sir Percival Cresacre, a Knight Templar, in 1477 fought a tremendous battle with a wild cat. The fight was long and bloody, raging from distant High Melton woods, via Harlington, to end on the porch of Barnburgh's church, where the dying knight finally succeeded in crushing the cat to death. The porch floor was said to be stained with blood which resisted all efforts to scrub it clean.

My morbid thoughts were interrupted by a friendly voice. A miner on his way to work had stopped by my side.

'Where's tha goin', lad?'

'I'm goin' to Doncaster. To see Bruce Woodcock training.'

'But that's five miles away! Where 'ave you come from, then?'

I told him.

'Well, you've done two miles already, and it shows: your face is as red as a tomato. 'Ere lad, 'ave a drink.'

I drank deeply and gratefully from the small tin bottle, which all miners carry.

'Me dad's a miner,' I said. 'He works as a hewer. Shifts fourteen tons a day from that pit.'

'He works much harder than me, lad. I work on the surface – much easier.'

It was time for him to move on.

'Well, then, to get to Doncaster, go straight ahead for about three miles, and then you'll find you're just outside it. In due course, you'll come to the first 'ouse. Ask your way from there to where Woodcock trains. If you get tired, promise me that you'll turn back. By the way, what's tha name?'

'Brian. Brian Blessed.'

'Oh, so you're Bill Blessed's son. I know him. I've played cricket against him.'

He started to walk away.

'Well, I'll have to hurry, take care.'

He waved goodbye and in a flash was gone.

The sun was now beginning to creep over the horizon, stirring deep feelings of doubt in me. Progress was so slow. Would I . . . could I, make it?

Woodcock . . . Woodcock . . . Woodcock . . . echoed in my brain. Slim waist . . . six feet tall . . . broad shoulders . . . His description, repeated again and again, lifted my spirits. Head low over the handlebars, I steamed ahead. I mustn't, I can't stop now. I must get there.

Pea fields, potato fields: I was in the flatlands now, mile after mile of it, running straight to the coast. With the breeze picking up behind me, legs wide open and feet high off the pedals, I whizzed downhill.

Wheeeee! Drunk on the sheer excitement coursing through me, at last I was getting there.

Must be a record, I thought to myself as I hurtled past Marr Thick, trying desperately to make up for lost time, yet allowing myself a moment's rest to take stock of my situation. Had anybody noticed that I'd gone? Would my mother be looking for me? Then again, what stories I'd be able to tell everyone on my return!

I pressed on through Marr, where bulls, safely shut in their fields, bellowed at me.

'Mooo, yourself,' I shouted.

Faster, faster, and there on the horizon: 'Donny'. Two miles of sheer hell. Soaked with sweat, I stopped for a pee. Doncaster. I'd made it. Where to now? Where's the Plough? Where's Woodcock? Slowly it dawned on me that I was utterly lost. Frustrated and tense, I relieved myself. I was one of the best at peeing. There was no wall that I'd encountered that was too high for me to pee over: seven, eight feet into the air! With my 'spadge', as we called it, back in its rightful place, I went on my way.

I stopped at the first main street I came to, and a small, curious crowd of people started to gather around me. I explained my problem.

'This lad wants to know where Bruce Woodcock trains.'

'What's tha want to see 'im for?'

''Cos he's goin' to beat Joe Louis and become the World Champion.'

'You ought to be at home, lad. Tha's a long way from Goldthorpe.'

'I know me way back.'

(There was no way that I was going to turn back now – not after that journey: my legs were red raw and exhausted.)

An elderly man offered vague directions:

'Go straight along that road and past that field till tha comes to a church. Go on from there towards Balby Road.'

'You're all misleading him. Shut up and let me tell him.'

My salvation arrived in the form of Gladys, who everyone agreed was the best person to help me:

'See this cut here? It's hard work, but it'll save you a lot of trouble. Go down it and then climb over a stile, then go on straight ahead and down the pathway. Climb another stile and you should come to a bit of a rough patch by a stream. Keep to your left, for as long as you can, and don't come off till you get to the main road: Balby Road. Turn right and follow it till you come to an estate, then ask again.'

For the next hour or so that is exactly what I did, asking the way again and again. This way, that way, up there, down there, I was told.

Eventually I found myself under a gas lamp. The gentle, friendly light did nothing to console me as I sobbed my heart out.

'What is it, lad?' A couple had come over and were kneeling by my side.

'I'm lost, I've come miles from Goldthorpe, me mam'll be mad with me and I'm hungry and thirsty. All I want to do is to see Bruce Woodcock train. They said that where he trains is around here, but I can't find it.'

'It's at the back of our house, just on the corner of the road. Look, lad, me and me wife are taking you inside our 'ouse. You can 'ave a cup of tea and some bread and butter and then I'll take you there.'

I couldn't believe what I was hearing.

'I know Bruce quite well,' he went on. 'But I know his brother Billy even better. Don't worry, I'll get you in.'

With that, the man lifted me up. I sat, feet astride his neck, legs dangling against his shoulders. His wife wheeled my bike at our side.

Never before had tea and bread and butter tasted so scrumptious; I devoured every crumb.

''Ow's tha feelin' now?'

'I feel much better for that,' I told him. 'I'm as fit as a flea!'

'Leave your bike here, lad. We'll walk over.'

It was a truly golden walk for me. All the while the man continued to talk reassuringly:

'We see Bruce running around 'ere nearly every day. 'E 'as a dog running with 'im. I think its name's Spot – looks a bit like a whippet.'

'I'd like a dog. But I've got a red tabby cat called Tibby, who's a smashing fighter.'

The inn loomed up ahead. It was the moment that I'd been waiting for; but suddenly I felt shy and very nervous: would I actually get to see him?

Bitter disappointment surged through me as we stepped inside, for there was nobody in sight – just a few big sacks.

'He's not here,' I whispered, my heart sinking.

A voice rang out sharply, directly above where we were standing.

'Last ten seconds, Bruce. Give it some 'umpy!'

Up there! They were up there in the roof. There was a second floor.

'There's a room up that ladder,' the man told me. 'That's where you'll find 'im, lad.'

It was a towering ladder; higher than the bridge at Goldthorpe. I wasn't frightened though – I was a champion at 'dasties'. Up, up, up, up we went, until our heads touched the ceiling.

Bang! The trapdoor flipped open like the lid of a jack-in-the-box, and harsh light hit us from all directions. A face peered out.

'It's Reg. 'E's brought a lad with 'im to watch.'

'Up you come, then,' said another, laughing voice. 'Come on, quick. Bruce hit one of his sparring partners so hard the other day that he went straight through that trapdoor.'

What a sight! Men were skipping and doing exercises: big men, small men. Hanging in one corner was a gigantic, home-made punchbag and then the most difficult piece of apparatus to train on: the swing-ball. Stretching from floor to ceiling, a length of tough rubber supported a hard, leather ball in the middle.

Difficult to time and hit accurately, this simple device could make even an experienced boxer look like a complete fool. Pounding it with colossal strength and speed, a boxer was firing punches with deadly accuracy.

Every time he hit it, the thing flew twelve feet and shot back at terrific speed, only to be met by a mixture of punches: straight lefts, straight rights, the like of which I'd never seen. He was god-like in his grace and power. My mind filled with images of Hector on the walls of Troy, the Amazing Mr X, Strang the Terrible; all of these giants paled into insignificance compared with this Titan.

The foundations of the room seemed to shake, as loud applause and shouts of appreciation came from all quarters.

'I pity Jack London when you fight him, Bruce!'

The exercise ended with a mighty right hand, and then the body in question turned around. I had my first front view of Bruce Woodcock. Suddenly the agony and the sheer frustration of my journey had been worth it.

Woodcock was enormous, with a magnificent, heroic, beaming face, thick, slightly curly hair and raised eyebrows. His shoulders were perfectly proportioned; his arms chiselled yet oak-like; his waist trim; his legs lean and muscular. His boxing stance was as natural as it was graceful. His eyes were full of concentration.

Feelings shot up my spine and burst in my head like a colourful cascade. My hands started to clap as they'd never clapped before. Tears of joy ran down my cheeks.

'By gum!' My excitement was making me jump up and down on the spot. 'Tha's the best fighter I've ever seen. Miles better than Joe Louis!'

Ripples of laughter filled the room.

'Who are you, lad?'

'Where's tha come from?'

Reg told them my story; how I'd cycled eight miles and that I was only seven years old.

'Good God! Tha's a long way from home.'

'What are you going to do when you grow up?'

'I'm going to be World Heavyweight Champion, just like Bruce Woodcock.'

A large, friendly hand touched my head. It was him.

'I've got a long way to go before I'm champion, lad. It needs a lot of hard work and dedication.'

'Do you like training, Mr Woodcock?' I asked.

'I do, lad. Otherwise there'd be no point in doing it.'

Somebody stepped forward – it might have been Woodcock's manager, Tom Hurst – looked down, smiled and asked me:

'Would you like to go in the ring with Bruce?'

'By gum, I would!' I couldn't believe my luck.

Before I knew what was happening, my shirt had been whipped off, leaving me in my vest and shorts. Gloves that seemed to be bigger than me were put over my hands.

Ding. Ding. Round one.

Moving forward, I was unable to take in the magic of it all. There was Woodcock, miles above me and ready for my attack, in his famous stance: left shoulder slightly raised as protection against a right-hand blow.

'I don't know what to do!' I cried out. I could see that I had no chance. 'I can only reach as high as his knees!'

'Well, hit his knees then, lad,' somebody yelled. 'That'll bring him down to size!'

This I did. The colossus crashed to the ground. Standing on his knees I pummelled his arms until I'd laid him out flat. The count came:

'Six . . . seven . . . eight . . . nine . . . ten! The winner!'

I had knocked out Bruce Woodcock!

Bruce was immediately on his feet again and, lifting me up in his arms, carried me to the exit.

'By God, lad. Tha can't half punch. I've got to continue training now, but these people will make sure that you get home to your mum and dad. You can come and see me another time.'

Everything was now a haze. The voices all around me blurred into a noisy echo. Far, far away in my mind, I was enveloped in cloud; this was a wonderful dream land. To this day I can't remember anything about my journey home, or even collecting my Mickey Mouse bike. My only faint recollection is that I travelled on a tractor: some of Reg's friends dropped me off on the outskirts of Goldthorpe.

It was very dark by the time I heaved my bike up on to the pavement and approached my front door.

'Where in God's name have you been?' rang out the angry voice of my father. 'The police and the whole neighbourhood have been out looking for you. They've searched everywhere. Sergeant Gruber's here, and you're in for a right tellin' off. Before he starts though, look at your mother. She's been like that for hours: worried stiff; crying her eyes out.'

Mother's face was red and her eyes swollen, but she put her arms out and held me close.

'Thank God you're safe. You frightened me to death.'

Her tears showered all over me as she wept, full of relief that I was safely home. Had I caused all this? The full horror sank in as I realized what I'd done. The deep, rumbling voice of Sergeant Gruber interrupted my thoughts:

'Now then, lad. What's tha been up to?'

Quietly but with feeling I poured out the details of my story, to the utter amazement of everybody present. Mrs Dancy was there from next door, as well as half the neighbourhood: they seemed to be poking their heads in everywhere. My old grandad was there too. At first I hadn't noticed his small frame, white hair and black eyebrows. He chuckled hoarsely as he blurted out his verdict on me:

'By gum, Brian. Tha's a rum lad!'

Sergeant Gruber, standing there with his blue eyes, fair hair, red face and stocky build, broke through the laughter grandad had set off:

'Next time you choose to go off without telling your mum and dad where you've gone, I'll take you on with a pair of boxing gloves! And let me tell you something, lad: you won't have such an easy time with me as you did with Woodcock!'

With that, he strode out of the house. Then they all left, except for Mrs Dancy and Grandad. Even though I'd been a naughty boy, a huge supper was put in front of me: Yorkshire pudding, veg, gravy and even a little bit of meat. I'll never know where my mother got that meat from, but I wolfed it down. Then came the blancmange pudding, which I ate till I felt full and contented.

Grandad turned to me:

'Don't you think you owe your mother a favour?'

'I do, Grandad, I do.'

'Then sing her a song, lad.'

The words of 'All Things Bright and Beautiful' flowed from my lips.

'It's worth all the tea in China, a voice like that!' Mrs Dancy commented.

'Come on, then,' said my father. 'Up the wooden hill to Bedfordshire.'

I scarcely had enough energy left to climb those stairs. The last image I had was of Mum and Dad kissing me goodnight and then there was the softness of my pillows and the cosy warmth of the soft sheets.

I fell into the deep, contented sleep of a child. But not for long. I awoke with a start. 'Bloody hell! I forgot to get his autograph!'

3

The *Flying Scotsman*

On many a summer's afternoon I would sit at the back of friendly Mr Parkin's house, which overlooked the London and North Eastern Railway line, watching the smoking engines go by: goods trains struggling with all their might to pull iron wagons loaded with ore.

One rainy day a train seemed to almost buckle its heavy wheels and pistons as it groaned with the effort of its task. Sparks flew as the wheels ran free, unable to grip the wet track. The sweating stokers, lit up by the boiler, shovelled coal at an incredible rate in an attempt to sustain the engine. The roar of the frustrated train and the massive eruptions of grey-black smoke from the funnel were reminiscent of some beleaguered dragon and inspired me to help their magnificent effort by cheering them to the skies.

The grimy face of the driver smiled broadly as he raised his L N E R hat in thanks and sounded his shrill whistle.

Gradually, the skill of the driver and the titanic effort of the stokers won the day: the steel dragon gathered pace and powered away.

Moments like this were memorable, but nothing compared to the sight of some of the great express trains. At that time the uncontested train expert in our gang was the tiny, bespectacled Tank Guest. Although he lived over the bridge, he was accepted as a full member of the Probert Avenue Gang. His little steel-rimmed glasses would steam up at the mere sight of a train. Out would

46

come his handkerchief to quickly wipe away the perspiration from the lenses, which he then promptly returned to his pink, cherubic face. His deeply treasured L NE R handbook would appear in a flash from his pocket. This contained the names and numbers of trains for the length and breadth of the country. Tank would carefully finger the pages, and in a reverential tone describe how he had seen a hundred of these steam trains. He had underlined each name and number with his pencil.

This devotion would take him to far-away places like Mexborough and Doncaster – and sometimes even to York! On occasion we would go with him to our little railway station, two miles away in Bolton-on-Dearne. We would stare in wonder at the colourful L NE R posters advertising trains to the dreamed-of seaside resorts of Bridlington, Cleethorpes, Redcar and Skegness.

One poster showed the famed *Scarborough Flyer*, with its blue livery. My mouth watered at the prospect of going by train to Newcastle, then by bus to Newbiggin, to stay with my Aunt Florrie and my Uncle George.

'What's yer favourite train, Tank?' asked Mike Burns, who was sporting a bright blue tie that enhanced his usual immaculate appearance.

Tank's eyes glowed like fires, magnified by his glasses. His chest started to heave and his whole frame shook with emotion:

'The *Flying Scotsman*,' he half roared, 'there's nowt like it. It's bigger than anything and faster than any train in the world. Whammo! Whammo!' Tank shrieked. 'When it comes towards you the sleepers holding the line together creak and shake. The whole embankment feels as though it's going to cave in. As it whizzes past, yer can be blown off yer feet or sucked in if you're not careful. Straight after, the line's red hot – hot enough to burn yer fingers off!'

Tank's outburst immediately sparked a heated debate, for various members of the gang passionately begged to differ, each having his own particular favourite locomotive.

The Doubting Thomas of our gang, Brian Lee, proudly proclaimed that the *King Arthur*, belonging to Southern Railways, was much better and bigger than the *Flying Scotsman*.

'Aye,' added chubby David Dunbar, 'and what about the *Mallard*?'

As the discussion gathered force, 'Wise Owl', Gerald Athey, gently interjected:

'I'm afraid I have to agree with David. The speed and vibration of the *Mallard* constantly breaks all the pots in the restaurant car. Also, its cylinders have been known to burst because of its great speed.'

Voices now were at fever pitch as famous engines' names filled the air:

'What about the *Cheltenham Flyer* and the *Cornish Riviera*?'

'Aye,' shouted Colin Picton, 'and what about the giant *Merchant Navy*?'

Poor little Tank was desperately under siege and couldn't get a word in edgeways. Fast and furious the names continued to be bawled out. I bellowed that the crack train and the best in the world was the *Red Dragon*, which went between London and Wales.

'What do you know about the *Red Dragon*?' growled a stocky lad called Clegg, who came from another district and was not part of our gang.

My hackles immediately rose, and I returned his growl, retaliating:

'Because, face-ache, I've seen it on a cigarette card and heard about it on the radio.'

Clegg grimaced and muttered:

'Tha knows bugger all, Blessed.'

'I know 'ow to put a fist in your fat gob! Yer great spawny-eyed pillock,' was my fond reply.

That lit the fuse and a scuffle broke out. This was brought to an abrupt halt by Gerald and Caldeon.

'You ought to be ashamed of yourselves,' hissed Caldeon. 'Now shake hands and let that be an end of it.'

Clegg and I, with looks that could kill, reluctantly obeyed the order. Once peace reigned again, Caldeon continued:

'Fair's fair, and Tank hasn't been given his chance to speak. So let's keep quiet and listen to him.'

The little train lover wiped his glasses and began quietly:

'All the trains you've talked about I know. You don't have to tell me what they are like! I know them and hundreds more. Trains you've never even heard of: the *Golden Arrow*, *Devon Belle*, *Brighton Belle*, *Capitals Limited*, *Queen of Scots*, *King Edward*, *Lord Nelson*, *Royal Scot*, *Princess Scot*, *Black Bull*. I could keep on telling you names from here to kingdom come, but not one of them is in the same class as the *Flying Scotsman*. It's bloody spiffin', that train. You can ask any stationmaster on the LNER from here to Scotland, and they'll all tell yer the same!'

'He may be tellin' the truth,' Caldeon interrupted, his blue eyes smiling under his blond, wavy hair. 'We must put him to the test and vote on it. Who agrees that we should find out about the *Scotsman*?'

No abstaining on this issue: all hands shot into the air like rockets.

'When will the *Scotsman* pass the embankment again?' asked Gerald.

Out came Tank's little red book:

'Two days' time, at about four-thirty p.m. It sets off from Derby station at three p.m.'

'On that day we must all run from school, as fast as we can, so that we're all here on time. So work hard and make the teachers happy,' ordered Caldeon.

'Aye, we won't want any bad marks, or we'll be late,' I added.

For the next two days Tank was as nervous as a jumping bean.

'Stop pesterin' me and stop frettin',' I said. 'Tha'll be all reet.'

When the big day came, we all arrived with sweaty red faces at the back of Frank Parkin's house overlooking the railway line. We perched ourselves on the wooden fence: an ideal spot for everyone to get a perfect view. Our mood was happy and expectant.

'There's a train coming!' shouted David Dunbar, who was already at the side of the track. It was good to see him smiling, brave lad, for his dad had died only two weeks earlier.

'False alarm,' said another voice. 'It's a bloody goods train!'

49

'Mind your language!' Mr and Mrs Parkin reprimanded us from their bedroom window.

'Shhh, no more swearing or we'll be sent away,' warned Caldeon.

Total silence and perfect stillness ruled. I whispered to Gerald:

'I'll bet Tank likes the new *Paul Temple* music on the BBC. *Coronation Scot*, it's called. It's nice, but Rimsky-Korsakov's *Scheherazade* is better.'

'Rip yer corsets off, did yer say, Brian?' Gary grinned.

'I'm trying to be serious, Gary. Shut yer gob and learn. It's a funny thing, Gerald, but there was a photograph in the paper of Marjory Westbury, who plays Paul Temple's wife, Steve. I never thought she'd look like that – very chubby! Her voice sounds like an angel. Still, she's good in the part, and so's Kim Peacock.'

Gerald smiled and, in that unique way of his, expressed his admiration for the new *Paul Temple* serial, feeling that 'The Madison Square Mystery' was the best episode yet.

'I like Richard Williams as Captain Blood in *The Spanish Main*,' Geoff chipped in.

'Indeed,' said Gerald. 'And the music, Walton's Symphony Number One, is perfect for that serial.'

God, I thought, I'll be glad when I'm as old as him. He knows so much!

Warming to the theme, I proclaimed with feeling that I thought *The War of the Worlds* was a smashing serial.

'That's good music, eh? . . . Mars, isn't it? . . . It's out of this world!'

This produced gales of laughter from Gerald and much back-patting;

'Yes, Brian, it's quite literally out of this world. It's from Holst's *Planets* suite.'

'I like *Happydrome*,' David chimed in. 'Do us the voice of Enoch, Brian. Go on!'

My voice rang out sharp and high-pitched:

'There's blue bloody blood in my veins!'

Amid the laughter that followed, Mrs Parkin called out from the bedroom window:

'You sound just like Enoch.'

'Well, young soldier,' Caldeon addressed Tank. 'How about starting the train song?'

In a quiet, tiny voice that slowly gained pace and rhythm, Tank began. The rest of us then joined in, all rocking sideways on the fence:

'Jicketi-can, jicketi-can,
The train goes running along the line,
Jicketi-can, jicketi-can,
I wish it were mine, I wish it were mine,
Jicketi-can, jicketi-can,
The engine driver stands in front,
He makes it run, he makes it shunt,
Down from the downs, down from the downs,
Up to the towns, up to the towns,
Over the ridges, and up the lea,
Down the ledges, and up to the sea,
With a Jicketi-can, jicketi-can,
Jicketi-can, jicketi-can . . .'

'Wooooaaaa, woooo,' echoed Tank.

David Dunbar had his ear to the track, and suddenly bawled out:

'There's another train coming! Not the *Scotsman* though – it's far too slow.'

'It's full of troops!' Caldeon's voice rang out. They're Yanks! Give 'em a cheer, lads!'

We immediately started singing:

'Over there, over there, over there,
Over there, over there,
For the Yanks are coming,
The Yanks are coming,
The Yanks are coming, over there . . .'

Waving our bayonets, taken from the local ammunition dump, we roared:

51

'Do you need any help, Yanks?'

'Sure do! . . . All the help we can get, young men!'

Our faces flushed with pride at the compliment. We all admired the Yanks and their marvellous 'Flying Fortresses'. We cheered our heads off.

'Hooray! Hooray! . . . Go get 'em, Yanks! Show old Hitler and Tojo what's what! . . . Mulicrush 'em! . . Pulverize 'em! . . . '

What with the train, the cheering and shouting, and Mrs Parkin trying to stop us from swearing, the whole place was in uproar. The singing rose in a crescendo:

'The Germans came in four by four,
Big fat Goering stuck in the door,
Singing Ooh-la-la-la,
Ooh-la-la-la,
Ooh-la-la-la,
Wee, wee, wee!'

The whole embankment was blanketed in smoke and steam from the engine, but we could just make out the shapes of various vehicles at the back. It was an impressive sight: Bren-gun carriers, big guns and tanks, one of which looked like a Sherman.

'Watch out for the German Tiger tanks!' warned Caldeon. 'Hit 'em in the belly where it hurts!'

'That's right,' cried another voice. 'You ought to ship over some of them Russian TR4s. That would fix 'em!'

Gradually the cheering evaporated, as the train chugged under the bridge and out of sight, bound for unknown frontiers of battle.

A gymnastics show followed, as we all performed handstands, vaulting, wrestling and piggy-back rides. Our energy seemed boundless until Mrs Parkin called us to come and get sandwiches and dandelion and burdock – our favourite drink.

She placed the groaning tray on the lawn and started to supervise us. We all found her beautifully graceful. Her angelic voice, her sexy, loving eyes, all her movements, charmed the pants off us. The sinking sun highlighted her pretty flowered dress and her perfume filled the air with the fragrance of wild roses. In an instant we were all like Botticelli angels:

'Thank you, Mrs Parkin.'

'Ta very much, Mrs Parkin.'

'May I have some more pop, please, Mrs Parkin?'

'These sandwiches are lovely,' I purred. 'What's in 'em?'

'Gooseberry jam made by Mrs Dancy.' Then came that delicious, far-away laugh. 'We would all starve if it wasn't for Mrs Dancy.'

Soon a sleepy haze drifted across us. We sat back to back, each supporting the other, and not for one second were any eyes diverted from the madonna before us.

'Enjoyed yer picnic, I see.' It was Mr Parkin: lean and angular, all six foot of him.

'Oh, yes Mr Parkin. Thank you,' Caldeon smiled.

All too suddenly the tray and our dream girl had gone. Mr Parkin was greatly liked by everyone, but we were intensely jealous of him because he was married to our goddess.

'When I'm grown up,' I choked out, 'I'm goin' to ask Mrs Parkin to marry me!'

'Tha's not the only one,' put in Geoff Green.

'Join the queue,' someone else muttered.

The extraordinary thing was that her eight-year-old son, Frank, was sitting right next to me, but never said a word. He just smiled.

'By gum!' David Dunbar exploded. 'We've forgotten about the *Flying Scotsman*!'

'I haven't!' Tank's plaintive voice called out from the fence. 'Please come back to the line or you'll miss it.'

During what seemed like hours, goods trains passed loaded with cows and rocks, and the odd express train went by now and then, but there was still no sign of the legendary locomotive.

'I'm goin' home,' a tired, bored voice said.

'And me,' added another fed-up voice.

'Oh, no! Please don't go!' begged Tank.

But his pleas were in vain. Excuses poured out:

'I've got to go, me mam'll be wonderin' where I am . . . '

'I have to fetch the bread . . . '

As the exodus gathered pace, terrible disappointment showed on Tank's face:

'Oh, please . . . I wanted you to see it . . . please stay, just for a few minutes . . . '

'No!' said Brian Lee defiantly, the sceptic's short supply of patience exhausted. 'It'll never come. I don't believe that it ever comes down this line.'

'It does! It does! It does!' the broken-hearted train-spotter wailed.

'Ah, stop bawlin' and shut yer gob! I'm goin'.' And with that, Brian Lee was gone.

The garden was now empty, except for Tank, Caldeon and me. Our respected leader put an arm around Tank's shoulder:

'Wipe yer face like a good soldier, and stand up straight. Brian and I will have to pop home for ten minutes, but we'll come back and stay with you . . . That's a promise.'

Tank smiled.

Hours later, armed with a bottle of pop and some K-Y powder – a sherbet dip – we sat patiently waiting for the 'earth trembler' to arrive. Nothing was said. The silence was as golden as it was sweet.

As the evening wore on Caldeon lit the candle in his jam jar and tied the makeshift night-light to the fence. But despite his efforts, the candle slowly melted down into a pool of gooey wax. The dim light flickered, spluttered and finally died.

In the all-consuming darkness, our eyes were as heavy as lead. It was Tank himself, mature way beyond his years, who plucked up his courage and turned to us and whispered:

'Sorry chaps. I think the *Flying Scotsman* has gone to bed for the night . . . '

'I think we ought to do the same,' smiled Caldeon. 'And on behalf of Brian and myself, thank you for a lovely day, Tank.'

We then marched off smartly in single file, whistling the Mozart piece nicknamed 'The Little Tin Soldier', which always introduced *Children's Hour* on the radio.

Days passed by before our gang gathered together again, this time outside Booth's shop in Goldthorpe. Brian Lee approached and said triumphantly:

'Well, the train never did turn up, did it?'

Caldeon stepped back for a second and then tore into him ferociously:

'Don't talk such absolute rubbish! You missed a rare treat. It came down the line like a smoking dragon! You could see the fires burning, roaring red, and the stokers shovelling coal in. It was gigantic! Massive! It made the whole embankment shake, just like there was an earthquake. A hundred and twenty miles an hour – so fast that it passed by in a flash! If I hadn't held on to a bush, I'd have been blown off my feet. After it had gone, you couldn't touch the steel line – it would have burnt your fingers off! Isn't that right, Tank?'

'Oh, yes!' confirmed the owner of the LNER handbook, standing there perplexed yet swollen with pride. 'The *Flying Scotsman* – there's nowt like it!'

On 5 April 1992 I picked up my sixteen-year-old daughter Rosalind from her school, Brooklands in Weybridge, and headed down the M25 towards a mystery destination. Swapping roads, we sped along the A4 and turned left down Heston Road, to arrive at Glade Lane. After crossing a tiny bridge that spanned the Grand Canal and following unsurfaced roads, we passed a two-acre field containing several ponies and a donkey. Then we found ourselves in a wide yard with a stocky, cheerful man with grey hair, called Mr Bellamy, who invited us to follow his car. A minute later we stopped and walked together to the main door of a warehouse which, when unlocked, revealed another door. We went in, and there, in pristine condition, stood the *Flying Scotsman*. After forty-eight years I had, at last, clapped eyes on our boyhood dream!

4

Arcadian Days

If you follow the railway line from Probert Avenue for two miles or so, nearing Bolton-on-Dearne, you arrive at the Seven Fields. In the early days of my childhood those distant pastures contained the most amazing hordes of frogs, toads and newts.

The fields dipped gently, and at the lowest point there was a narrow stream, stretching for miles, that everyone called the Gam. Lining it were a wide variety of bushes and trees, in particular weeping willows.

The Gam was slow-moving and held many forms of pond plants: lilies, potamogeton, marginals and oxygenating plants. Its depth varied from two to four feet and it exuded total peace and perfect natural balance. Of all the places of my childhood, this one gave me the deepest serenity.

Of course, on many occasions I would come with the Probert Avenue Gang – Colin, Geoff, Caldeon, Tank and the others – and we would spend an enjoyable day. But it could never compare to being on my own; only then would I experience complete bliss.

The summer sun would shine down brightly, energizing the earth, while a gentle breeze would stir the willows, creating movement in the branches, twigs and leaves, and producing a gentle, far-away music.

Blowing on a hand-made whistle made from a bulrush, I would find myself melting into the pastoral scene, like some child-like rustic Pan, oblivious of time.

During this idyll water beetles with glistening blue-black bodies would busy themselves, hurrying up and down the stems of the lilies. Water-boatmen would skate across the surface, skilfully avoiding the caddis fly. Newts would rise, blow an air bubble, then descend into the mysterious depths of the multicoloured weeds. Newts of the most gorgeous colours: brown, light-red, yellow, orange, black and even the odd albino. The smooth skin of the female common newt – what grace! Swimming ghost-like along the marginal plants, she would leave a trail of delicate eggs.

One day a deep-lying plant parted to reveal a larger specimen: the great crested newt. I put my hand gently into the water and then, finding myself in a position to stroke it, lifted it to the surface. What I saw took my breath away. Placing it in a very large jam jar, I was able to examine the creature at my leisure. It was male, eight inches long, and the most stunning great crested newt I'd ever set eyes on, with big, protruding eyes, a long, black body and a crest suggesting high black pinnacles. Its stomach, by contrast, was golden with large black spots.

The creature in the jar was slightly magnified by the glass, and held up to the sunlight it symbolized all the primitive magic of the animal kingdom. Another movement and it was in my hands again; then a gentle stroke and an effortless return to the water. Down he plunged, free, his legs pressed against his body as he dived out of sight.

The whole episode seemed like some secret ceremony. As I stared at the vision, a sensation of well-being enveloped me, and I could feel my eyes focusing with ever greater concentration. The odd green leaf or petal would float and circulate in the tiny eddies. The water's surface and what lay beneath it would beckon me, drawing me down to share in the mystery.

When the gang were with me, it was during experiences like these that I could hold sway over them.

'Tell us stories, Brian,' they would beg. Even Caldeon and the much older and wiser Gerald Athey would pour out the same request.

Slowly, in a tiny, hushed voice, I would elaborate stories about the great dinosaurs, using newts as a starting-point.

'In the history of the earth,' I would tell them, 'nowt was like those giants.'

Then I would rattle off the names at great speed:

'*Triceratops, Pteranodon, Antosaurus, Pterodactylus, Brachadon, Pliosaurus, Diplodocus, Allosaurus, Ichthyosaurus, Stegosaurus, Gorgosaurus, Brontosaurus* and the great thunder lizard, *Tyrannosaurus Rex*!

'They roamed the land around here, and they were like huge newts; all different colours. It wasn't long ago that they were still alive.'

'No, Brian,' said Gerald. 'Sorry to have to correct you, but they died out millions of years ago . . . '

'No, no, no!' I retorted. 'They died out sixty million years ago. That's not long . . . Look, Gerald, do you want to tell the story, or me?'

Gerald smiled.

'No, Brian. I'd rather you did.'

'Right then,' I replied. 'I'm sorry,' I said, addressing Cedric, 'you missed the last episode of *The Lost World*, by Sir Arthur Conan Doyle. It were great! There were a bit where the explorers came across an everglade where adult iguanadons were feeding in the grass with their babies . . . The music was lovely and the sounds were real . . . Yer see, dinosaurs could also be caring and loving.

'Don't forget: next Thursday, six-thirty p.m., the BBC Light Programme. The trailer says Professor Challenger gets kidnapped by giant apes. The man playing him, Abraham Soefar, has a great deep voice; he's just right for the part.'

'We won't miss the next episode!' they all shouted.

'I'll tell you what I do miss,' I lamented. 'That they're not alive today . . . '

Hours passed as I described how explorers maintained that prehistoric creatures still existed in certain parts of Africa. Even in Scotland there was the Loch Ness Monster. Mouths opened wide and drooled as I embellished on the theme.

'Go on, Brian . . . Go on!' they pleaded.

'Well,' I said, pausing for effect. 'We still don't know much about the Matto Grosso in Brazil. That's where *The Lost World* is set. In the BBC serial, Conan Doyle calls it Maple White Land. Isn't that a lovely name?'

A chorus of approval greeted this revelation.

'What do we do, Brian? What can we do?' Caldeon asked in a serious tone.

'With you as leader, Caldeon, and when we're a bit older, we should go there by plane, boat and then on foot, like Professor Challenger and his men. Not even head-hunters with poison darts and blow pipes, deadly snakes, anacondas that can crush a train [this image made Tank gasp with astonishment], quicksands and high precipices, should stop us from getting there . . . to Roriana!'

'Roriana? What's that?' asked Cedric.

'I keep telling you, it's the "Lost World". It really exists. Look at a map of Brazil!'

Everybody was absorbed in his own thoughts as I sat back and watched, satisfied and expectant. Their imaginations were filled with dreams of magical deeds to come.

Then the whole scene was ruined by a strident voice from the railway embankment. It was nine-year-old randy little Elsie Green, who was always showing me her knickers.

'Brian! . . . Brian Blessed!'

Immediately I sank deeper into the long grass.

'I can see you . . . yer mother says yer tea's ready, and if you don't come this minute, she'll clear the table!'

5

The Milk-top Baby

When I was almost eight Mum and Dad asked me if I could help them to get a baby. Their request made me jump up and down with excitement as I nodded an enthusiastic yes.

'But how?' I asked. 'Where do we get it from? What do I have to do?'

After giving it some thought, Mum said:

'We need you to collect as many milk tops as you can. When there's enough we'll take them to the 'ospital and get a baby.'

From that day onwards I started to collect every milk top in South Yorkshire! They were made of thick paper but with a soft centre, so that I could push my finger through and thread hundreds of them on a long piece of string. Up and down Goldthorpe I went searching for them until there wasn't a spare cupboard or drawer in the house that wasn't chock-full of milk tops. Yet there was still no sign of the baby!

Around this time my mother became very fat – through eating too much pudding, I thought. And then, all of a sudden, it happened! As we were leaving school one day, my dear chum David Dunbar shouted to me:

'Brian, yer mother's had a baby!'

Not since seeing Bruce Woodcock had I known such excitement. A baby! I couldn't believe it! Down the road I raced, skidded to a halt at our front door and thundered in. Dad stood at the top of the stairs, beaming.

'We've got a baby boy,' he said.

'Have you?' I replied, not daring to breathe. 'Where did you get it from?'

'From the 'ospital.'

'You had enough milk tops then?'

'Oh, yes. Thank you, lad. Now, come and see your brother.'

I rushed over to the cot and beheld the sweetest face I'd ever seen. He was so cute! I gently tickled each cheek and then his chin, which made him smile deliciously.

'Look, look, he's smiling!' I cried.

'No, no, it's just wind,' said my red-faced mother, with a grin.

I wasn't convinced, for he continued to smile.

'What shall we call him, Dad?'

'We like the sound of Alan.'

'No!' I protested. 'You should call him Tarzan or Zorro.'

My parents laughed, and stuck by their original choice. So, Alan it was, and he proved to be a right bobby-dazzler, smiling from morning till night.

Home life became one big frolic until, five months later, Alan developed a temperature. The doctor diagnosed pneumonia. The very word sent shivers down our spines: in those days it was a frightful illness to combat. Life became a nightmare as my parents and the district nurse fought for Alan's life. The neighbours took over when my mother could no longer keep her eyes open. My father was, of course, at work most of the time.

My brother had to be kept warm and so his cot was brought downstairs, close to the fire. Poultices by the dozen were applied to his flaming-hot body, but despite his pain he always flashed me a smile.

The crisis came late one Friday night. We all peered into the cot: Mum and Dad and me; the neighbours; the doctor. My mother wept dreadfully:

'Oh, 'e's such a little titch! It doesn't seem fair that 'e should die.'

Alan's breathing started to speed up and then for a moment seemed almost to stop. But at last it became regular again and the doctor smiled:

61

'The crisis is over. He's going to live.'

We all went to bed and slept like stones.

Our joy at Alan's recovery coincided with encouraging news on the war front. After their marvellous victory at El Alamein, the Eighth Army had now captured Tripoli. On 2 February 1943 the last German troops at Stalingrad surrendered to the Russians and this was followed by the Germans' surrender in North Africa on 12 May. On 16 May the RAF conducted its famous 'Dam Busters' strike with the aid of Barnes Wallis's revolutionary bouncing bomb.

Then the news broke that Mussolini had resigned on 25 July and later we heard over the radio that British and American forces had conquered Sicily. The year ended on a great note of optimism with the announcement that on 24 December General Eisenhower had been made Supreme Commander of the Allied Forces in Europe. What a Christmas!

The radio was the centre of our lives. The BBC continued to give us a tremendous service with programmes like *Band Wagon*, with Arthur Askey and Richard ('Stinker') Murdoch; *Monday Night at Eight*; *Henry Hall's Guest Night*; and *Workers' Playtime*, which was Ernest Bevin's idea. Then there was *Garrison Theatre*, with Jack Warner crying out, 'Mind my bike!' And if that wasn't enough, we had *Hi Gang!* with Ben Lyon, Bebe Daniels and Vic Oliver.

But *ITMA*, with Tommy Handley and his team, was the favourite programme. Ted Kavanagh took the title from the *Daily Express* which, whenever it printed a story about Hitler, headed it 'It's that man again'. There was also the 'Radio Doctor', Charles Hill, who later became chairman of the BBC. As for music, you could take your pick from Jack Payne, Mantovani, Geraldo and *Forces' Music Club*. Henry Wood, from the Proms, conducted the premier of Shostakovich's Seventh Symphony, 'Leningrad', the score of which was flown in on microfilm from the beleaguered Russian city. Those were great days!

My air-raid shelter was an Aladdin's cave. By pillaging the local ammunition dump, I was able to fill it with a fabulous collection of bayonets, jackknives, and German, English, American, and

Italian helmets. My favourite helmet was the German one, which was black and very frightening. Wearing this on my head, and sporting a moustache created with a burnt cork, one day I roared out my imitation of Herr Hitler and walked straight into my headmaster's study. He congratulated me on my impression and promptly removed the helmet. The school authorities were informed and, after I had been given a severe telling-off, all my booty was removed from the shelter. But at least I still had the wooden tommy-gun my dad had made me. And he'd built me a smashing model of an American 'Flying Fortress'!

It seemed, though, that the Allies didn't need my help. The German war machine was beginning to show cracks. On 27 January 1944 the Russians lifted the siege of Leningrad after 872 days. That summer, on 6 June, came the momentous D-Day, when the Allied armies landed in Normandy to liberate Europe. The enemy hit back at us with the first V-1 flying bomb attack on Britain on 13 June, but to no avail. The Allies liberated Paris on 25 August and pressed on to do likewise for Brussels on 3 September. But still the Germans continued to attack us, now with their new long-range V-2 rocket, starting on 8 September.

Like the rest of the lads in our street, I kept a diary of those events in my scrapbook. The Battle of the Bulge started on 16 December and the Germans' Ardennes offensive was finally defeated on 16 January 1945, marking the end of the war for them. Russian troops entered Germany on 20 January and, on 25 March Allied forces launched their offensive over the Rhine. Incidentally the last German rocket landed on Orpington, Kent on 27 March. A month later Russian and American troops linked up at the River Elbe. It was all over. Hitler committed suicide on 30 April and on 7 May the Germans surrendered to General Eisenhower. VE Day – Victory in Europe – followed on 8 May.

We all went crazy! The weather was perfect and, joining together in celebration, everyone brought out their tables and chairs to form one continuous table around Probert Avenue. Mrs Dancy baked bread for the entire street. There were speeches and dancing and bonfires that carried on until the early hours of the morning.

A week or so later King George VI and Queen Elizabeth came

through our village in their impressive black limousine. We cheered ecstatically and I managed to get to the front of the crowd to get a good look at them. They both smiled happily and the Queen looked as pretty as a picture. The King, though sensitive and handsome, looked surprisingly pale.

Very soon the air-raid shelters were torn down and gardens quickly made tidy once more.

After the turmoil of the war Britain somehow needed a hero. He came in the shape of Bruce Woodcock. Since my epic journey to see him, he had conquered all in his path. Victory after victory was vividly described to us on the radio by the great commentator Raymond Glendenning and his colleague W. Barrington Dalby. Throughout the war Woodcock had continued to fight and had beaten all comers. On 17 July 1945 he knocked out Jack London in six rounds at the Tottenham Hotspurs' ground to win the British and Empire Heavyweight Championship.

In Probert Avenue we sat around our wooden radios and cheered our heads off. Throughout 1946 it was the same story: a lightning left followed by a tremendous right, and it was all over. He won the European title and was matched against World Light-heavyweight Champion Gus Lesnevich. Woodcock won handsomely by a K O in round eight. It was now felt that he was ready to fight Joe Louis for his World title but he was to be given a final test against the huge American heavyweight Joe Baksi.

On 15 April 1947 the whole of Britain gathered around their radios to hear the fight. Most people believed that although Baksi was a formidable opponent, Woodcock would prove too fast and would win with his famous right hand. Bruce usually took a couple of rounds to warm up but it was obvious, from what the commentator said, that for this fight he was revved up and ready to go.

As the two boxers stared at each other, and the referee gave his final instructions, Bruce was already skipping on the spot. The bell sounded for round one and a strange silence fell over the spectators at the Harringay arena; a silence that filled homes throughout the land. I was sick with worry and held on tight to my mother.

Immediately Baksi, much to everybody's surprise, propelled himself out of his corner and went straight for Woodcock. Bruce sidestepped him smartly with his superior footwork and at the same moment jolted Baksi with a good straight left. As the American tried again he received a similar punch and grimaced, as if to say 'How many more of them are you going to throw?'

Suddenly Bruce let go a right which just missed Baksi's chin and brought an excited shout from the crowd. In the next few seconds Woodcock found himself tied up on the ropes with his opponent but fought his way out with a one-two high on the American's head. In the process my hero took a couple of punishing body blows which slightly slowed him up. Although the commentator described Bruce as smiling at these efforts, Baksi persevered and caught Woodcock with what everybody at the time described as a sucker punch: a big, slow left hook. The blow broke Bruce's jaw and he fell forward and rested on one knee. At that point I looked at my father with horror. I simply couldn't believe what I was hearing:

'Woodcock is down.'

I could just hear the count: 'Six . . . seven . . . eight . . . nine . . . '

'Oh! Stand up please, Bruce,' I shouted.

'Woodcock's on his feet at nine,' continued the commentator. 'But he doesn't know where he is. Baksi hammers him to the body and Woodcock is hanging on helplessly over the ropes. Baksi goes in for the kill and sends a crashing right hand to the jaw and Woodcock is down again.'

Up he got again. But at the end of the first round Bruce was still down when the count reached nine, and only the bell saved him. From that moment he hadn't a clue where he was as Baksi continued to savage him and hand out the worst beating in the history of boxing. The American was a big, heavy puncher with blows that could be measured on the Richter scale! He really was the white equivalent of George Foreman. We couldn't understand why the referee didn't stop it. I suppose, like the rest of us, he couldn't believe Woodcock could be defeated. The awful thing was that Bruce kept getting up; he just wouldn't give in. My weeping was upsetting my mother and my father himself was close to tears.

At last, in round seven, thank God, the referee stopped the slaughter and awarded Baksi the fight. A short while later I huddled with my chums under the gas lamp. We were devastated. It was the worst moment of my life. That evening, as Dad put me to bed, I said:

'He'll get better and come back, won't he, Dad?'

'Of course he will, lad,' he smiled, and persuaded me to go to sleep.

The headlines over the next few days said things like: 'Woodcock rushed to hospital' and 'Doctors fight to save Woodcock's eyesight'. Later, doctors confirmed that the operation had been successful but that Bruce would be out of action for at least a year. Like the little boy in the film *Samson and Delilah* who asked 'Why did Samson die?', I asked my dad:

'Why did Bruce lose?'

My poor dad remained silent.

It was reported in the local papers that Joe Baksi had kindly visited Bruce in hospital and, as he had once himself been a coalminer in Pennsylvania, he would visit the pits in the area, including our own, Hickleton Main.

Racing from school with my chums, I was already there when he arrived: a stunning giant with immense shoulders. So this was the conqueror of my hero! I barged through the large crowds and eventually managed to grab his hand and hold it tight, trying to hurt him. At the same time I shouted up at him:

'One day, I'll box yer head off. You were dead lucky to beat our Bruce.'

The colossus looked down at me and said:

'I was lucky, young feller. I'm sure, next time, it'll be a different story, and he'll beat me. Bruce is going to be all right. Don't anybody worry about him.'

Later that day my dad met Baksi and got his autograph for me.

Ah, well, I thought, he can't be all that bad!

6

Borstal Boys

'Earnshaw's coming! Look out! He's let his dogs loose!' Fred Dyson bellowed.

All the lads ran like the wind, hurtling towards the fence surrounding the orchard we were pillaging. Everybody was loaded down with plunder: Red Russets, Cox's Orange Pippins, Bramleys.

The fence was no obstacle; we cleared it with a mixture of front vaults, back vaults and the good old-fashioned dive. (It is amazing how adrenalin can galvanize the body into making superhuman efforts.) Down the railway embankment we poured, just like a waterfall.

Running, I still found time to berate Dyson:

'Yer stupid, great, gormless sod! This is not like you, Fred. Yer supposed to keep yer eyes open. That was no warning! Earnshaw's on us!' I belted him around the ears and booted him up the rear.

On and on we rushed, tearing across the railway line. At last we had put some distance between ourselves and the snarling dogs. Unfortunately, Fred had stumbled and lost his chicken feed, which had slopped out of its bucket. He was bound to be in serious trouble now. What would he tell his parents? That stuff was hard to come by.

Pain pumped through our bodies and exhaustion started to set in as we pushed ourselves up the opposite side of the embankment and headed for the security of our gardens. Here, in the obscurity of our beloved labyrinth, we could make ourselves invisible among tall, thick hedges, pathways and holes that we could tunnel into: ideal places to hide our scrumptious booty.

Emerging under the gas lamps of our street, we exploded with relief into bursts of laughter.

'Crikey, Frank!' I wheezed. 'Yer should have seen yer face when the dogs barked.'

'By gum!' Tommy Weston chipped in. 'I thought we'd really had it then.'

'Nah,' I said, full of confidence. 'They'll never catch us.'

The commotion was brought to a sudden halt by the appearance of Mrs Carstairs just across the bridge.

'You lot should be ashamed of yourselves. If I 'ad my way, I'd send the lot of yer to Borstal this instant! Yer've been stealin' apples from Mr Earnshaw, 'aven't yer? Come on, empty yer pockets.'

'We've done nothin' of the sort!' I protested. 'Just been playin', that's all.'

'Yer a born liar, Brian Blessed,' she snapped. 'One day yer'll end up in court and be sent to prison.'

Ah, shut yer mouth and give yer arse a chance, I thought to myself, staring at her contemptuously.

'Don't look at me like that, yer cheeky, brazen-faced little devil! Come on, empty yer pockets. Now!'

We obliged.

To her absolute frustration, she was faced with the fact that we were innocent of all her accusations.

'I'll catch the lot of yer red-handed one of these days, but never mind' – there was an almost sadistic quality to her smile – 'Mr Earnshaw's caught one of your gang, Gary Simmonds. He's already been caught three times for stealing. One more conviction and he goes straight to Borstal!'

Christ! I thought, Gary is one of my best friends: brave, true and lots of fun.

Having the courage of a lion, Gary would have attempted anything, but was always let down by the fact that he couldn't run as fast as the rest of us – hence the trio of captures.

'You should leave him alone,' I protested. 'He's done nowt.'

'Nowt? Nowt?' Her voice grew louder. 'Brian Blessed, you've

been seen coming out of that orchard, and not for the first time either. There have also been reports of you and your gang stealing beer bottles from the back of the Horse and Groom and then you go gettin' twopence back on the empties from Betty's Bun Shop! People said yer breath smelt of beer . . . disgustin'!'

'Not true!' I defended myself. 'It was only dandelion and burdock.'

'Yer can lie till yer blue in the face, but yer can't get away from the fact that yer thieve from pea fields, strawberry patches, pubs and orchards. Yer'll sink to any dirty, filthy little trick. And, as for your filthy habit of carrying a dead cat around the place – you'll end up catching something you can't get rid of one of these days and you'll give it to other people.'

'There's nowt wrong in that. Everybody has a dead cat now and then.'

This was quite true. There was always a dead cat somewhere that had just been killed on the road. Before it started to rot, which took five weeks or so, it made a marvellous real-life toy. You could play at being Tarzan with it, hanging it from the branches of a tree as if it were a lion or a leopard. When the smell got a bit too much, you'd bury it and then dig it up every couple of months, fascinated by its gradual transformation into a skeleton. It was a familiar sight to see two or three lads holding their dead cats by the tail and twirling them round in the air.

Mrs Carstairs looked as if she was going to burst a blood vessel:

'Yer'd do well to keep out of my reach, you filthy, disgusting little sod! I'll make yer bloody ears ring one of these days. Does yer father know about yer pretty behaviour at Mrs Shepherd's garden party? It was a disgrace, the way you embarrassed her daughter Anne on her birthday. The guests didn't know where to put their faces. You, hidden up their tree with that stinking cat, pressing its belly so its mucky filth fell on the people below!'

'Well,' I shouted back, 'they broke their promise. They said I could go to the party and then changed their minds.'

'Do you blame them?' Mrs Carstairs blasted back. 'Yer can't get away from the fact that yer a cheap, born thief.'

'Enough!' a voice rang out. It was Wise Owl, Gerald Athey. As always, he kept a detached yet loving eye on us. He had a quality of character that compelled all adults to listen.

'There's nothing wrong with these lads. They're just a bit high-spirited, that's all. They don't mean any harm. Have you forgotten what it was like to be young? If all the world were like these lads then it wouldn't be such a bad place. You might also care to remember how much they help out the old folk: running errands for them and cleaning their windows and gardens.'

'They still need a good thrashing,' Mrs Carstairs rapped out.

'Quite the reverse, Mrs Carstairs,' Gerald retorted. 'They need to be treated with a little understanding and humour.'

This was too much for her and she sped off, muttering as she went that Probert Avenue was going to the dogs.

'Now then, lads. It's all right,' Gerald turned to us and said. 'I've spoken to Mr Earnshaw and he's not going to prosecute. He says that if you'd only go and ask for apples he'd be happy to oblige. You really are overdoing his orchard. I know it's fun and a great adventure, but he says you're breaking his branches and ruining his trees. Look, how about goin' over there and sayin' you're sorry? Give his place a rest.'

Gerald's kindness affected us deeply and we were filled with remorse. We trudged over to Mr Earnshaw's house.

'Sorry, Mr Earnshaw,' we spluttered out. 'We won't do it again.'

'That's fair enough then, lads. Come and see me any time and you can have as many apples as you like.'

'Me mam makes lovely apple pies and that'll be a big help,' I added.

Luckily, Gary did not get his fourth booking. However, a few weeks later he was caught after falling through a skylight at Highgate Junior Mixed School. I wasn't with him at the time but met him as he was heading home, with a badly torn knee and blood pouring out of the savage wound. His socks were drenched red.

'Christ! Gary. What happened?'

'I lost my balance and fell straight through the glass. I landed on a desk, knees first . . . Oh, God! It hurts so much and I can't stop it from bleeding. Some staff saw me and they're bound to tell the police. I'm for it.'

'Put an arm around me and I'll help you home,' I said.

I rapped loudly on the front door of his house.

'Mrs Simmonds, Mrs Simmonds. Your Gary's been hurt in an accident.'

'Leave him with us, lad. Thank you, Brian,' she whispered, her face creased with worry.

Days passed by and there was no sign of Gary. Then, one day, terrible news filtered through the Probert Avenue grapevine: he was to appear in court in Doncaster. Shock waves passed through every house in the street. Good-natured people came forward in droves to testify to Gary's character; he was a much-loved boy.

Gary's words about the police haunted me. We all dreaded the 'boys in blue'. Whenever we were trespassing in a farmer's fields and the cry went up, 'Look out! There's a bobby!' everyone would freeze in fear. Panic would then set in as we caught sight of the dark-uniformed figure with the blue helmet. Not even an angry farmer armed with a blunderbuss could produce such abject terror.

Sergeant Gruber or PC Hawksworth visited the Simmonds household every other day, leaving them pale and tearful, and when the appointed day arrived Gary, accompanied by his father, was driven to Doncaster Court in a police car.

That evening Mrs Simmonds came round and sat drinking tea by our fireside. My mother and father were by her side, offering comfort and love. She poured out the details of that traumatic day:

'It was Jim who saved him.' She fought back the tears at the thought of what her husband had been through. 'He begged the judge to spare Gary.'

Jim Simmonds had a terrible stammer, and a situation such as this did not help matters.

'Please . . . p-p-p-please, give 'im one more chance. I promise . . . I p-p-p-promise, he'll not do any wrong again. He's such a good boy to his mother . . . he helps with errands and shopping . . . nothing is t-t-t-too much t-t-t-trouble for him . . . He'll do anything to help anybody . . . He's not a bad boy – just high-spirited! He's loving and k-k-k-kind, sweet-natured . . . Oh, please, judge . . . I beg of you, p-p-p-please . . . My wife and I haven't slept for d-d-d-days . . . It'll k-k-kill us if he goes to Borstal . . . Oh, dear God in Heaven . . . p-p-p-please take p-p-p-pity on him and release him . . . please.'

Sobbing with relief that it was all over, Mrs Simmonds finished by saying:

'That saved the day: Gary's been released on the express understanding that it'll never happen again.'

Weeks later the fields near the Gam were ripe with peas, awaiting our plunder. Hordes of us raced to the railway bridge leading to the rich pastures, vaulting and somersaulting over the fence. Halfway down the embankment I realized that Gary wasn't with us. My eyes scanned the bridge and focused on his tiny, dejected frame, sitting, with legs dangling, overlooking us.

'Come on, slowcoach,' I urged him. 'Tha'll drag behind and miss all the fun.'

His thin voice drifted back:

'Don't worry abaht me. I'm not feeling well. I'll wait till yer get back, and you can tell me all abaht it.'

7

The Brick Pond

Lord, Lord! methought, what pain it was to drown!
What dreadful noise of waters in mine ears!

Duke of Clarence
Richard III, Shakespeare

As I look out of the window of my tiny study this cool November
evening, I am confronted by the chapter that is the hardest to
write. I have already described in detail the pastoral beauty of
that heavenly stream the Gam, but in complete contrast to this
was a stretch of water situated two miles away and known as the
Brick Pond.

Mothers, fathers, grandparents, uncles, aunts, and teachers
alike, the length and breadth of the Dearne valley, were united
in spelling out the stern warning: the Brick Pond is forbidden
territory. Shuddering with dread, they would furnish all the
gruesome details:

'Its sides are steep, going way down beneath the surface of the
water. Down, down, deep down. There are ledges everywhere that
can trap your body. It's almost bottomless; even the best swimmers
have never managed to reach the bottom. Parts of it are choked
with clinging weeds, rubbish and refuse.'

The picture they painted was as vivid as it was threatening.

'People who haven't listened, who have taken no heed of the

warnings and have gone there, have paid for their ignorance with their lives. It takes the police hours, sometimes days, to find them. Never ever, ever go there!'

For children, especially our gang of heroic explorers, such advice merely added to the temptation. To us this sinister and dark place was an unexplored continent. There could be untold treasures and adventures there and the prospect of visiting this forbidden land soon became irresistible.

Guilty, yet impelled by the thrill of it all, we often ventured to this dark water. In fact, contrary to what our elders would have had us believe, shallow, friendly parts of the pond were infested with sticklebacks. A small branch with a length of string and a bent pin knotted to one end made a fine fishing rod! Small, wiry worms could easily be scooped from the clay for bait. They were irresistible to the fish, and soon our jam jars would be full of writhing tiddlers.

'See who can catch the most?' Caldeon would throw out the challenge.

Left, right and centre, boys stood with their makeshift rods. Subtle twists and jerks of the wrist were accompanied by ecstatic cries of triumph:

'I've got one!'

'I've got *another* one.'

'So 'ave I.'

'Tha's not the only one.'

'By gum, look at this one. It's twice the size of any of the others!'

All the keen competitors would line up at the end of the day, each boy proudly holding up his bulging haul. In his own mind each was the undisputed champion, convinced that he had caught the most fish. Gary Simmonds, me and a close friend from over the bridge in Goldthorpe, Les Eames, would generally win outright. But the losers quickly got over any disappointment and the day would end with a great amount of laughter, wet socks and friendly leg-pulling; the end of a perfect adventure.

When my parents casually asked where I'd been, I'd lie through my teeth:

'Oh, just the Gam.'

I never, ever went to the Brick Pond — at least that's what I told them.

To be accurate, there were two Brick Ponds. The other one had vertical sides of ash and coke and there never seemed to be any visible forms of life in it. There were reports of people drowning cats and dogs there: times were very hard, and the expense of feeding and looking after extra animals often put too much strain on a family's budget.

Alongside this foul place was the brickyard. To me this was a charmless, repulsive, dead place. Heavy metal tubs, brimming with slimy clay destined to be turned into bricks, were all over the place. Dragged slowly along muck-encrusted rails by thick, ugly, rusting chains, they trundled towards a battered shed where the winding wheel was housed.

It was almost as if the Clay Men from *Flash Gordon* were there, by the look of the men working hard, struggling against rain that made their mud-caked skin seem to ooze.

The roaring and clanking of the machinery, combined with the stench of baking bricks and the bellowing workers, was appalling. We had to clap our hands tightly over our ears to keep out the unearthly sounds of this hell-hole.

One day the gravelly voice of the foreman boomed out harshly:

'What the hell are you doing here?'

'Oh, we're just going over to the next pond to do some fishing,' I responded.

'Never mind fishing!' he roared. 'I'll break your bloody necks if I catch you!'

He was huge, muscles bulging through his torn shirt, and wore a mud-stained apron and trousers that looked as though they were made from canvas. Unhappy and bad-tempered, the foreman was always grumbling or shouting. He was clearly consumed with frustration at being unable to catch us.

Although I was only a little lad in short trousers I found nasty and pointless aggression intolerable, which provoked me to reply:

'You just wait till I'm grown up, you brussen, four-eyed pillock! I'll come back and gee you a right bashing!'

Immediately, he charged forward like a rampant bull, only to be met by a hail of stones and rocks, thrown with such accuracy that they halted him in his tracks. The shower faded, and when he looked up, like Macavity the cat we had disappeared.

Running like speeding bullets, we arrived at the Brick Pond panting, laughing and excited.

'By gum!' Frank Parkin wheezed. 'Tha's not scared of anybody, Bless!'

'Nah! Blokes like that don't frighten me. Me Dad would mulicrush him. I've got ten uncles as well, who could all flatten him any day. Next time I'll bring me German bayonet and stick it up his arse!'

We all laughed about my threat as we busily assembled our fishing rods.

Fresh spring days followed one after the other. Nature was at its peak and the pond was alive with familiar sounds, such as the 'Brevit . . . Brevit' of the common and natterjack toads. Black eggs clustered in their thousands, rippling gently in vibrating jelly, filled the entire surface of the water; so much so that our much-loved stickleback fishing was hampered and catches were few and far between.

Yet we didn't ignore the chance to collect as much toad spawn as we could. Greedy hands plunged deep into the sensual, oozing jelly, which we would hurriedly slip into one-pound jam jars, filling two at a time. Boots and socks discarded, paddling in the shallow end of the pond, we covered a considerable area; hunting, watching, splashing.

Suddenly there was rejoicing all round: a rare large, yellow frog had been found.

'Let's have a look, let's see!' came an excited chorus.

Tank Guest held the creature out, proudly displaying what was actually a unique find.

'By gum, Tank, that's a smasher!' I raved.

'Aye,' said Caldeon approvingly. 'I bet that's as good as having your LNER train book?'

'Oh, no. Nowt's as good as that!'

The train lover had got his priorities right.

'Good old Tank, tha's got the best catch of the day.'

'Soldiers,' Caldeon, our captain, said a little later, casting a stern eye over his troops. 'You're disobeying orders. Some of you are getting too cheeky . . . brazen-faced . . . You're getting too near the deep side. If I see anybody get within six feet of the deep end I'll put them on extra guard duty outside my air-raid shelter.'

Everybody sobered up after this terse but well-intentioned lecture. It immediately brought back ghostly echoes of the warnings our parents had given us.

A couple of weeks later something I'd seen at the Brick Pond led to an extraordinary confrontation with several of my teachers. My description of the toads' mating habits provoked an unexpected reaction.

'They're all dead,' I explained. 'I can't understand it. The little male holds on to the female and after they've mated they won't let go. They all gather together in a great big ball, bigger than any football. They choke each other to death.'

This was instantly and arrogantly dismissed.

'Nonsense, Blessed. This is another one of your fairy stories.'

The disbelieving teachers loomed over me, pouring scorn on my repeated protestations. The maths teacher, whom I loathed, was particularly vitriolic. As he bent down and pushed his pale face close to mine, his thin, metal-rimmed glasses gave him the look of Himmler.

'The word "pathological", Blessed,' he sneered, 'look it up in a dictionary, lad, because that's what you are rapidly becoming – a pathological liar who lives in cloud-cuckoo-land. Never paying proper attention in class, from day to day you fill the heads of other pupils with your ridiculous stories of dinosaurs and space monsters. This madness has got to stop, lad.'

'It's not madness. It's not. It's true,' I insisted. 'I got a big stick and prodded at them, 'cos some of them were still alive; but I couldn't part them. There's thousands of them, all over the pond . . . rotting.'

The teachers were amazed and furious at my stubbornness, and in turn their anger made me dig in further, as usual.

'That's enough Blessed. Put out your hand, my lad.'

With that I received 'six of the best': three strokes of the cane on each hand. It was very painful, but there was no glimmer of discomfort on my face for them to gloat over. After all, I was in the right. What I had reported was absolutely true.

'In future, Blessed,' 'Himmler' concluded, 'kindly confine your observations to the aquarium tank in the natural history class-room.'

'Confine, confine', I thought to myself, it's always bloody 'confine'. They'll never stop me saying and doing what I feel is right.

My story had an immediate impact on scores of the boys. After school a mass exodus took place, all heading for the Brick Pond. There they saw it for themselves, and on all sides a chorus of voices burst out:

'Bless is right.'

'They're all bloody dead!'

'My God!'

'Uuuuuuhhhhh!'

'They're all rotted.'

'They're all smelly and putrid.'

'Christ! Pull some to the side.'

The macabre scene seemed to strike some form of ghoulish excitement into their souls. Galvanized, they darted back and forth from one end of the pond to the other.

'Come over here!' cried a lad who had reached the steepest side, overcome by the grim spectacle before him.

'Careful, it's deep over there!' shouted others. The lads who real-ized exactly how dangerous the situation was tried to alert the more adventurous, but their shouts were drowned out by the cacophony of shouts and yells as more and more of us grew reckless. A group was gathering at the far end. Danger, deadly danger.

Of course, it had to be Tank. Poor, sweet Tank. The boy who loved railway engines and never did anyone any harm. He was swanking that he wasn't afraid of the water.

'I can swim,' he shouted, and moved out on to a narrow promontory that was directly over the deep part of the pond.

David Dunbar looked at me in alarm and joined me in bellowing out:

'Come back, you daft sod. You can't swim. For Christ's sake, come back!'

We might as well have saved our breath. Tank continued to behave in a bizarre manner. He actually began to act out a character called the 'Diver' from the familiar radio series *ITMA*. His impersonation was unerringly real.

'Don't forget the Diver, sir. Don't forget the Diver,' he joked.

As he spoke these words, his arms assumed the position of Tarzan about to make a dive. Whether he intended to plunge in or whether he simply slipped, we'll never know. In an instant he was in the water. Everything was still. Time stood still. Bodies were held in tight, as in a vice, unable to move. Eyes stared, fixed, unflinching, unbelieving. Mouths became parched. Screams, horrible screams, from all sides.

'Jesus! Get a branch, get a pole somebody!'

'Can't anybody swim?'

'You, Maurice, you can swim.'

'No, I can't. I can only do three strokes.'

'Help. Get some help, for God's sake.'

'Move, bloody move now, get some man. Quick!'

Lads moved like lightning, hurtling off in all directions, desperate to find someone; somebody who would know what to do.

'Where's Caldeon? He can swim.'

'He's not here.'

It was appalling: none of us could swim.

'Tank!' I yelled as loud as I'd ever done. 'Do the dog-paddle, try and do the dog-paddle. Head for the gully – we can reach you there.'

Did he hear? Could he hear?

'Get him, somebody. Jesus! Get him, somebody.'

'Oh, my God, he's going down . . . in the middle!'

Poor Tank's face. Convulsed with fear, white, terrified.

'Aaaaahhh . . . aaaaahhhhh.' Strange, strangled cries of horror and despair came from his lips. His arms flailed, flapped and splashed in all directions.

One moment he was down, the next he was up again, his hair matted and plastered to his face. Weeds clung to his face, drawing him down.

His glasses were now gone.

'Keep going, Tank. Keep going, for Christ's sake, keep going.'

Nobody was there to help.

'Can't anyone find a man. Bloody hell, there must be somebody.'

Branches and logs were hurled in from all sides – all to no avail.

'Come on, somebody. I know where there's a big log.'

Heaving it through the bushes, we hurried with it towards the edge. We stopped. Total shock. Silence; ice-cold silence.

Tank was no longer there. The surface was still and calm, as if nothing had happened: still, calm water with only the gentlest of ripples.

Sobbing broke the silence as lads fell to their knees, distant despair in their eyes.

'Gone, gone, gone,' came a terrible whispered chant.

'He's a goner.'

'Where?' I pleaded. All fingers pointed to the middle of the water.

'He just disappeared.'

I couldn't accept it.

'He might still be alive,' I said, trying to reassure myself. 'There could be an air pocket under one of the ledges.'

'No, he's a goner. There's nowt to be done.' There was an unnerving air of certainty about what they said. 'He's dead.'

Adults arrived in droves, but they were too late. Too bloody late.

'Back away from the sides now, back away,' said policemen as they fixed white ropes around the area. They barked savage, unfeeling orders at us:

'Keep clear . . . you. Back away. Do as I say!'

Interrogation followed. What had happened? How, why, who and where? Vicious accusations filled the air.

'Serves you right, you stupid little buggers. Now get off home and think yourselves lucky that you're not in jail.'

The eyes of the other adults burned fiercely: we were the objects of their scorn. Their faces were unforgiving and condemning.

'Aye,' they snarled, 'the whole lot of you ought to be sent to Borstal.'

I couldn't take this.

'It's all your fault,' I burst out furiously. 'You should fence this rotten place up.'

'Cheeky sod!' an adult snapped. 'You'd only climb over it.'

'Then you should have it electrified. That would have kept us all out.' I wasn't about to give in. 'It's all *your* fault. Tank would still be here . . . and we can't swim either!'

Eventually, hundreds of children from surrounding schools stood looking on at the watery grave, all getting smacked by their parents, angry at them for being there but relieved that it wasn't their child in the water.

Later that day I was back at home, nibbling quietly at my tea, not breathing a word of what had happened to my mother and father. With me were my friends Brian Lee and Caldeon, both absent when the calamity happened.

Rain fell as I returned to the pond. The crowds had thinned out. Men were diving into the water, poking and probing into the depths with curved wooden poles, reaching under the ledges, trying to find Tank.

'Aye,' a morbid elderly spectator whined, 'he's bound to be under a ledge, you know. I've seen all this before.'

'Turn yer eyes,' a policeman requested. 'They've found him.'

Faces looked away, quietly praying.

Tank's uncle stood there, screeching and howling like a banshee. His high-pitched wails cut through the murmur of prayers. People moved forward, embracing Tank's parents.

'He's at peace now. He's in the arms of God,' they said quietly.

I peered out, my face having been buried in a bush. My spine went cold with dreadful, foul horror. I shuddered at the sight: Tank's body was horribly swollen, lifeless and limp. His L N E R cap was no longer on his head.

The rain continued to pour down, making the surface of the pond ripple.

From that day on the swimming baths at Thurnscoe and Wath-on-Dearne were made far more available to us and so, in a way, Tank's death saved many lives.

A year passed. Lads of all ages from Bolton-on-Dearne, Highgate and Goldthorpe assembled by the Brick Pond. Standing in a long line and wearing our woollen swimming trunks, we waited for the signal. Our leader raised his arm slowly and with a single downward movement shouted:

'Dive!'

Instantly, with great resolve and power, we propelled ourselves into the air, hit the water and settled into a steady crawl: arms driving, legs heaving with great gusto.

Success! We'd reached the opposite side. We all roared triumphantly. Caldeon ordered us to head for the middle of the pond. Once there, we rolled over and dived straight down.

Down, down, down we went, to the murky depths of that evil pool. We touched the bottom and beat the bastard for Tank's sake.

8

The Lands Where the Jumblies Live

Tank's death heralded the end of my childhood; it also marked the end of my life at Probert Avenue. My parents decided to 'flit' and exchange houses with a family on the new estate in Bolton-on-Dearne, two miles away. I was sad to leave Goldthorpe but the new house was cheerful and was close to the Gam and the Seven Fields.

Despite constantly getting on the wrong side of the teachers, I had enjoyed my junior school well enough. And yet somehow I couldn't shake off the feeling of having been a stranger there.

Apart from the odd art class or English lesson, it is the day I imitated Bud Abbot and Lou Costello that has stayed most happily in my memory. For two hours I entertained the entire school with my impersonation. It was a shared experience of pure happiness and contentment.

Of course, I was entirely ignorant as to what it all signified. My appetite and energy for life was enormous, but from my guts to the top of my head I felt untapped and untouched by the teachers.

I am not blaming them: I was a strange, complicated lad. The occasional muttered, 'Oh, dear, what do we do with that Blessed boy?' was perfectly understandable. For me, too, the longing for some kind of breakthrough had been painful in the extreme.

For God's sake! Didn't they know that when they had crudely rapped my knuckles or pulled my ear to stop me dreaming, they had interfered with something rare that was developing in me? The same happened to other children too. How could the teachers not realize that we children were unique individuals, with original gifts that needed to be nurtured? We had brought something new from birth, as all generations do.

It is such a delicate age between seven and eleven, and the rigidity of school shocked me. It seemed to me that our teachers were out of tune with the song of nature. Their harsh objections stunted my progress, and on such occasions I instinctively returned to my core and quietly protected what I knew was real. In this state I was neither rude nor rebellious – simply happily silent!

How distressing that the teachers didn't want to know about the window I was looking through to the limitless landscape beyond, where knowledge and being could be one and lead to understanding.

The cursed, boring eleven-plus examination loomed on the horizon. Still, I told myself, it would soon be over and done with and then there would be six uninterrupted weeks of glorious summer holidays. Oh, what bliss! What larks!

Equally joyful was the realization that I would represent Highgate Junior Mixed School as their fighting champion, against Goldthorpe Junior School. The match was to take place immediately after we had sat the eleven-plus.

On the great day I doubt if any exam invigilator was ever as flabbergasted as when I announced with great confidence after twenty minutes that I had finished.

'Are you absolutely sure, boy?' the teacher asked incredulously.

'Yes,' I replied. 'It was easy, sir. A piece of cake!'

The truth was, I was so impatient to get outside and warm up for the fight that I had filled the exam papers with sketches of dinosaurs and noughts and crosses. Lads like me weren't interested in exams.

So there I was, shadow-boxing in the middle of the football field, pausing now and then to look at the purple haze on the distant horizon. Out there was Sir Arthur Conan Doyle's Maple White Land, full of giant white apes and thunder lizards; a countryside crammed full of great crested newts, slow-worms, vibrant shining yellow frogs, and radio sets buzzing with stunning BBC adventure series.

My face grew red as my impatience to fight increased. Out poured the other lads after the exam, all intoxicated by the prospect of seeing the scrap. They were drawn to me as to a magnet, and were so disappointed to find me on my own! For half an hour we killed time, but my opponent never turned up.

Eventually we decided to have a fifty-a-side rugby match. Our normal game was football, but we felt the alien game of rugby would best suit our pent-up, frustrated energies. So it proved! What a match! Thump, bash, swear, run! All with a little tennis ball. Never had I enjoyed myself so much, and to this day I regret never having played rugby!

A golden summer passed and it was now the autumn of 1947. I was in my eleventh year. The transition from Highgate Junior Mixed School to Bolton-on-Dearne Secondary Modern came as a complete shock. The regimentation of the junior school was replaced by an even sterner regime. Loud, cold commands from unfamiliar teachers and prefects echoed down the corridors:

'Keep in line!'

'No talking!'

'Hold your heads up straight, idiots!'

'March in a straight line, or you'll stay all day until you can!'

Eventually, in alphabetical order, we lined up in the assembly hall, numbering five hundred or so. Half the school was girls, the other half boys, and 'Ne'er the twain shall meet'. That rule was absolute.

The mood in the hall was quiet, still and utterly depressing. The headmaster, Mr Brown, a medium-sized man with gaunt features and far-away eyes, presided over us from a podium. His second-in-command, Mr Taylor, stood alongside him. A huge man with broad shoulders and a rather red complexion, he was also noteworthy for the fact that he was a 'Golden Gloves Wrestler'.

These two impressive personalities loomed over us, exuding total authority. In a strange, quiet delivery, Mr Brown slowly introduced the rest of his staff. To his left, stretching down the side of the hall: Mr Outhwaite, Mr Musket, Mr Bedford, Mr Mann and Mr Dalton. Each man's head nodded in turn, acknowledging his name. The roll-call continued on the opposite side: Mr Ogly, Mr Jones, Mr Donaldson, Mr Moran and Mr Hardy.

The last-named sported a drooping moustache which combined comically with his long face and thin body, rather reminiscent of Ichabod Crane in *The Legend of Sleepy Hollow*. His appearance generated a great deal of laughter, which evaporated as the 'Golden Gloves Wrestler' rasped out:

'If I hear any more of that, I'll have you all complete a two-thousand-word essay on laughter, *after* four p.m., in my study . . . and woe betide anybody who makes a spelling mistake!'

Silence held sway once more as the headmaster continued in his strange, detached voice:

'In this school you will find strict rules. These you will learn from your teachers, and I promise that if you do not adhere to them, you will have *me* to contend with. Within this framework of rules you will find ample opportunity for an enjoyable education. This school offers a wide range of subjects from English to sport and gardening.

'You see the large emblem behind me, depicting an eagle flying to the stars? That symbolizes our school motto: "To the uttermost". That is what I expect from you. Let us pray.'

His piercing eyes closed as he intoned the morning prayer:

'. . . to labour without asking any reward, save knowing that we do Thy will, Amen.

'Now, march in single file to your respective classes. And no talking!'

At last I found myself in Class 1C – the bottom class – under the watchful eye of Mr Dalton. We were considered somewhat hopeless, and the best that could be expected of us was that we should behave ourselves and possibly learn a few basics. In short, we were the dunce class.

Any teacher who found himself in charge of 1C considered himself to be doing some form of penance. Mr Dalton was no exception. He had a stocky frame, thinning hair and tired eyes that viewed us with a kind of weary fatalism.

Mr Dalton nodded to the prefect, who quickly and dutifully

planted the dreaded blank sheet of paper on each desk, heralding the start of an arithmetic lesson.

'We'll see what kind of standard you've arrived at,' our sleepy teacher muttered as he began to cover the blackboard with elementary sums.

Jesus Christ, I thought to myself. This is awful! What a boring pillock! Oh, God. I was so depressed by it all.

Except for a few friends from my previous school, there was not a friendly face in sight. My thoughts drifted to the recently departed summer and a splendid holiday at my Uncle George's. Bliss! My eyes closed. I could smell the sweet air and see the low-lying rock pools at Newbiggin, full of pretty fish and multicoloured crabs.

'What's your name, boy?' growled Mr Dalton, rudely awakening me from my dream.

'Blessed, sir,' I answered.

'Well, get on with your paper and stop gaping like a moon-struck calf!'

The days passed uneventfully. It seemed to me that our teacher had allowed something to die within him years ago. He was not by nature unkind; indeed, he possessed a gentle sense of humour. But, like his smile, it seemed to stop at a certain point on his face. Then the edges of his mouth would freeze and his face would collapse into a frown. I was to learn later that my hasty analysis was far from the truth.

Unfortunately for him, we soon discovered how to penetrate his defences and try his patience, which gave us no end of fun. On such occasions he would charge up and down the room screaming blue murder at us, doling out severe doses of the cane for good measure.

Of course, *we* were in charge. Whatever mood took our fancy would be inflicted on our unfortunate tutor. But even at this stage of my young life I realized that it was not something that I was proud of. A sense of ignorance and inadequacy pervaded me. Where was the magic now? In my genuine urge to improve and learn? The realization of my folly in not treating the eleven-plus with the seriousness it deserved, weighed heavily on my mind. Gradually, a slothful degeneration began to take place.

My first impression of our headmaster, as being a remote and cold man, was quite wrong; his watchful eyes and penetrating mind had observed it all. A tremendous change was about to take place.

It all started when he took charge of our class. We were on the edge of our seats, trying valiantly to please him, when he suddenly stood up, smiled mischievously and said:

'I think you need greater help than I can give you; someone of the order of a giant! Do any of you know what a giant is?'

'Yes, sir,' I spoke out. 'Someone five times bigger than a man.'

'Indeed, Blessed,' he replied. 'But I am thinking of someone even larger than that . . . a complete earth trembler! In a week's time you will all be confronted by it,' he smiled.

When the day arrived, we stood with bated breath in the classroom, awaiting the promised Titan. Mr Dalton was no longer there; his chair stood empty.

The tension was unbearable. Then, gradually, a faint sound grew louder. Light footsteps approached. The door slowly opened and Mr Brown, with a hint of a twinkle in his eye, quietly and proudly announced the name of our new teacher:

'*Mrs* Brown.'

Never can jaws have dropped so fast and so low in disappointment and shock. The expression in our eyes varied from utter disbelief to deep incomprehension.

My God! Women were not supposed to teach here. It was an absolute rule. We felt completely let down. Where was the promised giant?

Not only was this 'giant' a woman, but she was also quite old, in her mid fifties, and very small – no more than five feet tall – and with spectacles on the end of her nose. Two woollen cardigans festooned her upper body; large, thick woollen socks ran down into a pair of cushioned slippers. Her whole appearance filled us with abject despair.

There was a long silence as the woollen pixie surveyed us. Mr Brown coughed to clear his throat:

'I leave you in good hands . . . '

In a second he had vanished. An ominous silence reigned. Then there was a slight movement as she looked down her long nose to get a different angle on us. All the while absolute stillness prevailed.

Maybe she needs a mushroom to sleep under, I thought as I stared back at her.

Then, just like a real pixie, she did two pirouettes on the spot, drew a deep breath, turned her back on us (a dangerous thing to do) and began to wipe the blackboard clean. We all broke into quiet fits of giggles. Then Maurice Cook, one of the more eccentric members of the class, imitated the pixie pirouette, provoking even more suppressed laughter.

It is doubtful, in the entire history of warfare, that a missile has ever been propelled with such destructive force as the wooden board rubber that hit Cook on the side of the head. The pinpoint accuracy would have impressed William Tell!

In no more than a second, from within the folds of her cardigan, the Pixie brandished a small, thin cane, lashing out like lightning on the fists of the half dozen or so gigglers who had not had time to hide their smirks, or their hands.

Cook was holding his ear, shocked and in pain. He then found himself bent double as the Pixie, with amazing energy and speed, applied a vice-like grip to his other ear and propelled him through the classroom door, straight to the headmaster's study.

There, the Pixie informed us on her return, his dancing career was receiving great encouragement.

There was not a vestige of ill will or temper in her behaviour. The demonstration of discipline she had given in those few seconds was awe-inspiring.

As quickly as it had begun, it stopped. A great silence again filled every nook and cranny of the room. We all stood like ramrods as she moved her hand across the blackboard, scribbling scores of numbers.

Then, stopping abruptly, she pinpointed her aim with the remaining half inch of chalk and threw it into the waste-paper basket with great accuracy. We instinctively ducked our heads, thinking it was for us.

'Einstein.'

She spoke quietly.

'Albert Einstein: the greatest living scientist, the creator of the theory of relativity . . . But of course, I am addressing blockheads who are liable to confuse him with Frankenstein!'

We didn't laugh at this.

'You are all known throughout the school as "woodentops", and that at every turn of your heads you leave a deposit of sawdust . . . is that how you wish to remain?'

'No,' we replied weakly.

'Speak up, I can't hear you.'

'No.' The response was firmer this time.

'Very well,' she grimaced, 'I promise you this: in six months' time you will have a deep love and understanding of the likes of Einstein, and a knowledge and growth that will astound the rest of the school! I will use all my powers to drag you into the light so you can learn to hold your heads up.'

After another pause she gently requested that we should sit, at the same time nodding to the returning Maurice Cook to take his place.

'This is a maths lesson, I understand . . . normally.'

She smiled.

'Let's forget about this. Instead, I'm going to read you a story: *The Hound of the Baskervilles* by Sir Arthur Conan Doyle.'

We were transfixed. She read brilliantly, filling our minds with haunting mystery. The reading ended with the words:

'. . . it was the footprint of a giant hound!'

'Oh, please go on, Mrs Brown,' we begged.

'I will,' she smiled. 'Another day.'

Those 'other days' proved to be wonderful, and school became a place of exciting achievements. Mrs Brown's astonishing drive, determination and infinite capacity to bring out our individual gifts was awe-inspiring.

I found myself racing to school, in the knowledge that something completely original would be revealed to me. Shakespeare, Shaw, Wilde, Masefield, Keats, Wordsworth: these and many other writers we were to discover, and their influence was phenomenal.

When she spoke of the Greeks and their history, we could feel the stones of the Parthenon and the heat of the sun. The wanderings of Odysseus came alive when Mrs Brown recounted his adventures, tears running down her cheeks as she conveyed his yearning and loneliness.

For Mrs Brown we worked with integrity and zest, trying our utmost to please her and meet her high standards. She had a sweet way with incentives, giving presents and prizes of apples and oranges, comics, rare magazines and books on various subjects.

I managed to win prizes for English essays three times in a row! This, combined with good reading tests, edged out my fellow competitor, Raymond Finbow (incidentally a marvellous goalkeeper), by two points. For my efforts I won two *Eagle* comics, a stack of copies of *Hotspur* and *Wizard*, and a bag of oranges.

That was just fine, but I was not so happy when she informed me that I was to have the honour of accompanying her and the headmaster to the Picture House to see *Henry V*, starring Laurence Olivier. The film proved to be fantastic, but the ordeal of sitting next to the headmaster left my neck stiff with fear and tension.

My parents noticed the obvious improvement in my school work, which I now raced home to show them.

The year had been a strange one. My hero, Bruce Woodcock, was still fighting for his sight in the Leeds Infirmary, as a result of the Joe Baksi fight, and this had depressed and slightly undermined me. We all hoped he would soon recover and make his comeback.

Charlton Athletic had won the FA Cup by beating Burnley 1–0 at Wembley, and now my favourite team, Manchester United, were looking really promising. Players like Johnny Carey, Jack Ashton and Charlie Mitten were making their mark. Our local team was Dearne Athletic, a good, strong side who played in the Sheffield Association League.

In every field, meadow, road and backyard, balls were kicked high and low. Coalminers on their way home from the pits would find the streets full of boys playing football.

'Get on the wing, Mr Green!' we would shout, and he, like all the adults, would gladly oblige. My parents bought me a top-class football, which was expertly looked after and cared for: dubbin was rubbed into it and it was kept at just the right pressure. It glistened black, and when you kicked it there was a wonderful pinging sound.

Sometimes, on a Saturday, I would play from nine in the morning till five in the afternoon, after which my face would match my old red-dyed shirt: the team colour of Manchester United.

'Good God! Look at him, Billy!' my mother bawled out one day. 'He looks like a tomato . . . And don't bring those boots in 'ere. Take 'em off and clean 'em out there.'

'Right, Mam,' I smiled, taking good care to do it properly, for they were smashing, hard-toed professional boots with Frank Swift's autograph printed on the instep.

The confidence we now had as a class displayed itself on the football field, as we beat all and sundry, including teams that were older than us.

As Mrs Brown helped us to develop, other teachers also began to play an important part in our education: three new members of staff arrived: Mr Mills, Mr Longdon and Mr Quemanet. All proved to be outstanding, and I began to realize how lucky we were to have so many good teachers.

Mr Ogly, the gardening teacher (who was a priest in his spare time), constructed reinforced, glass beehives in some of the corridor windows. There, at our leisure, we could study the bees going about their daily routine.

Gardening interested me enormously, and Mr Ogly and I became good friends. He was a slightly off-beat character with a deep, crusty voice and a face that was always deeply tanned, because he spent so much time outside. One of his eyes seemed unable to focus properly and when lighting his pipe in class he had the strange habit of shouting 'Come out this boy!' before proceeding with the matter in hand. This varied from the attributes of compost and manure to the mileage that Jesus Christ must have put in when delivering his teachings.

Mr Donaldson, the art master, possessed a complex and mysterious personality. He was quite tall, with stunning black eyes, a light-brown skin and greasy black hair. When he smiled, his moustache highlighted his magnificent white teeth. He had a powerful, sinewy physique, displayed to advantage when he was teaching football and other sports.

The first time we met him he looked at us carefully before breaking the silence by saying gently:

'I enjoy a serene, quiet life, which is essential for the creation of art. In this classroom you will learn a new approach to life that, for a while, may make you feel that you are standing on your head ... This will soon pass. One word of warning: I have never had to call on the assistance of my friend Jeremiah!'

At this, he produced a massively thick stick from under his desk, which took our breath away.

'Looking at you fine young men, I'm sure that I won't need his help. As an introduction to my thoughts and this new way of thinking, let me say at once that there is no such colour as white: it is orange-grey!'

Among his many gifts, Mr Donaldson proved to be an astonishing actor. He seemed to possess voices within voices, and to my young mind, had a strong similarity to Sir Donald Wolfit. Seeing him perform at the Dearne Centre in Romberg's musical *The New Moon* was a revelation. He handled straight plays and musicals with total ease. In the middle of an art lesson he would deliver speeches from Shakespeare and Marlowe. I am in no doubt that he would have made a definitive Captain Ahab in *Moby Dick* and could have performed a fine *Othello* twice nightly.

Shortly before the summer holidays of 1948 we learned that Mrs Brown was to leave us. It was revealed that her stay had been intended to be a temporary one, to put us on the right road. We were devastated. She had become the light of our lives. Dear Pixie had led us to the rainbow's end, to the pot of gold. It is no exaggeration to say that she had shown us new frontiers and lifted us to ever-greater heights.

As unobtrusively as he had introduced her, Mr Brown gently took her hand, and led her away. She wept and laughed uncontrollably as the class begged in unison:

'Please don't go!'

Gradually her tiny frame disappeared from view and we never saw her again. I was, however, to hear from her many years later,

in no uncertain manner, when I was acting in the BBC TV series
Z Cars.

Around this time my beloved red tabby cat Tibby miraculously
found his way to our new house. Frantic scratching on the back
door alerted us. I cried and hugged and kissed him until he was
in grave danger of being loved to death. Quickly, food of all kinds
was put in front of him, and he set about the serious business of
expanding his girth.

That night, in front of the fire, with my long-lost friend curled up
beside me, life was perfect once again. And what was more, Bruce
Woodcock was beginning to make a steady recovery. Rumours ran
through the area that he would definitely fight again. The walls
of Troy were being rebuilt, and proud Hector would emerge once
more with his spear and handsome brow.

Despite my mother's disapproval, I continued with my boxing
and started taking tuition from some of the many professional
trainers in the area. As a result I ended up fighting for the
school.

I was a solid, six-and-a-half-stone fighter, although it was
impossible to go after the title of 'top dog' at my present
school as the boys in the higher classes were much older and
much bigger.

But the time would come, I thought, as I pounded at the
swing-ball and big punch-bags. Every day seemed crammed with
excitement and activity.

At school Mr Quemanet was taking us by storm, energizing us
by starting the morning's lesson with:

> 'Jicketi-can, Jicketi-can . . .
> The train goes running along the line,
> Jicketi-can . . . '

Our bodies swayed backwards and forwards each day to the
rhythm of the 'train song'. He possessed colossal energy and
the combination of a fertile imagination and versatility was
impressive and stimulating. His stocky physique, Continental

manner – he would wear shorts some days – and his broad, ready smile made you feel happy and free. Geography, history, drama, art – he invested all the subjects he taught with freshness and a much-appreciated simplicity. The headmaster had obviously taken a great deal of time in selecting him to fill the gap left by Mrs Brown.

That spring Mr Quemanet suggested that our class should put on a play and present it to the rest of the school.

'Find a tale,' he said. 'And put your own words to it.'

This excited us, but we puzzled over what to put on.

'Rumpelstiltskin!' I shouted out. 'That's a right grand tale, that is!'

So Rumpelstiltskin it was.

The two weeks of rehearsal were absolutely terrific, Mr Quemanet passionately urging us on and showing joyous appreciation of our efforts.

Maurice Cook, known as 'Mousie' to his friends, played the Miller's daughter, Billy Platt played the Miller and everyone else the villagers. I played Rumpelstiltskin himself. To this day I still remember the strange, deep-throated, frog-like voice I used for the part. This, combined with gymnastic leaps and bounds, seemed to work very well.

We performed the play only once, during a lunch hour, and the whole school attended. The headmaster kindly allowed my mother to come (unfortunately, my father was at work) and it was a sweet sight to see her sitting with all the lads in the assembly hall.

Our audience roared their approval throughout, thoroughly enjoying the performance. Suddenly I was experiencing the same ecstatic, wide-awake feeling that I had felt doing my Abbot and Costello act at junior school.

Afterwards the praise flowed, and Mr Jones, who was to be a major influence in my later years, told my mother that I was a good actor.

'What is acting, sir?' I asked.

'Well, you'd better find out, Blessed!' he smiled.

The following day, at lunch time, we all choked on our food as Mr Donaldson ordered us to stop eating. With one gigantic heave of his body, he turned to survey us with his fiery black eyes.

'What happened yesterday in the play?' he demanded.

Then, turning again, he targeted poor John Cox, who offered: 'Blessed was funny, sir . . .'

After a look of contempt, Mr Donaldson roared dramatically: 'Blessed did something of paramount importance.'

At this stage he was looking directly at me. I was praying that he wouldn't ask me what it was, for I had no idea what he was talking about. He continued:

'When the Miller's daughter finally guessed his name, during his mad laughter, what did Blessed do? . . . He paused! He paused! Probably the most important effect in dramatic art. That's what he did, he paused!'

Stillness reigned over the hall.

Mr Donaldson wrapped his hands around Cox's head, covered his eyes and at the same time and in a half-reptilian voice, recited:

> 'They went to sea in a Sieve, they did,
> In a Sieve they went to sea . . .
> Far and few, far and few,
> Are the lands where the Jumblies live;
> Their heads are green, and their hands are blue,
> And they went to sea in a Sieve.'

Then he quietly asked:

'What does it mean?'

Poor Cox was bewildered.

'I don't know, sir.'

After a long pause I jumped up excited and sang out:

'I know, sir. It's just like the polly glide – when you rub one hand round your tummy and at the same time keep patting the top of your head with the other. You have to be in the right state to do it proper.'

Mr Donaldson nodded, smiling mysteriously, and remained silent.

God! I thought, I love this school.

96

9

Dove of Peace

'You're not Picasso! You don't look like Picasso! If you're Picasso, let's see you draw something.'

The speaker was Yours Truly. It was 1950 and, along with scores of other lads, I was in the grand circle of Sheffield City Hall's Oval Hall, to confront the pretender with the tanned face and silver hair who claimed to be the great artist.

This fellow with the dark circles under his eyes didn't impress us as being a genius. On the contrary, he reminded me of the simple-minded feller who sold the 'Green 'Un', a football paper, in Mexborough on Saturday nights. This impostor was amiable enough and didn't seem to mind me examining his jowls with my hands, but what was a dead give-away was his false Spanish accent! You could tell, straight away, he wasn't from Spain. For my money he reminded me more of Carmen Miranda, who was famous at the time for singing, 'Ay, ay, ay, ay, ay like you vairy much', and that's exactly how this funny gentleman sounded. I ask you, Picasso indeed!

'That's not a real Spanish accent,' I said.

'Well,' he replied in a kind voice. 'It iss thee ... er ... how shall I put it? The best I can do. You must forgive me; my Engleesh is not a vairy good.'

We all stood about, now knowing what to say. Eventually, I shot back at him:

'If you're from Spain, how much did it cost you to come here?'

Again he smiled, and touched his head.

'Oh, much money. Many Engleesh pounds. All worth it, young man, to be here to celebrate peace.'

'You see: he doesn't know how much it costs,' said the lad next to me.

There was only one thing for it: we had to get him to draw for us to prove who he was. Out came a pencil and paper and he began to doodle. It didn't take him long and the results confirmed to us beyond any doubt that the feller couldn't draw properly.

'What's that supposed to be?' we chorused.

'It iss a Dove of Peace.'

If that was supposed to be a great drawing, by one of the world's greatest artists, then I was a Dutchman, and I said so.

But you certainly couldn't fault the man's patience as he smiled for the umpteenth time and said:

'Thees iss zee first time in years zat I 'ave a creetic.'

He then laughed so loudly that we all had to join in. The adults had been finding the encounter hilarious and they laughed too, at the same time taking us to task for doubting the great artist's word.

Gradually it penetrated our thick skulls that we had behaved badly and that the foreign gentleman in front of us was indeed Pablo Picasso.

The artist generously allowed us to copy his drawing as best we could. We had all brought books and bits of paper for autographs and these all came out as we tried to reproduce his strange drawing. When we had finished I asked him why the dove looked so unfinished at the bottom of its body. He was deeply amused by this and answered:

'I am trying to show zat someone is holding zee dove in zeir 'and.'

Picasso then added his signature, which we tried to copy despite the fact that it looked like algebra.

We were attending the Second World Peace Congress. Forty-eight thousand people had come from all over the world to Yorkshire to join hands in peace. Most of them were camped in Wortley Hall, a few miles away, which some days before Dad and

DOVE OF PEACE

I had already visited. It was a wonderful experience: young and old sang songs of brotherhood and peace by the camp-fires; songs that filled one's heart with joy and hope. Guitars were strummed to accompany everyone's favourite song: 'Ain't goin' to be no war, no war, no war no more, no more.' It seemed, at last, that mankind was on the point of achieving universal peace.

Now here we were, in the Oval Hall with over two thousand people, awaiting the arrival of the great black American singer and actor Paul Robeson. We were actually about to see him in the flesh! This was the man I'd seen in stacks of films. His powerful presence on the screen was extraordinary! Who can ever forget him in *Showboat* and *Sanders of the River*, and so many more fine performances? The great man's voice was never off the radio and his records were bought and cherished by an adoring British public.

We all sensed that we were now about to experience a miracle. What a setting it was too. Sheffield is proud of its magnificent City Hall, which was designed by E. Vincent Harris and opened in September 1932. During the Blitz Sheffield was targeted by Hitler's Luftwaffe, and eight Corinthian columns faced with Darley Dale stone, at the City Hall's imposing front entrance, are peppered with tiny shrapnel scars.

Through these columns there are intricate wrought-iron gates with glass panels depicting the coat of arms of Sheffield Corporation. Then, beyond these gates, the foyer has walls lined with Hopton Wood marble in two tones. The domed ceiling bears the coat of arms of the Royal Standard and is illuminated in colour and surrounded by a decoration of medieval design. It is through this foyer that access was gained to the Oval Hall where we were sitting.

As I looked out towards the stage, which was occupied in quick succession by speakers from all over the world, I was struck by the character and spaciousness of the auditorium. It was an oval enclosed in a rectangle with a curved floor and domed ceiling. The greater part of the ceiling was taken up by a huge oval light, and around the hall ran two horseshoe-shaped balconies. The honey walls, beige seats and carpet and rich walnut panelling gave an agreeable feeling of warmth.

Behind the podium were four more Corinthian columns and directly behind them were red and gold patterned pipes that belonged to a magnificent organ. Below, two carved red lions opened their mouths, and between them appeared the Titan himself.

The audience rose and their cheers reverberated all around the hall. The black ambassador of freedom smiled broadly, opened his arms wide and took in the applause. What grace and authority he had! His face shone with health and vigour and his broad shoulders and massive frame shook with emotion. It beggared belief, but the giant before us was even more impressive than on the screen!

Silence claimed the hall. Robeson was like a statue. He placed his left hand to his ear and quietly sang the first few words of the canoe song from *Sanders of the River*:

'I-ee-o-ko I-ee-o-ko. I-ee-o-ko-a jega-day . . .'

The deep majesty of his voice started to thunder out. Its awesome sound, which seemed to come from a god, penetrated our souls. My father bit his lip and my mother wept, her tears increasing as Robeson went on to sing 'Just a Wearyin' for You'. The entire hall seemed to have but one heart as our towering friend sang, for a further hour, negro spirituals and, of course, the stunning 'Ol' Man River'.

On and on went the applause. With a delicately raised hand, Robeson silenced the euphoria. And then once again, beginning with a tiny, fragile voice, he built up to an emotional climax that reverberated around the stage as his bass-baritone voice poured out:

'Your people, my people, all people together will win through to peace.'

In between such fine sentiments he sang out:

'I'll bring my people to freedom – yes! I'll bring my people to freedom – yes! and they'll never know slavery again – yes!'

These words throbbed out like the drums of the Congo, Zambesi and Limpopo. He ended by saying:

'My friends, I will never stop until freedom and peace have been achieved on earth.'

When the concert was over people embraced each other unrestrainedly. I raced to get backstage, dodging every official like a will-o'-the-wisp. When I was caught I said I was Bill Blessed's son and they let me through, for my dad was much respected. Pressing my way into the crowd surrounding Robeson, at last I reached the great man's side. Competing with everybody else talking to him, I managed to tell him that I had all his records and had seen all his films. I told him he had missed out 'Ah Still Suits Me'. On hearing this he roared with laughter, saying:

'Bless my soul, young Mr Blessed. That's the sweetest request ah've ever had, to be sure. It's a twosome, son. You know that? Maybe, son, you can sing the other part?'

'Oh, yes,' I replied, 'I know the words. They are sung by your wife on the record aren't they, sir?'

'Glory me! So they are!' said the surprised giant. 'Sit on my knee and let's be singing.'

It was a funny duet, with me singing the woman's part and Mr Robeson replying. Off I trilled:

'Does yer ever wash the dishes, does yer do the things a wishes, does yer do 'em – no you won't.'

Robeson sang back in a voice so deep it ran up my spine:

'No matter what you say ah still suits me.'

Overawed and out of my mind with excitement I stayed with him to the end of the song and received a hug that knocked me for six!

On the bus home I kept saying to Mum and Dad:

'He hugged me! He hugged me!'

With Paul Robeson now part of the peace movement it was inconceivable that war could ever happen again. Just think of it: no more war! Bloody marvellous!

A few weeks later life at home turned upside down. Looking through the front window one day, I saw my mother walking across the grass in obvious distress. On entering the house she screamed at me:

'He's dead! He's dead! He's dead! ... Oh, my God! ... He's dead!'

101

'What is it, Mam?' I choked. 'What are you talking about?'

'Oh, my God! . . . Lord, Lord God Almighty! He's dead!'

She gripped the sideboard as her whole body shuddered with horror.

'Your Uncle Bernard is dead . . . He's killed . . . killed . . . killed!' she shrieked aloud, tearing at herself.

I tried to hold her but it was impossible.

'It's all right, Mummy . . . It's all right,' I whispered.

'Oh, Brian lad . . . ,' she wept. 'They found 'im in the coalmine this morning, with a big rock on top of 'is 'ead . . . squashing 'im into the ground . . . and 'is legs were stuck out like dead twigs . . . 'E never deserved that, never in this wide world. 'E was only a lad . . . twenty-one, with all 'is life in front of 'im. There's no justice in this world . . . '

Her tears poured out as I held her as firmly as I could. Dad was at work and the only other person present was Alan, who was in the corner crying his eyes out, terrified.

My mother's voice was hoarse from hours of suffering, and she went on intoning the same words:

'Dead . . . dead . . . dead . . . and 'is wife is expecting 'er first baby . . . Oh, dear Jesus . . . Oh, God! . . . This will kill 'is mother. She won't live through this. Bernard was 'er favourite. I can't believe 'e's gone . . .

'I went up there, Brian, for the news. 'Is mother wants to die, Margaret and all the sisters are screaming and 'is wife sits there like a stone, 'er face as white as a sheet, rocking backwards and forwards and not saying a word . . .

'I've never been that close to Bernard but, dear God, 'e never deserved that. I couldn't stay in that 'ouse: the crying is terrible . . . what am I to do . . . what am I to do?'

'I'm going to make you a cup of tea. Sit down. Come on Mam, sit down,' I said. I managed to get her to the sofa, at the same time urging my little brother to come and snuggle up to her. Arms wrapped round each other, they wept while I made the tea.

Bringing a clean, wet rag, I washed both their faces and gently told my mother to drink.

'I never want either of you to go down the mines,' she said. 'Do you 'ear me? Never. They should pay them with gold for the risks they take. When yer dad comes 'ome, I always sigh with relief . . . anything can 'appen: gas, fire, roof falls, and those awful iron tubs that crush people. I've heard terrible stories.

'When that pit buzzer goes, my 'eart is in my mouth for what might 'ave 'appened. At the end of it all, what do they get? Awful lung and chest complaints, so that they can't even enjoy their retirement. As for money, they never 'ave any. If it wasn't for yer dad and yer uncles giving 'im a bit extra each week, yer grandad would 'ave nothing . . . I'm sick to death with talk of coalmines.'

'Don't cry, Mam. Please don't cry,' I whispered. 'Have another cup of tea.'

'Shall I put "Shanty Town Moon" on the gramophone, Mam? That'll make yer feel better.'

'No, lad, thank you,' she managed to smile. 'I've got to get goin'. There's housework to be done and yer dad's dinner to get ready. I'd best stir myself or nothin' will get done.'

It was a mark of my mother's marvellous spirit that she could pull herself together so well. There was nothing she couldn't face. Her greatest gift, besides her love for people, was her impressive common sense, which drew people to her like a magnet, as if she were some kind of Earth Mother.

Now, after this latest trauma, here she was getting on with life. Alan, sensing the situation was improving, asked if she knew where the old clothes were for the rag-and-bone man: he was coming any minute and he had promised him a goldfish in return. In an instant the clothes were found and, with a jam jar in hand, we raced down the street. The rag-and-bone man was on his cart, whistling away through his broken teeth and expertly examining the cast-offs of various people: a goldfish was hard to earn and the discarded clothes had to be of reasonable quality.

On receiving our rags, he made no comment. We stood there apprehensively, at the same time gazing with wonder at the dozens of multicoloured goldfish in glass globes on his cart.

'OK,' he finally said. 'Yer can 'ave this one!'

We cooed with delight. Our fish was black and gold and a good size. Back home in my makeshift aquarium, its pretty colours impressed Mother and seemed to take her mind off the tragedy.

She was right: after Uncle Bernard's death his mother rapidly became ill and died in a matter of weeks. What was more, sweet Uncle Tom had lost the sight in one of his eyes. It was a bizarre accident. Long rubber pipes were used in the mines, from which water was sprayed to keep down the clouds of dust that came from the conveyor belt. Tom was passing the nozzle of one of these pipes when someone inadvertently turned the tap on. The tremendous pressure of the water caused a whiplash effect and like a king cobra the pipe struck him in the eye.

At that time my father was working in the Parkgate seam of Hickleton Main Colliery, at a depth of 900 yards. Previously he had worked in what was the famous Barnsley Bed Seam, which had its beginnings at the turn of the century, and which Dad and another miner, George Harrison, were instrumental in closing down.

They had been alone in the seam, securing sections of the roof with wooden props and using a bow saw to cut them to the correct length, when they sensed something was wrong with the atmosphere. Miners develop a sixth sense in the mines and George and my father went to fetch their Davy lamps, which ran on oil. To their alarm, the light went out, indicating the presence of carbon monoxide. At the same time they both felt a bit dizzy.

'I don't like this, Billy,' said George, and they made a hasty retreat to report the incident. Experts were called in and discovered vast amounts of the lethal gas. As a result, the famous seam was sealed off for ever.

Shortly after my Uncle Bernard's funeral some neighbours raced to our back door with news that chilled us to the soul: my father had been hit by a roof fall. This was the news that all miners' families dreaded and now, suddenly, it had come to us.

The neighbour reassured us that my father wasn't dead but that, as far as they knew, he had a few broken bones. We raced to Mexborough Montague Hospital to find him pale and in extreme pain. He had been working with two other miners when the roof had caved in, hitting him with falling sandstone. This kind of rock is usually made up of large stones and several such pieces had fallen on my father, breaking his thigh bone and a rib and giving him a compound fracture of the leg.

Fortunately his companions escaped unscathed and went at once for help. Like most miners, my father had a basic knowledge of first aid, and realizing that he was in shock, asked the lads to cover him in his coat. After being carried out of the mine on a stretcher, he was brought by ambulance to the hospital.

Throughout this time my mother remained calm and practical: her energies went into running the house and visiting dad. It was going to take time for his injuries to heal. A Thomas splint had been applied to his thigh and leg and taped in place. Tags hung down, holding weights that stretched the thigh so that the leg did not become shorter as it healed. As it turned out, his leg lost about an inch and he always had to wear a built-up shoe afterwards.

Shock was the great danger. Dad told me that there was another man in the ward with a broken thigh and he had died of it. When the doctors considered him fit enough, he was moved to Purbeck Rehabilitation Centre, the miners' home provided by their trade union, close to Doncaster. He was to remain there for three months and was now on compensation pay, which, though not as much as his full wage, was enough for us to live on.

It was the beginning of my final year at school. Studying and learning had by now become second nature to me and to have to leave all this was completely unthinkable. The atmosphere of the classroom, with its inspiring teachers and its well-thumbed books, gladdened my heart.

While there is no doubt that I was a late developer, my progress was now obvious and rapid. I wanted school to go on and on. The thought of winning a scholarship entered my mind, and possibly going to university.

Mr Jones, with all his brilliance and style, poured English language and literature into me; he was an excellent teacher. His Drama Club lessons were instructive and inspiring. My progress was such that I spent a week at Barnsley Grammar School to help in my development. It was a week of pure joy! Incidentally, there I met a teacher called Peter Dens, who was later to direct me in the professional theatre and who was destined to become one of Britain's finest directors.

Mr Jones also arranged for me to attend a two-day drama course held at my own school. This was great news, and I was thrilled and full of anticipation. A professional director from the Bradford Civic Theatre, David Giles, would take the course. Through the years he, too, proved to be an outstanding director and coincidentally I was also destined to work with him years later, on television.

With his long, dark hair and dark eyes, David Giles possessed great style and flamboyance. His voice was smooth and resonant and conveyed a professional sophistication that fascinated us. He had an engaging habit of pronouncing the word 'much', 'mooch'.

I asked him a million questions about the theatre, which he kindly and painstakingly answered. The climax of the course was to act a few scenes from *Macbeth*, and of all the people there he asked me to play the title role.

God, it was exciting! In the same hall where I had played Rumpelstiltskin years before, we now started on the opening scene on the heath. The way David motivated everybody was terrific: he had the witches coming through the doors and windows, expressing his regret that there was not a trapdoor available.

When the course ended I was devastated. From that moment on I was determined to be an actor.

In the meantime school continued to be blissful. My earlier impressions of certain teachers proved to be inaccurate. For instance, Mr Dalton, whom I had judged to be very dull, revealed a charming warmth and sense of humour. Now that we were in our final year the teachers dropped their guard and invited us to join them socially. When I told them about my ambition to be an actor they warmly encouraged me, saying that there was nothing in this world I couldn't achieve if I put my mind to it. They felt that if I could work hard then there was a possibility of my going to the Schofield Technical College in Mexborough and taking O levels, and then maybe going on to either university or drama school. My mind buzzed with the prospect of it all.

One of my friends, a bright fourteen-year-old called Barry

Paterson, had already gained entrance to the Technical College. He was a marvellous pursuit cyclist and seemed destined to be a champion one day. His sense of fair play on sports day was inspirational: he and I always had ding-dong battles over the 880 yards but on the rare occasion that he was defeated he would be the first to offer his hand in congratulation. To him life was joyous and offered limitless possibilities. If ever I frowned, his bright-blue eyes would light up and he would shake me out of my lethargy.

But not even Barry could dig me out of the pit of despondency into which I sank when my mother informed me that I must leave school. I had turned fifteen in October and it was permissible, by law, to take me out of school at the end of the Christmas term. I simply couldn't control my despair as I implored my mother to let me continue. She fully appreciated my argument but urged me to understand her own predicament: my father was still receiving treatment and as a big lad I was eating her out of house and home. She was at her wits' end trying to make ends meet. Eventually I reluctantly agreed and on that black day in December I left school.

Apart from in the coalmines and farms, it was very difficult to find work in the Dearne valley. Accompanied by my mother, I traipsed about visiting various potential employers, only to receive the same answer each time: 'Sorry, nothing available.'

My parents were adamant that I would never go down the pit. A lot of miners felt that way about their children. Eventually my mother arranged for us to meet a local dignitary called Percy Phillipson. This gentleman had started his own business as a joiner and undertaker in 1924, and in those early days owned a workshop and stables. By 1935 he had sold the horses and carriages and bought a motor hearse and two cars. He had also served as a councillor for fifteen years. In the First World War he had been apprenticed to a joiner and had completed his training in the navy: he became a Chief Petty Officer on HMS *Cleopatra* and was joiner to Admiral Tippet. He was also awarded the MBE. We therefore approached his premises in some awe.

Mr Phillipson proved to be a really tough character. Six feet tall, fifteen stone, with massive forearms, he lumbered towards us as we approached the gate of his house, which adjoined his business premises. He appeared to be in his mid fifties, and had short, neatly combed grey hair. After the usual courtesies he addressed my mother rather harshly:

'I can take my pick, yer know, of any of the school-leavers in the area. What's so special about your lad? I'll tell you this: he'll have to work hard if I take him on. I don't give owt for nowt – the most he could expect is thirty bob a week. I'd expect him to work from seven-thirty until five, with an hour for lunch, and also to work half a day on Saturdays.'

My mother was having nothing to do with this, and said:

'Owt for nowt? Thirty bob is slave labour. 'E doesn't come 'ere for less than thirty-five bob.'

The big man looked at me with a scowl.

'Well, I'll tell you what I'll do. I'll take him on for a trial period. If he's not much cop I'll sack him.'

That seemed fair enough and we shook hands on it. I was now an undertaker's assistant. Out of my wage, my mother would take thirty shillings and I would have five for myself. Of this I kept half a crown for my pocket money and put the other half crown into a post office account.

My dad had bought me a fine second-hand Raleigh racing bike, and on a cold January morning I set off for my first day at work. When I arrived at Phillipson's my boss took me into a large workroom, about a hundred feet long by thirty wide. Dominating the centre of the room was a huge sanding machine, while to my right was stacked masses of thinly sawn wood, about eight feet high. The wood was in a rough state ready to be sanded, shaped and polished for coffins. At the other end of the room was a black hearse and large folding doors which could be opened to let the large limousine out on to Goldthorpe High Street.

In the middle of the workroom were two doors: the one we had come through and another leading out to a large courtyard where Mr Phillipson's son, Maurice, lived with his wife in a separate house. Maurice was in charge of the transport side of the business and ran a fleet of buses that took local workers to various factories.

The workroom was a depressing place: half a dozen hanging lights struggled to pierce the gloom and the floor was covered in dirty sawdust. My employer and the surroundings were equally Dickensian. Mr Phillipson had a reputation for being a tremendous worker, and it must certainly have required a titanic effort to build up a business like this. His only competitor now was the Co-operative stores, which ran an undertaking business of its own.

'Any good at catching rats, lad?' Mr Phillipson rasped at me. 'There's bloody hundreds here and I've got just as many traps and can't catch 'em. I'll give you cheese at the end of each day and you can bait the traps. Now, come 'ere. I'm going to put you to chopping wood all day. I want to see those muscles grow so that you'll be as strong as my son Maurice. Elbow grease, lad – I want to see you develop elbow grease! Get stuck in until it hurts.'

He pointed to a large heap of logs in the corner, placed a hefty axe in my hand and departed. This simple job gave me some satisfaction and after an hour I worked up quite a sweat. After a while I was aware of a crush of dozens of people outside trying to look in. They were pressing their ghostly faces to the large windows and blowing energetically to melt the white frost. Gradually they succeeded and I recognized my chums, who had kindly dropped in to see me on their way to school. I waved, smiled and enthusiastically shouted out to them. They returned my greeting, but after watching me for a while their smiles faded. Shock was written all over their faces. Is this what is in store for us? they must have thought to themselves. Here is Brian Blessed, our house captain, and look how he's come down in the world.

After a short time they waved their goodbyes and I carried on chopping wood. They never came again.

Mr Phillipson and I didn't get on well. It wasn't his rough manner that irritated me – that I could readily accept. What got my goat was his habit of slapping me on the shoulder if I did anything wrong.

109

The sanding machine proved to be a problem. This vast contraption had a long sandpaper belt, about eight inches wide, that went round and round and was supported by several spools. There were several grades of paper, starting with a rough surface to be applied when the wood was coarse and more refined ones to be applied as the wood became smoother. The machine itself was about fifteen feet long and eight feet high. The sandpaper, when not in use, would be wound up until the spools looked like giant loo rolls. When I set the sandpaper in position, having placed an eight-foot-long sheet of oak under it to be smoothed, and then pressed the button to start it up, it sounded like a massive power station.

Once it was running well I pressed down on the paper with a wooden float, rather like the one plasterers use. The trick was to not press too hard in one particular spot. If you did you created a long groove on the wood. Once when this happened Phillipson went crazy. All the while I remained perfectly quiet: I was a good lad and knew my manners.

After a few weeks I started to master the technique of sanding and I thought I detected a grunt of satisfaction from the former petty officer. That was the trouble: he was used to ordering people around. In the morning he would enter the workroom like a bear with a sore head. He was always on the move and had a noticeable permanent limp. This, I felt, gave him considerable pain, in addition to his feeling that the people of Goldthorpe didn't really appreciate him. This was particularly evident when the Co-op beat him to it to supply a coffin. One of my mother's sisters, Louise, died and he was incensed when the Co-op got the order. He whispered scornfully in my ear:

'What'sa matter? Aren't I good enough for your family?'

I couldn't help feeling sorry for the boss because you just had to admire the man's gusto and workrate. By contrast, Maurice, who was over six feet tall and raw-boned, seemed quiet and contented. His side of the business seemed to go smoothly and his staff seemed to be happy and relaxed.

Gradually I became proficient at making a coffin. First I would cut the wood to size and sand it. I would then place the wood on the circular saw and cut halfway through the part where the shoulders of the body would be, and then slowly bend it to shape. After this I put the whole coffin together and stained and polished it. I then nailed on the decorative beading and put on the handles. The final touch was to place the pretty white robe inside and secure it in place with a staple gun. When it was finished it looked like a million dollars and I was as proud as punch.

Percy Phillipson was an artist with wood. It was a joy to see him, in his faded pinstripe suit trousers held up by braces and belt, his striped cotton shirt with press collar removed and sleeves rolled up, painstakingly blending two different types of wood together for a unique cabinet. The tension on his face, followed by relief and satisfaction that he had succeeded, made me smile. On such occasions he would go into his house and return with tea and cakes on a tray. Smiling broadly, he would apologize for his manner and say:

'My bark is worse than my bite.'

I couldn't help but like him, despite the fact that the next day he would resume his irksome manner. Life seemed to have turned sour for him and no longer offered any horizons. Within the confines of his little world he seemed to be stagnating. One day, gripping my shoulder hard, he groaned:

'Fifteen years a councillor, lad! That's what I've been. Driven myself into the ground to give a good service to this community and there are still people who won't give me the time of day! I've had Goldthorpe up to here.'

All through these outbursts I would calm him down before knocking on the door of his house to get him a refreshing cup of tea. Mrs Phillipson seemed so different from her husband: she was a peaceful woman with a ready smile and a reassuring manner.

After about five months I would occasionally answer Percy back, particularly if he was rude about my father and his politics. The local elections had taken place and Dad, now home again and working hard, had been put forward as a communist candidate and had amassed only 207 votes at the local elections. Percy gloated about the defeat, saying:

'He didn't do too well, did he? If communists feel so strongly about Russia they should go and live there.'

To his surprise, I said:

'Shut it, Percy! I'm not interested in politics. If you want to discuss it I recommend you invite my dad over and he'll eat you for breakfast.'

It was then my turn to be surprised as Percy ended our brusque exchange with a laugh, telling me:

'Communist or capitalist, Brian lad – we've all got to work.'

Around this time I was amazed to receive a letter from Fred Lawson, a full-time youth leader for the West Riding County Council's Education Committee, asking me to be part of the new Dearne Youth Drama Team. I was thrilled, as I was getting nowhere in my endeavour to act. It was also the first time in my life that I had received a letter. I felt so important.

Mr Lawson had seen me act at school and felt I was just the chap for his team. It was a turning-point in my life and I could never thank him enough. The director was a gentleman called Johnny Adams, who ran the Adult Dearne Players and who was renowned for his versatile talent.

Life now took on a new meaning for me, and we entered our first production – a one-act play called *The Legend of Raikes Cross* – at a drama festival in Mexborough and came third. We were cock-a-hoop with pride!

My work became more bearable, since I had the youth group to look forward to in the evenings. Percy now referred to me as 'his lordship' and regarded the whole venture as a waste of time.

I occasionally had visitors pop in to watch me work. One day a retired boxer came in, Chibby Chubb, who shadow-boxed all around me, making the customary whistling noises as he applied the old one-two. He was short, grey-haired and had a flat nose, and stated that he was the Lightweight Champion of the North of England. When he asked what I felt about his style I replied that he reminded me of Ike Williams, who had been a great World Lightweight Champion in the late Forties. This seemed to please my new pugilistic friend and from that day on he was a regular visitor.

Percy frowned when he saw Chibby, and remarked:

'He's Lightweight Champion of bugger all.'

My employer was also sick to death of my failure to catch the rats. Little did he realize that I had made no efforts to trap them: being on my own most of the time, I enjoyed their company and watched them frolicking for hours, throwing cheese to them at every opportunity.

Trade was good and sometimes I would work late to get a coffin ready for the following morning. They all varied in size and once, sadly, I had to make a tiny one for a baby. Strange as it may seem, my job was a cheerful one. I rarely saw a corpse, but on one occasion I did have to visit a house to get a dead man's measurements. Unfortunately, when we came to put the body in the coffin he seemed to have grown a couple of inches. Percy was furious:

'What'sa matter with you Brian? Can't you bloody read a measure?'

'There's no point in arguing,' I replied, and set about squashing the body into the coffin.

Percy looked at me aghast.

'Well,' I continued. 'He can't bloody feel it.'

After this experience I made the next coffin six inches too long, and during the church ceremony somebody said:

'It looks as if he's taken his bloody money with him!'

Percy suddenly decided that he wanted to have his own morgue. On the day that it arrived all hell broke loose. The foundations had been built a week beforehand and the builders thought it would be a simple task to erect it. However, they had not taken into consideration Percy's constant interruptions. Chaos reigned. I kept well away and made tea for the workmen during the lunch break. They were furious and frustrated and said they didn't know how I could work for such a madman. The whole project amused me enormously.

Soon after the morgue was finished and operational we had our first body in it. Percy, red-faced and bad-tempered, asked me to go and measure it, adding:

'That's if you're not scared of ghosties.'

113

When I arrived at the morgue I opened the door and saw the corpse covered in a white shroud. Gingerly, I pulled it back and recoiled in horror: it was my friend, Barry Paterson!

'Oh, God!' I groaned, sinking to my knees. 'Oh, no. Not him! Dead? How could he be?' (I learned later that he'd been hit by a car while he was on his bicycle.) I was unable to get up, and slumped back against the wall, paralyzed with shock. After God knows how long Percy appeared and said:

'What the bloody hell do you think you're doing? This is not a charity, tha knows. I don't pay good money for nowt.'

'Shut your cake-hole, Percy,' I said softly. 'For God's sake shut your mouth and give your arse a chance.'

Percy was furious at my outburst and jumped in saying:

'Watch your mouth, lad, or I'll give you a good hiding.'

'Yeah? You and whose army?' I replied. 'I'd hit you so fast and so bloody hard you'd never even see it!'

I was on my feet now and meant every word of it.

'What'sa matter with you?' Percy roared. 'Have you taken leave of your senses?'

After an eternity I passionately explained to him about Barry and told him how he was my friend:

'Christ, Percy! He had a great life in front of him! He had such high hopes: he was going to be a champion; he was going to be a professor. He could be anything. Bloody hell-fire! Look at him! Dead as a bloody doornail! His blue eyes are rotting already. For God's sake, I'm fed up with you, your job and this fucking awful bloody world! There's no justice anywhere. I'll wash his body! Give me the white spirit and poxy carbolic soap. No one touches him but me and his family.'

After this tirade Percy showed me another side of his personality – the Chief Petty Officer of HMS *Cleopatra* side – and held me close and comforted me. We washed Barry together and he made me tea and drove me home.

It was impossible for me to do the job any longer and I arranged to join a plastering firm called Riley's.

Barry's body was moved to another morgue because Percy's

started malfunctioning. My last three days were spent making my friend's coffin.

Elbow grease! That was the expression, and that's what I applied to the job in hand. Never did a coffin look so impressive! It shone with a brightness to match the pursuit cyclist's brilliant blue eyes!

10

The Man with the
Sausage Fingers

'We must be bold and go to Mexborough to try and join the
Theatre Guild!'

My words made my acting chum, Harold James, stop in
his tracks.

'Christ, Brian! No!' he protested. 'They won't accept us; we've
no education, and they're made up of schoolteachers and the like.
Besides, they're all brilliant actors and grown-up people – they'll
eat us for breakfast!

'Have you forgotten how marvellous the Northern Children's
Theatre were, under that professional director, Esme Church, when
they visited Dearnside with *Smugglers' Cave*? Even Mr Lawson,
the youth adviser, made it plain as to what an uphill battle we
had to remotely compete with 'em. And they're nowt compared
to the Theatre Guild!'

Harold's long, thin frame shook and his gaunt, pale face and
dark eyes magnified his shock.

'Nah,' I persisted. 'They won't mind about our education and
we're sixteen: grown-up enough. They can only say no.'

Despite my well-considered arguments Harold remained unconvinced, feeling that we would be overstepping the mark: we were
learning a lot with the Dearne Youth Centre and to make overtures
to Mexborough was tantamount to treachery.

'But we only do a single, one-act play a year there,' I smiled.
'For the rest of the time we're just twiddling our thumbs. We've
got to progress and extend ourselves. God, Harold, I saw the

116

Theatre Guild's production of Noël Coward's *Private Lives*, and the standard was even higher than Sheffield Rep's!'

This brought more protestations from Harold. But for the next half hour I used every cheap trick I could think of to make him laugh. He had a hearty sense of humour and the ploy worked perfectly.

The fact of the matter was that I was far more scared than Harold. And the thought of going there alone terrified me, so it was only possible in his good company.

We ended the conversation by shaking hands on it and blurting out wonderful words of resolve. However, over the next few weeks our bravery dissipated, to the point where we were trying to avoid each other. The situation was only resolved by our colliding, head on, outside Bolton-on-Dearne's bowling green.

'Oh, my God!' we both groaned. 'We're a right pair of shitless cowards . . .'

After a long pause, we continued in unison:

'Ah, bugger it! We'll go!'

Late on Friday night, two days later, we approached the Schofield Technical College, where the Guild rehearsed. The caretaker at the front entrance demanded sternly:

'Who are yer? What do yer want? We're closin' in half an hour.'

'Oh,' I said. 'We've come to join the Theatre Guild.'

'Have yer indeed? So, yer want to be actors, do yer? I can tell at a glance you'll never make it. Never in a million years.'

Beaming with self-satisfaction, he chortled: 'My nephew, Kenneth Haigh, is taking it up professionally. He's an actor and a half he is, and he'd act you two off the stage. Anyway, if yer goin' in be quick and sharp abaht it! They're in the middle of a dress rehearsal and won't take kindly to being interrupted. So watch yer p's and q's.'

This upset Harold and he questioned the wisdom of continuing, but the caretaker's boastful manner sparked off my stubbornness and we stepped inside. Directed by much friendlier people, we made our way down a series of corridors to the hall where the dress rehearsal was taking place. We could hear voices and even

117

through the big doors could feel the energy and talent of the artists inside.

My heart sank, and I became unsure and nervous.

'Jesus, Brian! . . . They sound too good for us!' Harold gasped.

We were rooted to the spot. At that moment a beautiful voice sounded in our ears:

'May I help you?'

It belonged to a pretty girl carrying a tray of coffee.

'We've come to join the Theatre Guild,' I said. This is my friend, Harold James, and I'm Brian Blessed.'

'Pleased to meet you,' she replied. 'My name's Mary Carr. Please come in.'

I took the tray as she opened the door. The pilgrims entered. Oh my! Oh, my! This was indeed Shangri-La. The hall was a large gymnasium with thick ropes hanging down the walls. Acoustically, the place was first-rate.

Our eyes were immediately drawn to the magic ritual taking place at the far end: large groups of people were handling the problems of a dress rehearsal in perfect harmony. Sitting unobtrusively to one side, we watched their expertise with total fascination. The play was a comedy called *The Rotters* (I can't remember the author). The actors had a concentration and ease that profoundly impressed me. Their attention to detail of character, instinctive use of the stage, and sixth sense with props, were riveting.

At the centre of it all, playing the lead and directing, was a great bull of a man named Harry Dobson. His large, red face beamed with personality and warmth. Energy radiated out of him. One moment he was roaring, the next using delicate modulation.

'Give, yer buggers, give!' he bellowed, but seconds later he was gently encouraging a young actor:

'Find your light, Ken.'

Then his large frame grew as he took a deep breath, spread his arms, and silenced the stage with a sweeping gesture.

'Just a moment, everybody . . . Hold it, Jim, I think we need a little more light here. Can you give me some blue?'

'Yes, Harry, yes,' came the reply from the scenic designer and electrician, Jim Meek.

The problem resolved, the rehearsal galloped on. Harold and I found ourselves laughing constantly – quietly at first so as not to be noticed, then much louder as we became more and more involved. We were so wrapped up in it all that we failed to notice the time; the rest of the college was now closed and the caretaker had long gone home.

The play came to an end just after midnight, leaving us both wiping tears of laughter from our faces. But in an instant overcoats and scarves appeared and people were ready to go, shouting goodnight to each other.

Suddenly I felt like an intruder and hung back in a corner out of the way. At the same time I felt lonely and sad at not being part of such a splendid team and a wave of depression crashed over me as I reflected that it was scarcely possible for me to join such people.

Meanwhile Harold had been busy shaking hands and congratulating everyone, but he too now stood alone, in the middle of the hall. There were still a few people around as the lights were switched off and in the dimness I felt it was safe to venture out. Not so. A large, dark figure powered towards me, addressing me in a stentorian voice:

'I hear you want to join us, lad?'

It was the director, Harry Dobson. His direct manner left me excited and breathless.

'Oh, yes, sir!' I blustered.

'Sir?' he roared. 'My name is Harry Dobson. What's yours?'

When I told him, he laughed even louder.

'Blessed, eh? And Blessed by nature. Who's your friend?'

Harold was introduced, and Mr Dobson, as I now called him, pounded his huge hand into ours in turn.

'Glad to meet you both. Well, you've seen our society. What do you think of us?'

'Oh, marvellous,' we replied. 'We want to be part of the Guild with all our hearts . . . '

He pushed his great, grinning, red face into ours, his huge nose almost hitting us, and whispered:

'It means bloody 'ard work and sacrifice. If you're not capable of a hundred per cent effort, you can forget it. Goodnight to you both. You know where to find us.'

The next week *The Rotters* played to full houses, and the Theatre Guild collected its customary rave reviews.

As invited by Mr Dobson, I raced to Mexborough in the hope of becoming part of the group, but all to no avail: they were having a fortnight's break.

The days dragged by as I kicked my heels waiting. Harold decided going up to Mexborough two or three times a week would take up too much of his time and decided to drop out. In all fairness he had a point: Mr Dobson would want his body and soul; it was a tremendous commitment. Though my every fibre seemed to want such dedication, part of me felt grave doubts.

I had been taking speech lessons with a fine teacher in Rotherham called Frank Cooper because my accent was still very strong, and if I wished to interpret the classics this had to be rectified. In my speech lessons the aim was to lose my accent but never my Yorkshire style of expression. This had to remain at all costs or my speech would have had a dead quality. All this required gradual, sensitive work, from my teacher as well as myself. Of course, at the completion of it all, I could still use my accent whenever I pleased.

English regional accents are colourful and wonderfully expressive and deeply convey a sense of our people and tradition. Myself, I find the Yorkshire accent absolutely magnificent. Indeed, there are times when writers, particularly on TV, do not do it justice and I rage with frustration. They have a tendency to make Yorkshire people slow and dull-witted, whereas nothing could be further from the truth. The Yorkshire accent combines richness, pride and nobility. I have always done my utmost to defend my beloved Yorkshire tongue, and in no way do I wish to disparage it.

However, to return to the impending meeting with Mr Dobson, my doubts about attaining the required standard of speech and entering a higher standard of theatre generated genuine fears.

After the Guild's two-week break I found myself once again looking into the large, red face of Mr Dobson. He had sent instructions that I should arrive an hour earlier than everyone else and in this time he set out his well-considered ideas on acting:

120

Above: At the age of eleven with my four-year-old brother Alan.
Right: Alan at the age of five – as good as gold . . . though I did once spot him smoking behind the compost heap.

Most of the Probert Avenue Gang, also known as the Homecroft Wanderers – the scourge of South Yorkshire. The team's captain, Caldeon Williams, is standing third from left, with the goalkeeper, Cedric Webster, on his left and Colin Picton with the ball.

The Brick Pond. So peaceful and serene – who would suspect it of claiming so many lives?

Top: Aged nine. I tried to say 'cheese', but couldn't see the birdy.
Middle: Mum and Dad in their early forties, outside our new home in Bolton-on-Dearne.
Bottom: 'To the uttermost' was the school motto of the Bolton-on-Dearne Secondary Modern. I adored the place and its teachers.

Top: On a picnic with cousin G
Aunt Florrie, Alan, Mum and cousin Gary in Newbiggin-by-the-Sea. *Bottom:* Seasid
heaven – fish 'n' chips, sun, sand and sea and the magic of the Geordie people.

Top: I won this knobbly-knees
competition, with Alan a close second and Gill a pretty (close) third.
Bottom: Early morning in Newbiggin: time to explore the rock pools and observe the
distant church slowly crumbling into the sea.

The majestic presence of Paul Robeson. His deep, thundering voice reverberated around Sheffield City Hall's magnificent Oval Hall (*below*) at the Second World Peace Congress. Picasso sat in a central position on the first balcony.

...ith apologies to Picasso, whose drawing I copied in 1950 as I sat alongside him. It's ...t a bad copy; his signature looked like algebra. The original, drawn in red ink, can be ...en in the Graves Art Gallery in Sheffield.

No 19,957   MONDAY, NOVEMBER 13, 1950   A KEMSLEY NEWSPAPER.

CONFUSION RULES IN 'F
CONGRESS H.Q. For Problem Congress

'Forts
Bord

"CONFUSION worse confounded" became the trade-mark of the retreating Second World Peace Congress in Sheffield today.

Two coach-loads of delegates arrived from Buxton for the much-advertised "Torch of Peace" ceremony, but soaking rain drove them to shelter behind the pillars of the City Hall.

RUSSIAN NOTE

Bevin Will
Reveal
U.K. Reply

BRITAIN'S reply to the Soviet Note suggesting a meeting of the Big Four Ministers on the ...ation of Germany.

Veteran South Yorkshire Labour stalwart, Lady Mabel Smith, stood on the hall's steps to watch the arrival of the torch.

The bedraggled "torch" runner entered Barker's Pool, accompanied by a motorcyclist and propaganda loud speaker unit.

Phones Off

He ran round the War Memorial and came to a standstill before a crowd composed largely of newsreel cameramen and reporters.
Engineers, busy

PABLO PICASSO on arrival at Sheffield L.M.S. station on his way to the "Peace" Congress at the City Hall.

SUPERFORTS
—North Korea and road and ra
Forty bomb
Sakchu, five mi
Yalu River, and
of Chongju.
Other bomber
for rail and
Sinuiji, tempc
capital, and th
lakchu.

'NEARI
On land a
U.S. Marine
than five n
through icy hil
miles-of-the-Cl
in the north-ea
The advance
Marines comb
either side wl
U.N. troops
four miles on
front throu
Neither Br
Korean forc
tion

NEW

Weather MURDER CASE

Top: 'Give, yer buggers, give!' was his battle-cry: the man with the sausage fingers, Harry Dobson, who stormed and bullied, cajoled and dragged me into the light.
Bottom: My heart's delight, the Mexborough Schofield Technical College, home of the Theatre Guild.

'It's all about giving,' he insisted. 'The more you give in life the more you get out of it. I can see that you're passionately determined. That's fine, but be careful. Your very determination can blunt you and create extreme tension. Being competitive can stunt you artistically. Balance, you must learn balance. That's the key. Of course, you feel you have a lot of ground to make up and you are impatient to get on. You simply have to trust me to help you approach the task with grace. Remember, the maximum effect with the minimum of effort – that is grace.

'The basis of all is love. You say you want, eventually, to enter the professional theatre. This, of course, is a fine ambition, but it has its problems. The commercial theatre is tremendously competitive and in that atmosphere you can, at times, lose your way and forget yourself. In a nutshell, you can bury your conscience. You will always have to remind yourself to constantly love and honour your fellow actors.'

It was at this moment that I felt the majesty of this wonderful grey-haired man (he was possibly fifty). His blue eyes shone vividly: two pools of infinite depth glowing with the fire of one who was truly awake. But it was his hands, his huge, red, sausage-like fingers, that stunned me into silence. They opened and closed with vibrant sensitivity, pointing upwards towards heaven, reaching for the right word or idea and then, on receiving the correct blessing and information, they conveyed the secret message to me.

His powerful voice ranged from bass to tenor, the different registers serving him by turns as he made his point. On and on his voice sailed, taking me with him on his odyssey.

'Honour talent wherever you go and never criticize your fellow actors. Don't be afraid to make a fool of yourself – everyone should be allowed to do that. Progress is like a stairway: when you've taken one step there will always be a slight interval as it flattens out. But don't lock yourself in a cupboard when this happens. Have the courage to keep your heart open, so that you may share with your fellow artists. You will come to understand just how much you need other people – you can't do it on your own.

'Well, lad!' he laughed. 'I've said a bellyful. Let's hear you read

121

Robert in the play in front of you, *The Silver Cord*. Don't look so nervous – I won't bite you!'

Gradually I relaxed and managed to read with some conviction.

'Not bad at all,' nodded Harry. 'You've a hell of a lot to learn, but you have a naturally good voice and basically know how to use it. Your lessons with your speech teacher are beginning to pay off. Right, you big ape! I'm goin' to give you your first part – the one you've just been reading – Robert in *The Silver Cord*. But, by God, you've got to work, lad!'

I was completely stunned; unable to move or speak.

'Well, lad? . . . Well, what do you say?' he roared.

'Oh, thank you, sir.'

'Sir!' he bellowed back. 'Call me Harry.'

'Oh, thank you, Harry, sir!' I replied.

That mighty mentor put me into overdrive. I sped down Adwick Road on my racing bike, plunging into the misty valley, my legs pumping and the dynamo pouring energy into the front light until the beam reached its zenith!

From that day on my trusty steed took me back and forth to rehearsals, as my life assumed a new meaning. Up hill and down dale, with a puncture here and a puncture there, but nothing delaying me for long.

Rehearsals took place three times a week, and in addition Harry devoted Sunday afternoons to giving me private tuition. Dressed in my favourite, navy-blue blazer and grey flannels, as the mature summer sun's rays penetrated various corners of the rehearsal room, I moved and responded to Harry's direction.

Gradually I began to learn how to relax and smile.

'That's better, Brian, lad,' he laughed. 'You do sometimes become quite grim. Perfectly understandable, having shut yourself in your room in your desire for knowledge; though don't forget: an actor draws from life. All work and no play does make Jack a dull boy.

'You also seem to feel that there's a massive difference between natural, everyday expression and that which occurs on stage. You are quite mistaken; it is rather like singing being an extension of speaking. Hamlet's advice to the First Player, for instance, is to be recommended to all actors. I sense you have buried your sense of humour but this will automatically and quietly return.

'What would you say is the most important thing you have learned so far in your life?'

'Oh,' I gasped. 'When I was a child, up to the age of fourteen, I felt as if I was outside, looking in on the adult world, never to be part of it. I was simply an observer. The world of entertainment, in particular, seemed another sphere altogether: remote and inaccessible. Then came the astonishing realization that that viewpoint was only a mirage; transition was possible. This was followed by the realization that I did have something and I could participate. I felt marvellous.'

'Yes, you big ape, but your main problem is that you feel you have to take a sledgehammer to a nut. You feel you have to push and heave and make a gigantic leap to be part of it, instead of simply opening a door and sitting down. You'll learn, Brian, you'll learn. Just as you'll learn that Edgar Wallace doesn't compare with such as Chekhov and Shaw.'

The weeks went by and Harry's magical teaching continued into the early autumn, right up to the first night of *The Silver Cord*. The play was a splendid success. My mum and dad sat in the audience, proud and astonished that I should be part of such a fine company.

There was then a break before casting took place for the next production. Harry went off on holiday and I found myself in no man's land. My blood was up and my mind was bubbling with ambition.

Unknown to anyone, I had written a letter to the Bristol Old Vic Theatre School stating that I was twenty years old, had completed my National Service and had won a scholarship and was therefore eligible for drama school. A pack of lies! I simply couldn't help myself; I dreamed night and day of going to the Old Vic School.

But it seemed impossible! If only I could be back at school again, especially where they taught drama. I knew I was potty but I longed for it so. The very image of Bristol and the West Country made me want to sing: scrumpy, Somerset, the university, Clifton suspension bridge, the Avon Gorge, the old Theatre Royal, King Street, Long John Silver, the port, *Westward Ho*! and the Bristol Channel pointing the way to the trade winds and far-distant lands. Not to mention a legendary movement teacher called Rudi Shelley, who taught at the Old Vic School.

Open up the pearly gates and let the pilgrim in!

The answer to my letter arrived and I was invited by the principal, Edward Stanley, to audition for the school at the Theatre Royal, where the Bristol Old Vic Company was based. I was really terrified, and what was more, I had barely enough money for the train fare: it would have meant drawing out my entire savings of three pounds ten shillings from my post office account. Fortunately Dad gave me two pounds; otherwise I would have had to have made the journey by bicycle!

Of course, there remained the problem of convincing the theatre school that I was twenty when I was really only sixteen. As for my National Service, there were rumours every day that it was about to end and so I didn't see this as a problem. Whatever the ifs and buts, I was determined to see it through. If I could only gain a place at Bristol I could then apply to the South Yorkshire Education Authority for a scholarship.

My parents were totally unaware of these problems, though I sensed Dad smelt a rat and had doubts about me embarking on the venture without Harry's blessing.

I was soon on the train and speeding towards my destination. The early morning was bright and the smoke from the funnel sent small, fleeting clouds across the meadows. The train's motion was friendly and seductive: jicketi-can-jicketi-can-diddly-dee-diddly-dee-diddly-diddly-diddly-dee.

The poet's words danced deliciously in my mind:

Faster than fairies, faster than witches, bridges, houses, hedges and ditches. And going along like troops in a battle, there go the horses, there go the cattle.

A quick glance in the mirror to check my collar and tie. Face is fine, I thought. Complexion pale and smooth with rosy cheeks. Hair, with correct side parting, smooth and neat. Laurence Olivier himself had nothing on me, I mused. Not so, for Olivier and his contemporaries were professionals. Wow! Professional! Would I ever be part of that world?

As the journey progressed I became more and more uncertain that it was such a good idea after all. My mind drifted back to several months earlier, when I had made several efforts to get to London to see shows there. My objective then had been to get to Waterloo to see the Old Vic Company.

My job as a plasterer involved working right up to midday Saturday, and so the only time available for such enterprises was Saturday afternoon. Most of my wage, three pounds fifteen shillings, went to my mother, with five shillings for myself. Two shillings and sixpence of this was needed for my speech lesson, leaving me with half a crown. One shilling and sixpence of this I put in the post office, keeping the remaining shilling for pocket money. The train fare to London was quite beyond my means. So I stole rides on goods trains, in cattle and coal wagons. Despite the pee and crap, I preferred travelling with the cattle as they were friendly and warm. It was much more uncomfortable sitting on coal and being open to the four winds. I also did a little hitchhiking. Nottingham, Derby and Birmingham would go whistling by, yet each time I would fail to get to London. When I returned home at God-forsaken hours, filthy, bruised and cold, my mother would think I was out of my mind and complain bitterly about my torn clothing.

Once, I did manage to get to the Old Vic but the show was long over. After inspecting my filthy clothes a bemused attendant showed me around the foyer. That was enough for me. I had actually been in the foyer of the Old Vic!

Now here I was trying to get into the Bristol Old Vic School.

'Temple Meads,' shouted the stationmaster. I had arrived.

It was midday and my audition was at three o'clock: plenty of time to walk the mile or two to the theatre and take in the scenery. Temple Meads was a delightful station, built of light-brown sandstone, with graceful, towering arches.

For a while the route was dull, but then the scenery changed and I found myself among impressive Georgian buildings. Unexpectedly, there was the inner port, with its brightly coloured yachts and seagulls screeching everywhere. The air was fresh and vibrant.

On reaching the city centre I was directed to nearby King Street. Wonder of wonders! There, at last, was the Theatre Royal, home of the celebrated Bristol Old Vic Company. Feeling myself on hallowed ground, I walked slowly, with head slightly bowed, holding my breath.

There wasn't much time to spare, for it was now two-thirty. Luckily, there was a café next to the theatre, where I fortified myself with several cups of tea as I was in a frightful state of nerves.

In next to no time I was being escorted by a smart young lady to a seat in the foyer, where I found myself in the company of several young men who were also auditioning. Their manner was assured and their speech impeccable, but the most disturbing thing about them was that they were clearly much older than me.

As each performed, his voice filtered through the half-open door. They were terribly good – there was no doubt about that – but they all seemed to be doing the same part: Hamlet or Richard II. Their voices also sounded rather similar. Despite my nerves I felt I could compete favourably.

Soon I was ushered around the graceful, green and gold auditorium to the stage. A slim, sensitive-looking man in his early forties stood in the front row and introduced himself:

'Hello, Mr Blessed, my name is Anthony Holland and I am the assistant director of the school.'

'Please to meet you,' I replied, and much to Mr Holland's amusement I handed him, in small change, the fee for the audition: ten shillings and sixpence.

Within seconds I plunged into the opening chorus speech from *Troilus and Cressida*, followed by Aaron the Moor, from *Titus Andronicus*. I was then beckoned down into the auditorium.

'What an unusual choice, Mr Blessed. Very exciting. Is that really your voice? Rest assured, I could offer you a place immediately but, if you don't mind my saying, you do appear a great deal younger than twenty.'

With that I confessed everything and received a slap on the back and hearty encouragement from Mr Holland. Two days later I received a letter from him saying that he was most impressed but felt I should complete my National Service and then apply for the school again.

Several weeks later the hair at the back of my head was being held in a vice-like grip by a massive hand with sausage fingers. It was Harry, feigning fury. Nevertheless, the pull was forceful enough to bring more than a suggestion of tears to my eyes. The whole scene was watched with great amusement by the assembled Mexborough Theatre Guild company of twenty or more people.

Harry's throbbing, bass-baritone voice seemed to transmit its energy right through to his fist as he strengthened his grip and shook my head like a rag doll.

'I am wasting my breath,' he growled. 'Patience, you bloody great ape! Patience! I ought to knock your fat block off. Takes himself off to Bristol, without so much as a by-your-leave. Takes himself off in a time machine to a landscape which, as yet, has no place for him. As Kubla Khan so aptly puts it, "The caravan to nowhere". God in heaven, Brian lad, you haven't even mastered the basics yet! Take a good look at your mother and try and acquire a little of her common sense.'

At this point the ladies laughingly begged Harry to take pity and to release me from my agony. This he agreed to do on receiving my assurance that from now on I would be a good lad.

What a relief! I was beginning to see stars. Comments and more laughter from the fair sex prompted the comedians of our outfit, Jim Meek the lighting man and his assistant Geoff Myers, to whisper:

'The ladies think you're right sexy. They dun't half fancy thee.'

I blushed profusely as ladies were still a complete mystery to me.

Harry's voice rang out like the bull of Basham:

'Right, you big ape, I've decided there's only one way to keep you out of trouble and that's to give you the lead in our next production.'

I choked.

'But aren't I too young, Mr Dobson?'

'Too young? My Aunt Fanny!' he roared back. 'You're play-ing Jack Hardacre in Walter Greenwood's *The Cure for Love*, and you'll be bloody marvellous, or I'll want to know the reason why!'

I shook my head in silence.

'It makes a change to see him quiet,' smiled Margaret Myers, a fine character actress with a warm personality.

In that silence all eyes surveyed me, enveloping me in warmth and kindness. (What I didn't realize at that moment was that I wouldn't experience that same feeling of unison again until I embarked with a team of people in 1990 on an expedition to climb Mount Everest.) The Theatre Guild members were very special and my hand was pumped and pounded from every direction.

The read-through was effortless and intoxicating, and after-wards Harry remarked:

'You're all going to be spiffing.'

We sped out into the night air happy and resolved. Imitating the style of Reg Harris, the champion pursuit cyclist of the time, I tore around bends and pedalled like fury down winding Adwick Road. Reaching the bottom, I stopped abruptly as the emotions that I had suppressed during the evening now overcame me.

Joy! Oh, joy! They like me – respect me, I thought. Confirma-tion. I do have a gift. Thank God! No worries now – I'm real. Yes! Really real!

The doubts thrown up by my earlier education – being in a 'C' class, a reject heading for oblivion – now finally disappeared.

Oh, God! This is bloody marvellous. Home! Home! I must get home!

Exploding like a Chinese firecracker, I poured out the events of the evening to my parents. Standing in front of the fireplace, Dad began to speak:

'Well, Brian lad, I've always said – and I know yer mother agrees – that there's nothing in the world you can't achieve if you set yer mind to it. We've watched you for some time now working 'ard on your speech, studying till all hours, to the point where we've been worried that you may 'ave been overdoing it.

Watching you develop with the Dearne Youth 'as been a joy. Johnny Adams 'as done you proud and you owe a great deal to 'im and Mr Lawson for backing you up. Your speech teacher, Mr Cooper, 'as performed wonders and now you've moved on to the Theatre Guild under the guidance of Mr Dobson. Harry informs me, by the way, which I've kept a secret until now, that your dreams of becoming a professional actor 'ave gone a stage further. Mr Hyles, the Chief Eduation Officer, has said that at the right time the South Yorkshire Education Authority will give you a scholarship to go to drama school.'

My mother burst into tears.

'It all makes me proud, Brian ... but I don't want you to leave home.'

After swamping her with hugs and kisses, I whispered:

'It's all too much to take in.'

'Aye, and it's time you hit the wooden hill, lad, or you'll have circles under your eyes,' Dad said, smiling broadly.

About this time I underwent a rather stringent examination for the Adult Gold Medal of the English Speaking Board, a tough bunch, in Sheffield City Hall. Christabel Burniston, a lady with classic good looks and fiery eyes, was the chief examiner and it would be fair to say that throughout the length and breadth of Yorkshire few applicants looked forward to her deadly scrutiny. However, this fine lady was profoundly respected by all.

In contrast, another organization, the Poetry Lovers' Fellowship, appeared to make allowances for our shortcomings, offering an encouraging smile here and an expression of rapture there. I always came away from them with high marks and even higher expectations.

Not so with Miss Burniston; burning Miss Burniston. Her eyes bore into me as I stood my ground. For two days she had examined my written papers and shredded my theories on Shakespeare's *Othello*. She roasted me when it came to my speeches and, as if that wasn't enough, paid scant regard to my acting ability. My offerings ranged from Henry V and Othello through to poetry: Laurence Binyon, Gerard Manley Hopkins, John Donne and Emily Brontë. Nevertheless, I was thoroughly enjoying myself, every bit of the way. By and by, I was learning.

I was attracted to Miss Burniston. During a moment of chastisement she sensed this and smiled faintly, but this instantly evaporated as she observed my cheeky twinkle. Her words poured out with even greater vigour:

'You must get it out of your head that you have a beautiful voice. You seem to have allowed yourself the luxury of falling in love with it. This is a frightful and counterproductive habit and I strongly urge you to set about getting rid of it. It is a common fault but, if it is allowed to develop and set in, it can prove to be the devil's own job to rectify.

'Stop listening so much to the sound and pay attention to what you are saying; concentrate on the sense. In your speeches follow the through-line and tell the story. What is your overall objective? Who are you? Where are you? After your vocal exercises let the voice look after itself. The voice is not your master: you are the rider and your voice is simply the horse. It serves you; you seem to serve it.

'Mr Blessed, you frequently get your priorities wrong and, worst of all, you love emotion for emotion's sake. Quite honestly, I simply can't judge your work, as it is just a long self-indulgent ramble. Yet, because you have presence and undoubted ability, I am willing, if you are, to examine you again tomorrow. In all fairness it will give you time to digest what I have said. You may think me harsh but this shock treatment is what you need.'

Throughout all this I had been vaguely aware of a small group of people watching me and writing. As Miss Burniston nodded a friendly goodbye, one of them, a tall man who had been partly obscured by the rest, rose and addressed her:

'Would you mind, Christabel, if I popped out for a breath of air and a few words with young Mr Blessed here?'

'Of course not, Michael.'

'Michael! Michael!' The name reverberated in my skull like Big Ben! 'Michael'! Bloody hell, it can't be! Not him. I'm going barmy – seeing things. Not here, not now, not when I'm so bad. Jesus Christ! Oh, no, no, no.

The gentleman stepped forward and stood directly in front of me, smiling and offering his hand.

'Pleased to meet you, my name is Michael Redgrave.'

Oh, yes,' I spluttered. 'Oh, yes, you are, I know that, sir. Where do you want to walk?'

At that moment a young lady informed Mr Redgrave that he was needed on the phone. Nodding an apology and asking if I would wait a few minutes, he moved off.

I was tempted to skedaddle: it was all too much for me. He was an acknowledged and celebrated actor – a professional! I had witnessed with awe his renowned performances in films, not to mention the glowing accounts I had read of his stage performances. The images and thoughts of all this fizzed in my brain.

Pacing ever faster round and round a small side room, I tried to get a grip on myself. The mixture of panic, excitement and shyness continued to bubble up inside me as I built up to the rhythm of a whirling dervish. And yet the concoction of feelings also had a rare sweetness. Intermittently I slapped the stone walls and then strained my ears at the door in case the tall star should inadvertently sweep in and catch me on one leg!

Destiny kindly let me finish the ritual before footsteps heralded the actor's approach and his smiling eyes, full of sensitivity and magnetism, focused on me. The voice, slightly cloudy with gentle darts of light, sang a further apology and beckoned me outside. My private dance had relaxed me and my smile and stillness delighted him.

'I'm positively starving!' I said.

'Feel like a cream tea or something?' he answered, laughing.

I nodded enthusiastically and words tumbled out of me like the waterfalls of Wharfedale!

'Oh, God, Mr Redgrave, you were wonderful in *The Browning Version*. When you cried, your lungs heaved so powerfully that I thought your back would break. Oh God, sir. Oh God, what acting.'

In the space of three hundred yards I covered half a dozen of his film performances and at the same time peppered him with questions about his Hamlet and King Lear. My intense joy and flood of queries gave my listener no chance to reply. His eyes simply widened and his smile increased.

Onlookers recognized him immediately but were most perplexed at the sight of me hurrying along backwards beside him. Moving ahead and galloping down a flight of steps, I stopped and looked up as Mr Redgrave approached way above me. He too became still as, my voice electric with youth, I fired up at him:

'Why doesn't Hamlet kill Claudius after the play scene?'

The great actor gripped his face, either suppressing a grin or containing his shock, but after several moments his fingers separated, revealing his searching eyes. Eventually he replied, with surprising melancholy:

'Oh dear me, Mr Blessed. To give an answer of this magnitude in a Sheffield street! I feel that Hamlet needs his father from page one. I suppose he never, totally, believes that the ghost is what he says he is. Throughout the play he simply misses his father; without him he is incomplete!'

Wiping his perspiring brow and running his hand through his thick hair, he went on:

'I played the role when I was as young as you, at Cranleigh. There is no doubt whatsoever that when you play the part it constantly invades your private life. In the morning you feel detached and happy, with an imaginary clear blue sky above you. By noon you are aware that small clouds are beginning to gather. In the afternoon these clouds thicken and intensify in your mind and the intensity increases as you accept that there is no getting away from the fact that, by evening, you will have to don the black clothes and face the complexity of that young man's nature. I have no hesitation in suggesting that actors commit themselves to this role for a limited season only. It is most exacting. After each performance I felt as if I had died a little.'

At this point Mr Redgrave arrived alongside me, laughing light-heartedly and cursing himself for being so solemn.

'Forgive me,' he continued. 'It all sounds rather morbid, which couldn't be further from the truth. There is tremendous joy and great satisfaction in playing the role.' He then added, with much merriment: 'Of course, you know what they say about satisfaction? It is another ladder in the same stocking.'

As I laughed we meandered down a side street and came upon a charming café. Over toast and tea, hastily consumed, the conversation was matter of fact. He asked about my home life and aspirations, which all rather intrigued him as he came from an entirely different background. Regarding my exam, I spoke of the difficulties of doing solo speeches and how easy it was to overemphasize, although the problem disappeared when one was doing an entire play.

He readily agreed, remarking that in his youth he had experienced the same difficulties. (Looking back on the conversation now, he was obviously being kind and generous to me.) He said he felt that the objectives of the English Speaking Board were splendidly sound. It obviously gave him great pleasure to be involved with it. But he expressed exasperation at the way certain people spoke, having no tolerance for stiff, pretentious speech, which he termed 'chromium Mayfair'. Speech had to be vigorous and alive, he maintained. The smile immediately returned to his face as he quoted an extract from an article he had written concerning that great, long-departed actor, Henry Irving, whose advice to the actor was, 'Speak clearly, speak clearly *and* be natural.'

'The italics are mine,' Mr Redgrave whispered conspiratorially.

For the next half hour we continued to stuff our faces with sandwiches, cakes and a steady stream of tea. If my worthy companion attempted to draw breath I immediately beamed in on him, like a maniacal Mekon, with another burning question. But it was not only one-way traffic, for he instantly responded in like fashion, forcing me to dig deep in myself to satisfy his searing blue eyes.

Our conversation embraced a multitude of topics, leaping from the neglect of Schiller to the possibility of George Bernard Shaw being more appreciated in the future. I was particularly fascinated by his comments on the role of King Lear:

'You'll play it one day, Mr Blessed. Look out for the comedy

— I fear my Lear was too much on the rack. Though, again, I played it when young. Larry Olivier was right: he discovered the comedy in it.'

With the speed of a laser beam he homed in on the achievements of that amazing artist Donald Wolfit.

'How does he do it? Hamlet, Richard III, Lear, Macbeth, all on alternate nights. A *tour de force*. What colossal energy!'

Energy was indeed the keynote as our discussion flowed on. The barrage of questions gained momentum until we collided in mid air, both speaking at the same time. Even our apologies collided and order was only established by one or the other offering a sandwich. I was milking him for all I was worth, which he wholeheartedly approved of, saying that that was what he was there for. I asked what was the high point, so far, in his life.

'Oh, without doubt, meeting the great Featherweight boxing champion Nel Tarlton, and having my back washed by him after working out in his gymnasium.'

Joy welled up inside me. Never was a Yorkshire lad so blissfully happy, and I began to talk at length about Bruce Woodcock.

All too soon our talk was over. But, horror of horrors, I hadn't the money to pay the bill! I had been so engrossed in the magic of the occasion that the matter had never entered my head. Christ! When the waitress added up the bill it came to three shillings and sixpence and I only had one shilling and threepence. I was mortified. Why, I couldn't even go Dutch! Shamefully, I explained my predicament.

My noble companion waved aside my worries and said, with a handsome smile:

'Oh, my dear fellow. There's no problem. I'll tell you what, when I'm on the way down as an actor and you're on the way up, you can buy me tea.'

We shook hands and bid farewell.

'This is the most agreeable hour I've spent in years. You'll get on famously in the acting world. Don't hesitate to come backstage to see me any time. Please keep in touch and bring me your news. Good luck tomorrow for the exam. I'll keep my fingers crossed.'

With that the great actor moved off, smartly adjusting his tweed jacket and flamboyantly entwining his scarf around his neck. As he gave me an elegant wave, he shouted:

'Please don't come and see me as Antony in *Antony and Cleopatra*. I have terrible difficulty with the lines – can't seem to grasp the part. Come and see me as Lear.'

The following day the exam went without a hitch, and after quiet deliberation Miss Burniston passed me with credit. To be given this by the austere lady was tantamount to receiving gold dust! She even flashed me a full smile.

At teatime I showed the medal to Mum and Dad, who were tickled pink. Mum cried her eyes out.

Later that evening I rushed over to Harry's house, bursting to relate the events of the last two days. My excitement knew no bounds as I all but sweated blood to recapture it all. Harry's red face beamed with mischief and devilment as he digested my news. As my passions got the better of me and almost rendered me incoherent, he hushed me until I finally wound down and fell silent. During this silence he chuckled away like a demonic Father Christmas, at last exploding into a huge belly-laugh. Pulling my face close to his, he whispered in the tiniest voice:

'You see, you big ape, people like Redgrave are just like you and me: flesh and blood.'

Two weeks later and the opening night of *The Cure for Love* was drawing closer. One day, during the last week of rehearsal, I arrived home from work, dusted myself down and vigorously brushed the loose plaster from my overalls. Dried plaster is insidious stuff and, if not carefully removed from work clothes, can spread into every nook and cranny. In spite of my diligence I frequently failed in this task and my mother gave me blue hell – the blue being the bruises on my elbow produced by the skilful application of a frying-pan. The only way to avoid the problem was to strip to my underwear in the outhouse and then I would be allowed in. The ritual concluded with a hot bath.

Plastering was tremendously hard work, rivalling some of the hardest jobs in the pits. As a result, plasterers and their labourers were immensely fit, with well-proportioned and powerful bodies.

This distinction I shared with my colleagues and it gave me great confidence. My chest, expanded, measured almost forty-five inches; my shoulders were wide and strongly muscled; my biceps shapely and impressive. Oh, yes! I didn't half love myself. I was the bee's knees, and why not? There was no harm in it.

That particular night I felt like a million dollars. My skin glowed with health, my hair responded perfectly to the brush and my mind danced with expectation and impatience to get to the Theatre Guild.

For eating my dinner at breakneck speed, I was scolded by my mother, as of old:

'I don't know, Brian. Gulping food down at that rate is no good for you. When you get older you'll pay for it. There's nothing worse than stomach trouble.'

I gave her a whopping great kiss, gripped my grinning dad with a hefty wrestling hold and, with my free arm, boxed my young brother's head. I shot like a speeding bullet out of the kitchen, grabbing my custard-pie dessert on the way. Cocking my leg over my bike, I plunged my gnashers into the lovely custard.

Slowly, with consummate ease, I pedalled up the road, the reliable dynamo humming its happy tune as it powered the lights into life. The last mouthful of pudding just gone, I noticed my chubby, short-haired, eight-year-old brother by my side, attempting to forge ahead of me. It was no race as I tucked my head down and applied the necessary power. A hundred yards further on I stopped with my arms wide open to embrace him. He ran his socks off and catapulted into me and, as always, ever since he was a baby, I covered him in kisses. It's still the same, even today, and Alan's now forty-eight!

I pressed on, out of Bolton-on-Dearne, up beloved Adwick Road to the outskirts of Mexborough. A mile further on I reached the hospital where I was born and turned right to complete the last half mile of the journey. Suddenly I stopped. A chilling, unearthly scream cut through the air – it was quite horrific. Odd moaning then followed, gradually developing into further high-pitched screams. The noise was coming from the hospital.

'What in God's name is it?' I whispered to several shadowy figures who stood by me on the pavement.

'They are all dying, lad,' said a woman. 'Poor buggers, poor bloody coalminers, caught in a fire. They've been pulling their bandages off all day. They've been begging the nurses to kill them. They bloody ought to kill 'em. They're all going to die anyway. Poor buggers. They should put 'em out of their misery.'

'What about painkillers?' I asked softly.

'Lad, lad. You can only give so much. Their bodies are burnt to a frazzle. Gaping, weeping wounds. Oh, lad! It doesn't bear thinking about. My husband and son are both coalminers.'

'So is my dad,' I said.

'Then let's pray to God they never suffer like these miners. Go on lad, on your way. There's nowt anyone can do here.'

Like a snail, I dragged myself up the hill, wheeling my bicycle. I felt as dead as the dynamo. The growing darkness conjured up the haunting nightmares of the past: images of coalmining tragedies that would never leave me. My mother's anguished words sprang to mind, ugly and alarming: 'Your Uncle Bernard's dead! Dead! Dead!'

What happened to the evening? There I was, happy as a sandboy, and now this. Oh, God! Coalmining! How much suffering has taken place to provide the nation with fuel.

When I arrived at the rehearsal room the Theatre Guild were aware of the situation and we rehearsed for only a short time before calling it a day.

A few days later, as the nights were shortening and keen frosts pinched our cheeks, it was opening night. During the previous two weeks I had spent a great deal of time selling tickets. They were reasonably priced and, with tremendous backing from friends and relatives, I was able to sell more than four hundred seats.

Aunts and uncles from both sides came, and my Grandma and Grandad Blessed defied their doctors' advice in order to attend the production. My grandmother, who was twenty stone, being supported by Mrs Cook, who was also a large heavyweight, was a sight that didn't bear witnessing. Added to this, to see the frail little frame of my grandfather, pausing and coughing – he had silicosis from working in the pits – would have made a stone weep.

The Schofield Technical College was awkwardly situated at the top of a long hill and not served by the local bus. But these magnificent people, with the rest of the mass pilgrimage, made their way there, somehow. People urged Grandad to turn back but he would have none of it:

'Stop yer fuss and palaver, I'm reet enough. I wouldn't miss seeing our Brian for all the tea in China!'

My Aunt Elsie told me later that she thought he was coughing up blood. Despite all this he stubbornly and cheerfully refused to be deterred, struggling slowly up the hill until it levelled off near the entrance to the school.

With that kind of spirit in the audience, the atmosphere in the hall that evening was inspirational. The cast sensed it, and rose to the occasion, so that the play was a great success. Bravos echoed everywhere. My parents were beside themselves with joy and how sweet it was too to see Grandad wiping tears of laughter from his face at the curtain call.

The rest of the week followed a similar pattern: happy audiences and contented artists. You could not fault the production. My concern at not being able to cope with a lead role alongside such experienced actors finally disappeared. Harry, holding my neck in a vice-like grip, whispered:

'You got the part just right.'

I was as pleased as punch.

After the final curtain had come down and the crowds had gone home, I sat in my dressing-room still and quiet. Harry sat beside me, smiling and giving me that sidelong, mischievous glance that I liked so much.

'Well, lad, how do you feel?'

'Fine,' I nodded. 'I only wish I could do it all the time.'

'Indeed,' beamed Harry. 'It's all in front of you, lad. All you have to do is work and be patient.'

The thought of being patient churned my guts.

'Harry,' I moaned with frustration. 'I'm only sixteen. I've got to wait four years before I can go to drama school, and I've still got to do my damned National Service.'

Harry's big red nose rubbed into mine. Pushing his great sausage fingers through my hair and gripping it tightly, he said forcefully:

'Be bloody patient.'

At that instant the door flew open and the room filled with happy faces urging us to follow the music to the stage, as the party had begun. The Russian philosopher Ouspensky once said that parties are generally a waste of time unless they have real meaning. On this night the meaning was crystal clear: a total celebration of life. Eyes were alive, voices sang and bodies moved to the rhythm of the music. Though still shy with women and generally unsociable, I could nevertheless feel my uncertainty disappearing. A step here, a step there; it was the first time in my life that I had danced:

Off to heel, and here we go,
Heel for heel, and toe for toe.

Round and round the stage we went; the intoxication of it all consumed me. Hair flowing and naturally blond, belonging to my beautiful partner Gladys Jarvis, dramatically became shining black as another beauty, by the name of Ethel Hatton, took my hand. These two, thrice blessed, were the Guild's leading ladies. More partners followed until I found myself dancing with our neat props lady, Mabel Redman, and then lovely Rhoda Brierley, who had stolen the show with her performance as Mrs Doorbell.

'This is wonderful,' I shouted to Harry.

'Aye, lad,' he smiled. 'They are the salt of the earth.'

I found myself back to back with our leading man, Arthur Thomson, who whispered:

'We're all proud of you, Brian.'

I felt just like Tubby the Tuba when he first played in the orchestra, or Mole in *The Wind in the Willows*:

'Up I come, up I come – pop! Oh, my! What a wonderful day.'

My last recollection was of Harry wrapping a scarf around my neck and covering me with a borrowed overcoat. Then I sat behind him on his motorbike and we roared off into the Yorkshire night.

11

The Speech Lesson

It was no secret that I felt like an alien among the building sites of South Yorkshire. Not that I felt any animosity to my fellow workers the plasterers; quite the reverse, in fact. They were a smashing bunch of men: full of fun, hard-working and with an appreciation of world affairs.

It was simply that I did not enjoy the job. How could I, when my heart was set on acting? But I had to do something to contribute to the family budget and, with no qualifications whatsoever, I was extremely fortunate to get work as a plasterer.

All this sounds rather harsh on the art of plastering, for an art it was. When my boss, Chris Riley, applied the first coat of sand, lime and cement, it was sheer poetry. The application of the finishing coat of plaster of Paris and lime was likewise a joy to behold. Add to this his skill in spreading 'pink thistle' plaster on the ceiling and covering the joints with a bandage-like material called scrim, and you have almost all the dexterity of a Michelangelo! Chris had my unstinting respect, as did the other lads.

There was always a great deal of ribbing and friendly competition between the groups of plasterers, brickies, plumbers and carpenters, culminating twice a week in a lunchtime football match. It was us, the plasterers, versus the rest of the building site; that is, the workforce of the firm of Watford's.

These were hard-fought games, with victory sometimes going one way and sometimes the other. Dripping with perspiration, we would afterwards continue our afternoon's work.

It was at this time that the write-ups for *The Cure for Love* appeared in the local newspapers. I devoured every line in eager anticipation. There was no doubt at all that it was a complete success. The critics were unanimous in their approval – all that is except John Broxton, the accepted leading critic, who found fault with my performance.

Quite simply, he loved the production but felt I had overacted my part. He implied that I had allowed the joy of playing the lead role to unbalance it and therefore to make it somewhat unreal. Broxton had a phenomenal knowledge and love of the theatre and consequently demanded the utmost respect.

A few days later, with Harry, I found myself in the critic's company. He proved to be a sensitive, kind man, and was mildly surprised when I asked him to explain what he meant, as I did not understand. The whole meeting was accidental and splendidly constructive. He ended by saying that in retrospect he could have been wrong, and instructed me to take his review with a pinch of salt. Over the next two years John Broxton was to prove a positive influence on my development as an actor.

Some days later, arriving at work, I was surprised to see many of the Watford's men sniggering and whispering behind the page containing Broxton's write-up.

'What does it say?' one gentleman asked leisurely.

'Overacted his part,' I answered. 'I'm pleased to see it gives you so much pleasure.'

They moved back as I took a step towards them.

'Incidentally,' I continued, 'what he says is true. If you disagree with him, I suggest you stick it up your arse . . . or would you rather I gave you some assistance?'

'No, Brian . . . we meant no harm!

'That's fine, then,' I smiled. 'No harm done.'

Nevertheless, in the distance, I could see more figures half-hidden behind newspapers, their pathetically disguised voices taking up the theme:

'Overplayed his part?'

'Take no notice of them,' Chris kindly suggested as I began plastering, driving my trowel into the wall.

'I'm all right, Chris. Don't worry – it's water off a duck's back.'

My job that morning was to work my way over the big walls, spreading the lime and sand coat (this was called roughing or floating) while Chris did the angles around the windows. His job was not as physically demanding as mine, for he had arrived at the age when you take things a little easier, and he was the boss. People were a little nervous working with him because of his position, but I genuinely enjoyed his company. He had a rare wit, a nostalgia for the war years and a kindly wisdom. Beneath his calm exterior he seemed to harbour a deep sadness which I always attributed to a long-lost love. He was forever quietly singing love songs. Kurt Weill's 'September Song' was a particular favourite of his:

It's been a long, long time from May to December.

It was noticeable that morning that I was working with a different edge.

'Ease up, Brian,' Chris smiled. 'You're going to leave me behind. Anyway, don't forget: there's a football match against Watford's.'

'Yes, Chris. Indeed there is,' I replied, staring back at him. 'Ow many goals are you gonna score, Brian lad?' roared out Jack Jarvid, nicknamed Jarvo, our labourer, as he emptied his load on the board.

'A hundred,' I grunted.

Jack roared with laughter at this. He was an incredible physical specimen: about eighteen stone, six foot three, with massive, hairy arms and giant shoulders. Each day I would try to tire him by working myself to a standstill, but all to no avail: he never even raised a sweat keeping up with me. Sometimes I felt he may possibly have given me a hard look, but then his face would break into a smile and I would feel that I had imagined it.

Football was a sport I loved and our team, Riley's, played hard and well. On this occasion we hammered Watford's 7–3. Bathed in sweat, I returned to my trowel with renewed vigour.

'Beat the bastards, Chris!' I roared.

Over the next few weeks I became noticeably quiet. My mother became increasingly anxious, constantly asking if I felt well. Nodding, I would murmur:

'Nothing's wrong, Mother . . . nothing to worry about.'

My reply was far from the truth. In fact, the previous day I had physically attacked a man at work. There had continued to be a constant stream of abuse from Watford's workers about Broxton's write-up; they went on teasing, always from a distance and out of sight. But on this occasion a bricklayer named Percy chanced his arm and confronted me face to face. He was a man of twelve and a half stone and medium height, in his mid forties. He wasn't very bright, but I found him hard-working, kind and easy to get on with.

It surprised me then that he should choose to be so insensitive. His guttural speech rasped out as if he had some contagious disease:

''Ow now, brown cow. You're not much good, people tell me. Tha overacts thee part. The paper says tha stinks!'

He then began to prod me in the chest with his finger and at the same time to pour out further abuse. As quick as a flash, I slammed a short left hook into his solar plexus. As he doubled up, I ran my left hand over his shoulder and on to his spine, locking my other hand around his rear end, lifting him into the air, and put him head first into a full water barrel. Holding on to his ankles, I heaved him up and down in the water. Finally, I pulled him out and released him from his misery. He coughed, spluttered and swore, his nose bleeding.

'Shut it, Percy!' I said. 'You asked for it. Tell your friends they'll get the same. Now scram!'

Later, when thinking about it, I realized just how easy it was to cause serious injury. Fortunately he suffered no more than a few scratches but, although it was quite common on building sites to get into the occasional fight, I felt like a common bully.

After all, I had spent several years being taught to box and he had no idea how to defend himself. The sad thing was we never spoke to one another again.

After that confrontation the teasing gradually faded away and life took on its old pattern once again. The Theatre Guild, after the production of *The Cure for Love*, now had a rest period of a month or so before the next production was decided upon. It was rumoured that it could possibly be John Davidson's play *The Brontës of Haworth Parsonage*.

My moments of quiet now developed into hours of non-communication; I purposely avoided people. My mother and father were beside themselves with worry. They simply could not understand what was the matter with me.

'Please tell us, Brian, lad,' Father would plead.

Even my mother's pleas fell on deaf ears.

'Oh, Brian,' she would whisper. 'It frightens me to see you like this, yer eyes are big and staring . . . there's no expression in them . . . You must get out of that chair. You sit in it day in and day out . . . '

Every cell in my body wanted to speak out and explain to them, but I couldn't. My condition was as incomprehensible to me as it was to them.

The last thing in the world I wanted to do was to cause suffering to my parents. A week later, while washing my hands in the kitchen sink after finishing work on a Saturday afternoon, I managed to blurt out to my father what had been said by the Watford's workers on the building site. After a long pause he turned to me, put an arm around my shoulder and said:

'Take no notice of them, they're pig-ignorant and don't know their arse from their elbow.' He continued gently: 'You don't think the likes of Harry Dobson, Johnny Adams, Mr Lawson and Mr Hyles would invest so much time in you if they didn't think you were worthwhile, do you?'

'Yes, you're right, Dad,' I nodded. 'I'm being absolutely silly. Sorry for all this. I should know better.'

'You should indeed,' he smiled, rubbing my hair and affectionately punching me in the ribs. 'Go for a walk, then come and 'ave yer tea and we'll go to the cinema . . . it's abaht time we went out for an evening together.'

All this kindness brought a smile to my face for the first time in weeks, but after a couple of days this disappeared and my morose, withdrawn mood returned.

It wasn't just the unkindness of the Watford's men that had entered my subconscious, but certain friends and neighbours had implied that I was getting above my station and I had bitten off more than I could chew. They maintained that my speech had become false and that it had affected my whole personality. Broxton's write-up in the paper was a timely reminder that I was quite ordinary, with no special gifts, and that going to the Theatre Guild was a pretence and that I was deceiving myself.

My reaction to this criticism was intense and passionate. I declaimed in a grandiose manner that they were just unimaginative, cretinous fools! Of course, despite my protestations, the damage was done. My mental condition continued to deteriorate.

My normally good eyesight seemed to weaken slightly, and I had the feeling that people, when speaking to me, were far away, as if at the end of a tunnel. Their voices seemed vague, as if penetrating a thick cloud. On other occasions they sounded metallic and thin. When I answered them they noticed that I seemed to be having trouble with my hearing.

Then I began to experience the feeling that life was slowly ebbing away from me. Stupid advice from outsiders would ring in my ears:

'Get yer feet on the ground!' or 'Pull yerself together!'

Time passed so slowly. The world seemed like a picture that was gradually losing its colours, fading and darkening at the edges.

Then, quite unexpectedly, it all changed dramatically.

Suddenly everything speeded up at an alarming rate. My thoughts raced, panic gripped me and my heart beat painfully. It seemed absolutely impossible to control the awful negative thoughts that rushed through my mind. Round and round they went, like some dreadful electric windmill.

'Stop! . . . Stop! . . . Stop!' I would shout as I walked alone across the Seven Fields. 'For Christ's sake, go away.'

The more I tried to silence these thoughts, the louder they became. My condition was beyond parental help and I knew instinctively not to involve them.

I was beginning to find it impossible to talk to anyone. In the blackness of my despair I yearned for Harry's guidance, but his work had taken him away for several weeks. As far as the other members of the Theatre Guild were concerned, I was only a recent acquaintance.

What was more, I had no real friends. This was mainly attributable to my having shut myself away in my room for a year or so studying, to make up for my lost education.

The crisis was worsening. I found myself sitting in a ditch at the bottom of Wells' Field, near my home, rocking to and fro with my head in my hands . . . descending into oblivion.

Then one evening my mother automatically sponged my face, adjusted my tie and murmured:

'It's about time you went for your speech lesson or you'll be late.'

In my somnambulant state, I put on my cycle clips and set off on my green racing bike for Rotherham, fifteen miles away.

What the hell did I care about a speech lesson? Hell! I thought, Frank Cooper does not deserve the likes of me arriving on his doorstep.

Frank was a sensitive, natural tutor with a neat, sweet wife and an orderly home. His only knowledge of me was that I was hard-working, obedient and quiet. Deep inside myself I felt as though I was about to invade his home with my alien, ugly, negative presence.

Anyway, how could I possibly keep my composure?

God! I thought, after three miles, I ought to turn back.

But something inside me rebelled, reminding me that it was important to hold on to the artistic course I had set myself. However, as I pressed on, the negative thoughts began to take over again. The action of riding itself seemed to amplify them and make them more tangible and torturous.

Mexborough passed by as I plunged down Roman Terrace, past Manvers main colliery and up to Swinton. It was uphill now, but eased off as I approached the usually enjoyable straight road to Parkgate and Rawmarsh. The damned road went on for miles and the air started to reek from the vast industrial sites all around. I was dripping with sweat and the beginnings of a high fever, while the scene around me tormented my reverberating brain and a goblin voice tore into me:

'You are no good!'

'You are ordinary!'

'You have no talent!'

'You look like a fool with those Guild people. Give it up! . . . There's no hope of you getting anywhere as an actor!'

'Poor! . . . Poor! . . . Poor! . . . That's you!'

The wheel of negation spun faster and faster, bearing down on the centre of my brain.

Jesus Christ! I thought. I'm drowning!

Sparks of resistance flickered in me.

'I'm all right,' I replied to the voice.

That great actor, Michael Redgrave himself, had said I was powerfully talented.

'He did! . . . He did! . . . He did!'

Repeating this over and over again, I desperately tried to regain some balance. Dr Ellis of the Poetry Lovers' Fellowship had told me I had an amazing voice with a wonderful range.

'He did! . . . He did! . . . He did!'

More and more such protestations raged around my tormented brain.

Pressing heavily on the brakes, I brought my bike to a halt, the lights fading as the dynamo stopped. Then I realized that I had lost my bearings. To my right a rolling mill and a power station lit up the skyline. Clouds of black smoke contrasted with the volcanic red of the blast furnace. Men, with robot-like helmets, holding blue-flamed rods, cut through the steel, pouring cascades of sparks in every direction.

Rumbling bass sounds shook the buildings as powerful engines and giant chains clashed. I stared at it all in numb silence: a scene from Dante's *Inferno*. Black smoke belched out, and then I heard a bellowing voice behind me:

'What's tha doin', man? Tha shouldn't be here!'

'It's all right,' I shouted. 'I lost my way.'

With that, I cocked my leg over my bike and rode off again.

God! I've gone straight past Rotherham! I realized. Gradually I found my way back and forced myself unwillingly up steep Broom Road to 30 Broom Terrace, where Frank lived.

As the front door opened, a gentle light from the hallway shone through the mist. Frank's gaunt, handsome face expressed relief and at the same time his hands swept over his black hair in bewilderment.

'Good heavens, young man! We were getting worried about you. It's not like you to be late.'

Frank's sweet, clear voice and cheerful manner temporarily put me at ease. Sitting me down in his study, he frowned in consternation at me.

'I think you should relax, have a cup of tea and tell me all about it . . . ,' he gently but firmly suggested.

There followed a huge pause, during which I paced up and down the room. Then I rasped out:

'I'm sorry, Mr Cooper, but you can't help me – no one can.'

Then came an unbearable, even longer, pause, which I finally broke by crying out:

'God Almighty! . . . Jesus Christ! . . . Jesus! . . . Jesus! . . . '

Then I let out a long, drawn-out:

'Jeeeeesusss Chrissssssst! . . . Please forget the speech lesson . . . here's my half crown . . . keep it for nothing . . . my throat is dried up with smoke and cold. Anyway there's no point . . . I'm finished . . . finished! I have nothing to give any more!'

I tore around the room like a mad bull, pouring out all the filthy, negative dross that had accumulated in my brain. My body pulsated and heaved as emotions were unleashed that I had never experienced before. Arms flailing and hands clutching at my stomach, I pressed myself helplessly to rid myself of the pain that seemed to be destroying me.

My veins felt as if they were bursting and a feeling of intense heat sent me into paroxysms of violent shaking. Deep vents of emotion gave way to loud crying and sobs as I sank to my knees, lost in despair.

My voice gradually became more meagre and small, tiny and impotent, as I emitted, with barely the strength of a mouse, the words:

'They say I'm bad and untalented.'

Then the room closed in and I became semiconscious.

After some time I felt a cool, wet flannel being applied to my temple and Frank's hands sensitively and gently running through my wet hair. His expressive voice cooed various sounds in my ears:

'There, there, there ... now, now, now ... shhh-shhhh-shhhhh ... '

He whispered soft sounds, which developed over the next half hour into loving and wise poems; these he subtly interwove with simple songs.

His voice seemed far away and yet hauntingly clear. John Donne's words from his poem 'The Sun Rising' kissed my brain. Oh! those magical words:

> Love, all alike, no season knows, or clime,
> Nor hours, days, months, which are the rags of time.

I knew the words, of course, and Frank encouraged me, like a baby drinking medicine from a spoon, to say them with him.

Time passed and Frank's soothing voice turned to Shelley's *Prometheus Unbound*.

'Come on Brian,' cooed my teacher. 'Whisper with me:

> "To suffer woes which hope thinks infinite,
> To forgive wrongs darker than death or night."'

Now I had become still, my eyes staring and vacant. Frank continued with more Shelley:

> 'This, like thy glory, Titan, is to be
> Good, great and joyous, beautiful and free;
> This is alone life, joy, empire and victory.'

The repeated application of the cool flannel, and Frank's subtle tones, started to blow away the throbbing negation I had suffered. What funny songs he chose to sing: 'Beautiful dreamer, wake unto me'; 'Tempest'; 'Where the bee sucks, there suck I, In a cowslip's bell I lie'.

Gradually I found I could sit up on the sofa and enjoy the warm tea and delicious sandwiches that his wife, Thelma, provided.

My face broke into soft smiles as the tears ran down my face. This made Frank roar with laughter and shout out:

'That's better, young man!'

My eyes red-raw, I stared back at him in utter disbelief. Who would have thought he could have cured me? For cure me he had. How does one explain such a profound experience? It was as if he had put all my loose nerves back in place. His voice, hands, care and heart had penetrated my darkness and relit the candle with a surer flame. His capacity to give so simply had saved my life; quiet confidence and love, combined with a new strength, ran through my heart and body.

My route home, which still involved smog, city lights and bleak rolling mills, had the ambiance of Shangri-La. As I arrived home the delicate strains of the song 'Shanty Town Moon' echoed through the house. There, in the kitchen, in happy embrace, swaying to the music, were Mum and Dad, with little Alan smiling rapturously.

'This is an "excuse me", Dad,' I interrupted, putting my arm around my mother's waist and waltzing her around the living-room. At the end of the song we all clapped enthusiastically as if we were at a ball.

'Yer know,' Mother smiled, stepping back to look at me. 'Our Brian is quite grown-up!'

12

Hoober Stand

The late autumn of 1953 was full of mists and magic. Even my endeavours on the building site gave me a great deal of satisfaction. After work on Saturday afternoons, with my father, I would climb the disused railway embankment at the back of our house.

The view stretched for miles across the Seven Fields. On the horizon, in a purple haze, you could make out the edge of the Yorkshire Moors. To our left, about three or four miles away, higher than any other object, stood a stone watch tower. This monolith had always intrigued and puzzled me.

'What on earth is it, Dad?' I asked one afternoon.

'Uberstan,' he replied.

'Uberstan?' I echoed. 'But what does it mean?'

'I don't know, lad,' he smiled. 'I think it marks a central position for surveying. It's situated close to South Melton.'

'It looks so high,' I said. 'And the name sounds vaguely oriental, or Russian.' Grinning, I muttered: 'Maybe Fu Manchu and his followers live there. Or the mythological Els – the Elders. The Golden Race. Masters of Time and Space residing in pristine subterranean chambers underneath its structure.'

Remarks such as this were guaranteed to bring a quaint, wry smile to my father's face. He responded by saying:

' "You are old, Father William," the young man said,
"And yet you continually stand on your head."
"In my youth," Father William replied to his son,

152

"I thought it might injure my brain,
But now that I find that I have none, I do it
again and again." '

We burst into laughter, and took off on colourful flights of fantasy. Sitting down and contemplating the world around us, we would ease into our favourite topics of conversation; politics, art, natural history, philosophy, religion and astronomy. The whole dialogue was hugely enjoyable and constructive, full of careful thought, energy and vivid images. Dad remarked that he had always looked forward to me growing up and exchanging ideas with him.

We were both avid listeners to the astronomer Fred Hoyle's lectures on the BBC Home Service, which we found thought-provoking and inspirational. But as often as not the discussion would end with me showing my father one of the latest wrestling holds and attempting to pin him down on the grass. This would usually have him jumping to his feet, exploding with laughter and bawling:

'Any more of this and I'll give you the old one-two!'

'Will you indeed?' I would reply. 'You and whose army?'

'Never mind an army,' he would retaliate. 'I'll put this right on yer snitch!'

'If that's the case, let's see how fast you are,' I would shout, speeding down the embankment and grabbing Alan, who used to watch it all from behind a bush.

Within minutes we would all be at the tea table wolfing down salmon and salad with huge chunks of bread. God, I loved my family!

Saturday nights I adored. The choice of entertainment was limitless. After all, we had two local cinemas offering fabulous entertainment and the engrossing *Saturday Night Theatre* on the radio to choose from.

During these days a sweet, gentle stillness inside me harmonized with my surroundings. Harry told me that he wanted to play Branwell Brontë in *The Brontës of Haworth Parsonage*, and this news filled me with a contented glow. My speech lessons progressed and I received a distinction and a special commendation. On

153

learning of this, my mother and father hugged me affectionately, smiling and nodding happily.

Musical evenings were a regular occurrence at home, each member of the family appreciative of the others' tastes. My parents were intrigued by my love of such composers as Sibelius, Debussy, Mozart, Bach and Stravinsky. Introducing my mother to Butterworth's *Shropshire Lad Rhapsody* proved an instant success, for the music reminded her of a childhood holiday spent in Little Rollright, Oxfordshire.

Late one night, my father and I donned our warm winter clothing and walked to our beloved embankment. He was in a thoughtful mood and asked me questions about acting. Strangely enough, it was a subject that I rarely discussed, explaining to him that actors can be very boring when they talk about it.

Nevertheless, I explained, and I have never diverted from this conviction, that I felt acting is simply a must. If you are an actor you have no choice. The pathway is obvious and you are compelled to follow it, drawn like a magnet to a possible, attainable goal which contains a central core of mystery. It requires, like all the arts, tremendous courage, sacrifice, total commitment and a serious mind. But the serious mind must also embrace a generous sense of humour.

We turned our eyes and thoughts to the night sky. Our frequent dates with the universe were both intoxicating and compulsive, each of us regaling the other with the latest cosmological discoveries and theories. The young night covered us with its friendly cloak and the stars and planets seemed to light up in celebration.

The drama of the universe unfolded, with its gracious curve, the Milky Way, soaring across the backdrop; the Great Bear pointing the way to the North Star; and Venus, so bright that we felt it could cast shadows in a room. On and on and on it went; more and more galaxies and heavenly bodies.

Stars, we learned from Fred Hoyle, were red, green, blue, yellow and even brown. And among them were unseen black ones, awaiting motivating energy to form their dead material into new life.

It intrigued us that the suns varied in size from dwarfs such as our own sun, to the medium ones and giants.

'There they are, Dad,' I mused. 'Billions and trillions of them, all no doubt surrounded by planets and moons: the outriders of myriads of forms of life. The whole Milky Way must be teeming with life.'

'God, Brian . . . How privileged we are to have eyes to witness it.'

'Yes, Dad . . . Yes,' I smiled. 'You know, this is my deepest love: Outer Space. It even eclipses acting, this yearning to explore beyond the solar system. It causes me intense frustration and deep pangs of nostalgia. A feeling, Dad, of wanting to go to a different home.'

'Yes, lad, yes,' my father nodded. 'I think I understand your feeling.'

'Sometimes the throbbing of my pulse and the leaping of my mind cause me to propel myself out there. It's rather reminiscent of John Masefield's thought in *Lollingdon Downs*.'

Gently, slowly I spoke the lines from the poem:

'I could not sleep for thinking of the sky,
The unending sky, with all its million suns
Which turn their planets everlastingly
In nothing, where the fire-headed comet runs.
If I could sail that nothing, I should cross
Silence and emptiness with dark stars passing;
Then, in the darkness, see a point of gloss
Burn to a glow, and glare, and keep amassing,
And rage into a sun with wandering planets,
And drop behind; and then, as I proceed,
See his last light upon his last moon's granites
Die to a dark that would be night indeed:
Night where my soul might sail a million years
In nothing, not even Death, not even tears.'

As I finished, we both stood still. The vast tapestry of the heavens appeared to smile down on the stillness of the South Riding of Yorkshire.

13

Rite of Spring

My bedroom-cum-sitting-room was a square box. Except for the odd picture the walls were completely plain, and yet within the confines of these walls my imagination ran riot.

My pride and joy was a second-hand Bush gramophone, and over the years I had painstakingly acquired a fine collection of records. There were books everywhere – even cramming the drawers of my large, yellow dresser – ranging from Shakespeare to every conceivable tome on adventure. Oh my God, yes! Adventure unlimited! Daring tales that, as the ghost in *Hamlet* says, 'Make thy two eyes, like stars, start from their spheres; Thy knotted and combined locks to part, And each particular hair to stand on end, Like quills upon the fretful porpentine.' Tales such as the exploits of Mallory and Irvine on Everest and Thor Heyerdahl's voyage on the *Kon-Tiki*.

In my imagination I journeyed with these intrepid explorers. Brimming with pride, I accompanied the renowned Baron von Humboldt in Ecuador as he attempted to climb the mighty Chimborazo, and then shared his anguish as he ultimately failed. I sailed with him as he triumphantly bade farewell to that continent when the majestic volcano, Cotopaxi, erupted, as if in celebration of his astonishing achievements.

The deeds of the explorers leapt out of the pages, their bodies almost taking form on my bedstead and enacting their adventures before my very eyes. My brain would then fuse from too much excitement, and at the snap of my book the Lilliputian forms would reluctantly flee.

My window also looked out into a world of wonders. Of all the places on God's earth, I doubt if any room received the afternoon sun quite like mine. Some days it glared, chillingly white, and at other times it smouldered, a warm blood-red. No two sunsets were the same.

One evening, when altocumulus clouds appeared to be static around the flaming orb and its rays penetrated every corner of the pink sky, I pressed the button of my gramophone, watched the needle find the first groove, and crept back to the window. With the setting sun pouring golden light into my room, I waited breathlessly. Gradually and almost imperceptibly the sounds of Ravel's *Daphnis and Chloe* filtered through the air. The haunting sounds kissed the deepest reaches of my brain and carried me off to far-distant lands.

Over the moors I went, heading south-west, past magical Tintagel, then west across the grey, stormy Atlantic until, plunging and driving on, I could make out the undulating eastern seaboard of the USA. As it tantalizingly revealed itself, I followed its jagged contour until the fresh breeze whistled up the warmth of the south. Then, as I skirted fast and low around the Gulf of Mexico, my senses quickened with the promise of Maple White Land.

Up, up, high above black nimbus, I soared towards a cyclopean landscape of fiery volcanoes. Before the cloak of night enveloped me I peered down, down into the cone of already sleeping Cotopaxi, until powerful currents tore me away to the confines of ever-watchful Chimborazo. I hovered here in blackest night, in darkest Ecuador, a Yorkshire condor humming the hymn, 'Chimborazo, Cotopaxi, took me by the hand'. Surrendering to faith, I floated and soared on jetstreams of joy and alighted, at dawn, on the emerald canopy of the Matto Grosso.

Oh, Brazil! Oh, dawn of delight! Green, green mansions and a haven of long-lost temples. A never-ending carpet of trees, broken only by the cascading water and ethereal mists of the Angel Falls. Jaguar, ocelot, margay, jaguarundi and our rare friend the kod-kod: all growling, hissing and moving back before the honk-honk of the greedy anaconda. The hum of life! I swooned as my senses, dizzy with delight, sizzled with ecstasy among the flowering aromas. Pollinating powder-puffs leapt out from stems and dense clouds of morpho butterflies rose in the morning light, their electric-blue wings incandescently reflecting the sun's rays. The cacophony of sounds rose up – the jungle was alive with celebration.

Reader, I hope you will forgive this flight of fantasy, for it is intended to give you an accurate insight into the way my mind worked at that time. Without doubt I was desperately lonely, which seems a strange and ungrateful thing to write when Harry, Frank and the Theatre Guild spared no effort to encourage and care for me. The problem was that they were older; the young enjoy the young and I didn't have any young friends. Between plays and exams I buried myself in my room, seeing no one, and assumed the guise of a monk of Athos.

Physically I was far from frustrated, working six and a half days a week like a ten-bob horse. But my whole being simply yearned for young people who throbbed like me; who could soar and dance with me and burn the midnight oil. Youngsters who could race across the Elysian Fields with me and ascend the lonely heights of Parnassus.

Whereas at one time I'd had such an affinity with the Probert Avenue Gang, now each had gone his own way, deepening my loneliness. To a certain extent the air-raid shelter of my childhood had now been replaced by my room and the tag of Baron Frankenstein still applied. My mother, aware of my growing isolation, urged me to go out more. But although I would frequent the dancehalls, waltzing and jitterbugging my partners to a frazzle, I would return home as empty as a drum.

It was around this time that I first kissed a woman. The instructions from my elders were clear and simple: incline the head slightly to the right or left, at the same time place a friendly arm around the waist to pull the lassy closer, then plant a delicate smacker on her lips! I had rehearsed this action alone for days.

But when the tumultuous moment arrived, as I inclined to the right the lady moved to the left. An embarrassed scramble ensued as we adjusted our positions to try again. In an endeavour to please we both propelled ourselves forward, causing a mid-air collision.

Our noses took the brunt of it and with tears of pain we both apologized profusely. It was a disaster!

After this initial set-back my technique improved slightly. On one occasion I was walking a young lady home and, after much deliberation, began a bout of innocent necking. All was hunky-dory until we came up for air at half-time, and struck up a conversation. Within minutes the young lady, jumping to the conclusion that she had been snogging with the man from Mars, rapidly developed a headache, bid me a hasty goodnight and sped down the pathway to the safety of her home. This sequence of events was reversed when I was coerced into dating a rather hot young siren: as she inspected my flies I, too, complained of a headache and beat a retreat.

Generally, young ladies were perplexed by my personality and concluded that I really was the 'Man from Planet X' (a film with that title was doing the rounds of the cinemas at the time). Whenever I played football a bevy of sixteen-year-old beauties would hover close to the touch-line and enthusiastically applaud my every movement. These pretty stalwarts were determined to bring this alien back to the confines of humanity. Taking a free kick would sometimes mean walking a few paces off the pitch to get a better angle – into girl territory! As delicate hands confirmed that my buttocks were indeed firm I would make a complete hash of the kick. At such moments my rubicund, Martian face would look heavenward for guidance from the red planet; I was completely hopeless with the female human!

In fact, this suited me fine for, like many other young men, I had a horror of making a girl pregnant. In the village a young lad and lass of sixteen had recently married for just this reason. Giving ourselves a moment's respite from football one day, we saw them walking up Highgate Road to the cinema – a haunting sight as they both looked so grim. Dark stories of dark deeds made us cringe with trepidation, and in quiet panic we would head for the chemist's for the indispensable French letters.

Outside the shop we would draw lots to decide who would go in, and whenever it was my turn I would return with the customary bottle of lemonade or dandelion and burdock. Of course, if by some devious means I actually managed to buy some condoms, there was absolutely no possibility of me ever using them; I simply hadn't the nerve to go that far with a girl. Eventually I would blow them up into white balloons and hang them on the doorknob of the local vicarage.

We knew nothing about sex. Up to the age of fifteen we believed that if you even touched a woman's breasts you would make her pregnant. Then we were told that if you actually did the dastardly deed and managed, by a miracle, to pull out in time you had to be extremely careful about where you ejaculated: if you fired away within three feet of the woman and the slightest breeze caught the seed she would be 'in the pudding club'.

Our reliable informants also told us that it was compulsory, by law, for the occasional condom to have a hole in it! This government directive apparently took into account the moral perspective of the church and at the same time sympathetically encouraged nature to occasionally burst the rubber goods! For the life of me I could never understand this reasoning, but all the same we meticulously examined our rubbers for this minute dot. With zeal that would have impressed Sherlock Holmes, we applied our magnifying glasses to each and every condom.

In desperation one evening, when my parents were out, I tied a condom to the tap to see if the water would reveal a compulsory hole. Alan watched with fascination. Alas, the water pressure proved too strong, for the article ballooned gigantically and then exploded, drenching us both to the skin.

Quite apart from dealing with suspect condoms, there was also the whole problem of venereal disease – better known to us as the clap. Once again our trusted experts surpassed themselves, stating that the dreaded gonorrhoea could turn your penis into a cabbage! Crabs, the creepy-crawlies of the public toilets, were said to be capable of completely devouring your testicles. The only cure was to remain upside down on a pulley system for weeks, as laughing nurses painted liberal amounts of blue unction on the gonads. As for the ultimate horror, syphilis, abandon all hope if you contracted that. There was the faintest possibility that a thin, red-hot poker with nodules on it, inserted into the penis and then pulled up and down for hours, might just save you, but it was very doubtful. Generally the victim died of galloping knob-rot.

Also, as sure as God made little apples, if you got a lady into trouble you would have to marry her, or pay two pounds ten shillings a week for the rest of your life. It seemed to me that the only possible protection against all these hazards was to wear half a dozen condoms surrounded by several layers of best-quality roofing felt. To hell with sex! I would do without it.

The other option, masturbation, was also taboo. It all seemed so ridiculous – the whole thing had to be a spoof. We had been told something of the 'facts of life' at school, but I only half believed it then and over the years have continued to question its authenticity. I ask you, it can't be true, can it? I'm afraid it has always given me the giggles. Don't get me wrong: my sexual drive was as strong as the next man's – a naughty gust of wind toying with a lady's skirt could, and would, send me into deliriums of delight.

At work on the building site the conversation was often about sex. There was a time when my pale complexion was interpreted as a sure sign that I was playing with myself. Reminiscent of the Prime Minister at Question Time, I loudly proclaimed that I didn't wank, which produced hoots of laughter from the plasterers. The eldest of them was a seventy-year-old Irishman called Paddy Slavin, of whom I asked:

'Do you still wank, Paddy?'

'Oh yes, Brian,' he chuckled. 'Old habits are hard to give up!'

My answer to sex was simply, when the mood came over me, to work harder, play harder and to take the occasional cold shower. I let myself be guided by the sentiment that seduced dear Pinocchio:

'Hi-diddle-dee-dee, an actor's life for me.'

And when sex reared its ugly head I heeded the words of Pinocchio's little friend, Jiminy Cricket: 'Give a little whistle, and always let your conscience be your guide.'

It seemed to me at the time that everybody and everything was whistling: trees, bushes, grass, telephone wires, all musically responding to the urgency of the west wind. The longed-for spring, delightfully, caught us all napping, its message of hope and rebirth stirring our hibernating bodies into life once more. Out of my room I came and, with everyone else, joined in the Rite of Spring. The whole Dearne valley rejoiced in harmony to the rhythm of the season. Everywhere, in town and country, people swayed and moved to spring's song. The gardens on wash day vibrated with lines of dancing fabrics, whose rapturous movement attracted fluttering, newly hatched cabbage white butterflies. The energy of Nature gave confidence to young and old alike and people would burst into song at the drop of a hat. Old-fashioned radios, and suspect modern types, poured out popular songs such as:

Mr Sandman, build me a dream, make her complexion like peaches and cream.

Red buses, running between Sheffield and Goldthorpe, throbbed in musical accord as travellers solicited 'Mr Sandman' for romantic help:

I'm so alone, ain't got nobody to call my own.

On the radio the voice of the BBC announcer rang out: 'Friday night is music night, and here to sing to you are Anne Ziegler and Webster Booth.'

These words heralded the song 'We Are in Love with You, My Heart and I' – a sentiment that was shared by millions.

On the building site in Thurnscoe, a big, handsome labourer named Arthur Bromley could scarcely contain his admiration for Mario Lanza and every day exploded into a fine rendition of his song 'Because You're Mine'. Bromley's fine, open nature was full of love and expectation, for he was soon to be married. Engagements and marriages blossomed everywhere and people seemed happy and confident. There was work and there was a future. We had a young Queen, recently crowned, and here we were, a nation, embarking together on a new Elizabethan age. Throughout the land there was a feeling of expectancy, a sense of destiny.

In addition, the brightest jewel of courage and endurance had finally been plucked. For, only months before, mighty Mount Everest had at last been conquered by a British expedition led by Colonel John Hunt. The two successful summiteers, Edmund Hillary and the Sherpa, Tenzing Norgay, had become legends in their own lifetime. Everyone, everywhere was swept up in the emotion of it all. The whole team had performed brilliantly and the world rejoiced in their success.

A gentleman of five feet ten inches and thirteen stone five and a half pounds was the new Heavyweight boxing champion of the world – Rocky Marciano. Every challenger he fought was bigger than he was, yet, with his awesome power, he terrified them all. His famous right hand, which kissed all comers asleep, was affectionately known as 'Suzy Q'. He was to remain unbeaten for the whole of his career.

As a nation we had breathed a sigh of relief as that great old wizard of football, Stanley Matthews, had at last, in 1953, won an FA Cup medal with victorious Blackpool. But now, in 1954, the team to beat was West Bromwich Albion. In cricket, Fred Trueman and Brian Statham, two demon fast bowlers, were the pride of the North.

On the railways the great steam locomotives still graced our lines with their majestic splendour. The Class 7P *Britannia* and *Oliver Cromwell*, each weighing 94 tons, were frequently seen, as was the mighty Class 8P *Duke of Gloucester*. The much-loved *Green Knight* – Class 4MT, 67.9 tons – had made its debut for East Somerset Railways and the steam engine's survival was assured for the foreseeable future by the planned introduction of the Class 9F series, which included *Morning Star*, *Evening Star* and the impressive *Black Prince*. From the safety of a railway bridge, during that memorable spring, my little brother and I marvelled at these steaming dragons, sharing their joyful exuberance as they thundered across the countryside.

One day, imitating the action of an engine's pistons, our legs pumping away like billy-oh, we powered our bikes up the hill towards Highgate Junior Mixed School. We had cause for celebration for little Alan had at last learned to ride a two-wheeler. To mark the occasion Mum and Dad had dug deep in their pockets and bought him a new one and though half the size of my green racer, its bright, cherry-red frame and shining silver wheels commanded admiration from everyone.

Alan was as proud as punch. Ring, ring, ring, went his bell, accompanying his battle cry of 'Geronimo!' The weather was perfect too: blue skies with not a cloud in sight. On reaching the top of the hill we got off and made our way down a narrow path alongside the school and out to the remote fields beyond. Our destination was a place called the Windcover, a dense, dark little wood with a sinister reputation for being haunted. People seldom went there, for the farmer who owned it didn't take kindly to trespassers. (His nickname, Blunderbuss, gives a fair indication of his belligerent nature.) Leaving our bikes safely by a fence, we heeded the countryside code and walked around the fields to a half-hidden pond near the wood. The objective of this expedition was to find a great crested newt. Alan had never seen such a creature and I had promised him a sight of one.

For weeks I had fascinated him with stories of the many specimens of newts I had discovered in the Gam as a boy. As that lovely stream had now been destroyed you had to search far and wide to find such creatures. But there was no going back on my word, for Alan expected me to come up trumps.

We were well equipped with two home-made fishing nets, but at the back of my mind I had doubts about my chances of success. (Once you become a young man you lose some of that sixth sense you enjoyed as a child.) This particular pond was deceptive, promising much but yielding little. Bulrushes adorned its sides and the water, between two and four feet deep, was mature and clear. It was festooned with oxygenating plants which, when parted, offered hope of finding the denizens of the deep but, on further inspection, merely brought disappointment.

As time went by, I managed to scoop up a few water beetles and leeches to ease Alan's disappointment, but there was still no sign of our quarry. My little brother's face gradually assumed the fixed expression of a depressed monkey, with tears not far away. In quiet desperation I removed all my clothes and foraged in the deeper parts of the pond, where, after an age, success finally came my way.

Unseen by Alan, I hid the specimen before drying myself and getting dressed again. I then enacted a scene that I had experienced in my childhood: slowly I lowered a two-pound jam jar, with its prehistoric eight-inch occupant, directly in front of his face. The great crested newt's vibrant, orange-spotted belly, gaping eyes and impressive black crest took his breath away as, with a grin the size of a pancake, he shouted:

'By gum, Brian, it's a right smasher!'

With eyes bulging and lungs fit to burst, Alan gavotted and jumped up and down like a yo-yo. I received enough hugs and kisses to last a lifetime. Finally he stopped and quietly did what he has always done: held me close, whispering, 'I love you, Brian.'

His warm, dark-brown eyes glowed with ecstasy. He was still quite tiny for eight and his cropped hair made him even more endearing.

'I wish we could keep it,' he murmured wistfully.

But he knew the rules and, after admiring the lovely creature for another ten minutes, he had the honour of returning it to the pond. We watched with wonder as its beautiful form glided effortlessly out of sight.

For a while we had been aware of a figure slowly approaching us. As he drew closer his purposeful, direct approach made his identity obvious: it was Blunderbuss. At a distance of fifty yards he stopped, his gun held loosely by his side. He was tall, with features like a hawk, and he stood as still as a statue, barely seeming to breathe. It was like a scene from *High Noon*. Alan was nervous but he needn't have worried, for Blunderbuss's face broke into a warm smile as he asked in a crusty voice:

"Ave yer 'ad any luck? Did yer get anything?'

I nodded and described our success.

'Yer lucky. Once the tadpoles are gone, there's nowt much to see. Ponds don't 'ave the same amount of life as they used to 'ave. I recognize yer. Brian Blessed, isn't it? Saw you in a play in Mexborough last year. Yer were right grand. I wish yer fans could 'ave seen yer a few minutes ago with no clothes on! By gum, Brian, but tha's a right rum fella. Any road, yer can come here as much as yer like. On yer way back take the long path up there. Since they left the ponds yer'll find thousands of little yellow frogs in the fields. Anyway, I'd best be off. Cheerio.'

With that he disappeared as quickly as the great crested newt.

The whole meeting had proved to be quite contrary to what I had expected: Blunderbuss was a sweetie-pie and the Windcover free of ghosts. Indeed, as we made our way along the trail recommended by our host, the wood resounded cheerfully with the mating call of multitudes of magpies.

To our astonishment and delight we found the fields teeming with tiny frogs, as Blunderbuss had described. In all my years of roving the countryside I had never come across anything like it. We couldn't stop laughing as we filled our hands with the little fellows, but we had to be extremely careful where we put our feet. The frogs' minute, cold bodies could only tolerate the heat of our hands for a certain amount of time and on realizing this we put them down at once. We continued to watch this staggering scene in disbelief.

An hour later we were once more on the top of Highgate Hill. It was getting on for teatime and I knew that mum would be growing anxious. We plunged down the road leading to Bolton, with me leading the way.

I have done some stupid things in my time, but nothing compared with that day! There I was, the personification of Reg Harris, the world-class pursuit cyclist, hurtling down the hill, with my baby brother imitating my example and trying to keep up with me. God in heaven! What was I thinking of? The hill is long and very steep. Halfway down, as always, I stopped pedalling and started to coast – unlike my inexperienced brother. Twiddling ever faster, he passed me before veering horribly out of control. His front wheel spun at right angles to the frame and he flew straight over the handlebars, his lovely bike smashing into a wall and ending up bent double.

If that was horrible, it was nothing to what happened to Alan. He hit the road with his face and bare arms, bounced on its surface like a rubber ball and came to a smacking stop against a wooden fence. 'Oh, shit!' was all I could say. He was an awful mess: blood everywhere, his legs a mass of torn skin, and the appalling-looking wounds caked in dirt. His arms were the same, with one elbow dreadfully swollen. His face was wretched. In a frightful panic I sped to his side and tore off my white shirt in an attempt to stem the flow of blood. My gentle dabbing must have felt like hammer blows, for he begged me to stop and to get him home.

'I want Mammy, Brian,' he moaned deliriously. 'Is my new bike OK?'

Poor little sod, he was my responsibility. One eye was already closing rapidly and his face was swelling by the minute. Frequent tremors shook his system as the reality of it all hit home. With demonic strength I tossed him over my shoulder, mounted my racer and rode home one-handed.

Alan's injuries proved to be outwardly dramatic but not, thank God, really serious, although for several days he was in intense pain. When my parents learned the facts they said not a word. It wasn't a case of 'if looks could kill' – they simply stared at me in disbelief. I was to remain two inches tall for a considerable time.

That evening I sat in bed cradling Alan's swollen, bandaged form. But for the liberal amounts of yellow iodine, he could easily have been mistaken for an Egyptian mummy. Back and forth, in rhythm with his murmurings of pain, I rocked him, occasionally breaking the momentum to apply a kiss. His one eye viewed me with concern as he tenderly whispered, 'Tha's not to blame, tha knows. Tha munt blame thysen. I love you, Brian.'

Miraculously, two weeks later, Alan's wounds had healed up completely and his skin was as smooth as a baby's bottom. His bike had been lovingly restored to its pristine splendour by an army of caring uncles, and all was well again. I was back to my normal height once more!

It was then the second week in May and the sun had increased in warmth. Playing hide and seek with Alan, I sped like lightning down our garden, across the allotments, up the disused railway embankment and down to the Seven Fields beyond. There I lay in the long grass like a dead man, but in no time at all I had been discovered and Alan's little body nestled alongside mine, sharing with me the spectacle of tiny clouds fleeting across the azure sky. Skylarks hovered everywhere, their distinctive song trilling vibrantly in the warm morning air.

'See that one landing?' I said, pointing. 'People think that's where its nest must be but then always find they're wrong. The skylark is simply leading them away from the exact location of its nest, which is well hidden hundreds of yards away and well camouflaged. It then makes its way home.'

'By gum, Brian, tha knows a lot,' said Alan, his eyes out on stalks.

'Oh, yes,' I replied, flamboyantly stroking my eyebrows. 'Einstein's got nothing on me!'

Days later similar words of praise came from my mother, as we walked along the embankment one sunny afternoon.

'Oh, no, no, Mother,' I smiled. 'I'm quite ignorant really, I know so little. But I'm loving learning.'

She returned the smile and we continued our walk.

'As you know, Brian, I never went to school and I can't read. I'd 'ave liked to 'ave learned but I've never 'ad the time.'

We walked on, arm in arm, the sun's rays dancing on her wavy, light-brown hair and forcing her to shade her dark eyes from its power. Whenever she was deep in thought she had a way of looking down and sideways. It was a most endearing habit and always moved me to stroke her hair and kiss her temple. As I did so on this occasion she gave me a great hug and we sat down under the shade of a large bush.

My mother was now in her mid forties. In looks I strongly resembled her, both of us having rather big features, but like all mothers she had the loveliest face in the world. Now she was pensive, which always intrigued me. In hushed tones she said:

'Yer know, Brian, when I was nobbut a lass of thirteen I went outside of Yorkshire to Oxfordshire, on my 'olidays. It was lovely. I went with my cousin, Toocha, and stayed in a little, old-fashioned cottage belonging to my Uncle Harry's father in a small village called Rollright. The countryside was a fairy land of rolling 'ills, orchards, and sweet-scented yellow fields. Lying there with Toocha in those meadows, the scent was so beautiful it almost put you to sleep. Just like Judy Garland in that poppy field in *The Wizard of Oz*. There was Little Rollright and Great Rollright, though I could never tell any difference in their size. We once visited Chipping Norton, which was very daring, and had tea. The folks spoke in a quaint manner, all rolling their r's. They were always giving us apples and sweets.

'The summer was warmer there than 'ere in Yorkshire and it seemed to go on for ever. At night Toocha and I would climb down from our bedroom window to play "Jack, Jack, shine a light" with all our friends. Oh, they were the 'appiest of days! We went each afternoon to Long Compton to 'ave tea with our Aunt Thora and to listen to 'er stories. Once she took our breath away when she told us about the Rollright Stones. "You must visit them," she said. "And listen to the Whispering Knights. The stones date back to over a thousand years before Jesus was born. The largest stone is the King Stone and the other stones are knights. People say the King ordered his knights to stand there and protect England and others say they were turned to stone by an angry witch." '

My mother paused for a second and then continued:

'Well, Brian lad, we couldn't wait to see the stones even though we were a bit frightened. There were quite a few visitors there when we arrived, who explained to us that they were magical stones and that no matter how 'ard you tried you could never count them. This was true, because whenever we tried we always came up with a different number. Visitors to the stones were also sometimes affected by an 'igh-pitched buzzing in their ears. Toocha and I sat for ages alongside those stones. It were an 'ot, muggy day with a slight breeze. You know Brian, as sure as I'm sitting 'ere. I could swear we 'eard those knights whispering.'

The next day I had a young Dewsbury lad of fifteen visit me. He was a charming fellow and as determined as me to be a professional actor. We'd met the year before on an annual one-week drama course at Calder High School, near Hebden Bridge, and had got on famously. The drama course had proved to be a little intimidating for both of us since practically everyone there had seemed to be somewhat older than we were. In two weeks we were to attend the same course again, and this time we felt much more confident about it.

In my room we listened to Walton's music to Olivier's film of *Henry V*, and acted out various Shakespearian scenes together.

My young visitor had a strikingly powerful face and a fine voice. His potential was tremendous and there was no doubt that his dedication and talent would take him far. In fact, it took him very far – to the far reaches of space, as Captain Jean-Luc Picard of the US Starship *Enterprise* in the popular TV series *Star Trek: The Next Generation*. For this shy, self-effacing young lad in front of me was Patrick Stewart. He possessed genuine humility and grace. His eyes, I felt, had a slightly oriental look, which combined mysteriously with his rather serious, introvert manner. When he smiled, which was rare, his face lit up like the big lamp at nearby Thurnscoe. When he roared with laughter, which was an event in itself, the universe broke asunder. He was a terrific fellow and I loved his company.

Even though Patrick was over a year younger than me, he always seemed much more mature and it was amusing to watch his bewilderment when I vigorously wrestled with my father in our sitting-room; likewise his astonishment when my mother stopped the contest by hitting me on the elbow with a frying-pan! This kind of familiarity was new to him. When I visited his house the atmosphere was much more formal.

The next few days at work dragged on laboriously until my annual holiday arrived and I was free at last to attend the one-week drama course in the Calder valley.

The day before I left I stood on the embankment outside our house surveying the vista. The weather was inconsistent; not quite sure whether it was spring or winter. The wind blew with a keen freshness, carrying with it tiny particles of ice that peppered my face, making my eyes weep with the cold. During periods of respite from the sleet I looked to my right towards Doncaster – this large town marks the beginning of the flat fenlands that stretch for many miles to the east – on over the Rivers Don and Trent, past Normandy and New Holland to the far reaches of Grimsby, Hull and Spurn Head. Pounding my fists to keep warm, I turned my eyes northwards, conjuring up in my mind picturesque Knaresborough. I daydreamed of sailing from there along the River Nidd to enchanting Pately, Lofthouse, Masham and Ruckdon Pike, finally resting with King Arthur and his knights at historic Richmond. What a lovely county of contrasts! I turned now, head-on, into the west wind, which with renewed fury, tore at my clothing, forcing me to take a step back as my mac billowed like a kite. Surely this blast could come from only one place. Permit me to take you to its source.

Follow me then as I scoot through streams and valleys, over the undulating countryside that heralds those ancient Nestors, the Yorkshire Moors. Stay with me past Penistone, Shipley, Bingley, Otley and graceful, mystical abbeys. Let us climb even higher to proud Ilkley, the gateway to the Dales, and float in the waters of the Wharfe as it laps the land leading to Skipton, Burnsall, Grassington and Simon's Seat. Be patient now as our swift journey nears its destination. Pass the intriguing house of the Brontës and Haworth village and use your last reserves of energy to mount the hills beyond and reach the source of the wind. Yes, it is that strange, uncanny, derelict house, Top Withens: the very soul of *Wuthering Heights*.

Look up and see the dark, threatening clouds break and yield to the pure rays of light. Listen to Emily Brontë's words:

> No coward soul is mine,
> No trembler in the world's storm-troubled sphere:
> I see Heaven's glories shine,
> And faith shines equal, arming me from fear.

Early next morning, after a sleepless but happy night, I boarded the red bus for Barnsley and from there to Wakefield, Huddersfield and Halifax. The second bus I travelled in, green and yellow, blended in cheerfully with the rolling hills as we trundled towards the Calder valley.

My heart skipped a beat when at last I glimpsed the Calder High School, delightfully situated halfway up the hillside. The moment the bus stopped I leapt out and ran up the winding path towards the front entrance. Pausing for a moment I took in the surroundings below me: a steam train leisurely approaching Mytholmroyd before pressing on to Hebden Bridge; the hills on both sides of the valley rising steep and green; the hillside where

I stood, sprinkled with groups of thick, low-lying trees. The friendly-looking school, with its many windows, blended subtly into the delightful green landscape, beckoning me on.

The sun was warm, the sky clear and there was no wind. I took a deep breath: the still air tasted pure and alive with energy. For a brief moment I knew something original for the first time in my life. This experience was new yet familiar.

My heightened senses were suddenly jarred by a chorus of friendly hellos from a gathering of boisterous teenagers outside the front entrance. Everyone appeared to be excited about the prospect of the drama course. Animated exchanges developed into a cacophony as all and sundry shook hands and whooped with delight. Despite not knowing any of them, I joined in the fun and to add to my enjoyment Patrick Stewart was also there, hugging and pummelling me as he shouted:

'It's going to be bloody marvellous, Brian. The tutors on the course are terrific.'

We burst into the reception area and, after scribbling our signatures in the visitors' book, beetled down a long hallway, as mature overseers attempted to bring some semblance of order to the proceedings. Suppressing our giggles, we managed somehow to assume an air of respectability, and awaited our instructions.

It was all quite simple: girls to the left and boys to the right. The dormitory I was in was spacious and cheerful, the tall windows giving us a marvellous view of the valley.

Handshakes continued as my dozen or so companions blurted out their names. We were all sixteen or seventeen, some still at school and others, like me, at work. As for background, we were unmistakably a group of working-class lads, all eager to learn. Equally keen were the rest of the students, who numbered, in all, about a hundred.

That evening, in hushed reverence, we sat in a semicircle in the assembly hall, mesmerized by the tutors in front of us; for they were professionals or, as the poet Sir Henry Newbolt would have described them: 'The Dons on the dais serene'. On our left was a white-bearded patriarch called Mr Spradberry, the expert on stage design. Further along the row stood out the beautiful, haunting face of a woman in her early thirties called Ruth Wynn Owen, who would be directing and teaching drama. Next to her sat a young professor named Heuger who, with his lovely wife, would lecture and also direct. Alongside them was the chief drama adviser of South Yorkshire, Gerald Tyler, whom I had met many times before when attending his adjudications at youth festivals. A formidable man in his late forties with a thin, stern, sensitive face and devastating intellect, he was terribly demanding and hard to please. He had selected the tutors and was in charge of the course.

The last in line was a medium-sized gentleman with dark, searing eyes and an air of tremendous authority. His pale face was long and gaunt with a strong nose. He possessed a lion's mane of hair, wavy and dark brown. His voice was bass-baritone with an intriguing ability to soar into the tenor region. He spoke slowly and clearly, with a Continental accent. His delivery was an object-lesson in the meaning of grace: the maximum effect with the minimum of effort. This quality extended to the way he dressed. His elegant, black, flared trousers were firmly supported by a wide leather belt, and his slim waist emphasized his fine torso, which sported a green, cowboy-style shirt and darker green waistcoat. The final flourish was a large burgundy, silk handkerchief around his neck, held in place by a ring of hide; this cascaded romantically down one shoulder. He was none other than the great movement teacher Rudi Shelley, of the Bristol Old Vic Theatre School: the school on which I had set my heart.

In a flash the week's schedule was explained to us. This involved numerous rehearsals of extracts from plays, which were to be presented to the public on the last day of the course. The urgency of the situation was underlined by the tutors, who began at once to audition us. We were flabbergasted and thrilled to bits. Patrick, sitting next to me, pounded my ribs like a five-year-old.

Scripts floated around the room like taffeta. Never backward in coming forward, I seized on one called *Hiss the Villain*, a Victorian melodrama which focused on the fiendish lead, Mr Straker. Following Michael Redgrave's advice, I concentrated like hell on familiarizing myself with the text. Assuming authority and control, I gave a good account of myself, feeling as I did the full benefit of my speech lessons and Harry Dobson's guidance. When I had finished the speech there was a short discussion and I was given the part.

I eased back in my chair, happy as a sandboy. Patrick was generosity itself as he unobtrusively shook my hand.

'You lucky bugger, I wanted that part,' a lad behind me whispered. The voice belonged to a grinning youth called Trevor Parks, who shared our dormitory. He was a great character, with a mind of his own, and was destined to become the comedian of the group. The casting continued and everyone demonstrated their splendid individual talents, to be quickly rewarded with cracking parts.

Mr Shelley told me years later that the course had given him immense satisfaction. His own production of the York Mystery Cycle play *The Last Judgement* would take place the following day.

After dinner we enjoyed a leisurely stroll around the school gardens. It felt like being in ancient Greece: the tutors dotted about the terraces like Plato and Aristotle in the Parthenon, with us students buzzing around them like bees, as if they were some Hymettus laden with the honey of sweet knowledge. We were already a team united by happiness. As the sun sank out of sight and homes lit up the dark, distant hills, we reluctantly made our way to our dormitories.

After an hour of giggles and stories we slept. My last memory was of Patrick's face in the moonlight, looking up at the ceiling, with a glow of bliss in his oriental eyes.

Reveille was at seven a.m., and we were up like jumping beans and fighting for the showers. The large dining-room was a sunny delight with large French windows leading out on to a spacious balcony that gave a panoramic view of the valley. Conversations were at fever pitch and food was subconsciously pushed aside to allow some impatient enquiry to be pursued. Oh God! Oh God! The fun of it all! This is what I'd missed so badly since leaving school. Thoughts and emotions bubbled away as teachers and students came together in pursuit of the mystery of Art.

'Neglect the Arts at your peril,' Sir Charles Groves once warned an incoming government. That great conductor would have approved wholeheartedly of the dedication in our dining-room that day. Alert minds behind expressive young faces fired questions that tested the tutors to the limit. The flaming torch of enquiry was passed around at the speed of light.

The build-up of bodies around the main table, much to everyone's delight, gently crushed male and female together, creating a rhythmical wave effect. This resulted in a face disappearing, only for another to take its place. Such a flux heralded the appearance of the striking Ruth Wynn Owen, who announced, with a twinkle in her eye, that Mr Shelley was waiting patiently in the gym to put our energy to good use.

Ten minutes later we received a severe dressing-down for being late. Mr Shelley made no bones about it, maintaining that it was the first rule of the theatre never to be late. After allowing us time to take this in, he instructed us to watch him doing what he called basic exercises and to attempt to emulate him. We were to have one hour of movement with him each day, he said, and as we had only one week we should concentrate like hell and hope that something would sink in.

It would take a series of books to describe the work and teachings of this master. For a start, the term 'movement teacher' is misleading, for his tremendous talent, in addition to that particular art, embraced a whole range of accomplishments. These included: mastery of the history of theatre, acting and directing and an amazing knowledge of music. How privileged we felt to be in his presence. This lithe figure suggested cat-like agility and when still conveyed the impression of being balanced and centred from the middle of the solar plexus. The man seemed incapable of making any movement that was not, in itself, beautiful.

After half an hour's exhilarating exercise to the music of Don Gillis's *Symphony 5$\frac{1}{2}$ for Fun*, we sat panting and sweating on the floor while our teacher scarcely drew breath.

'You all have ghastly deportment,' he said in a deep voice. 'This has come about because of bad habits from your childhood. It can be rectified by intensive work and discipline but, my God, you will need to work hard and how! See what I mean?' he said, pointing to a young lady slouching in a corner. 'Huh?'

The 'huh' was low and rumbling and made us all immediately sit up straight. This caused him to smile broadly and give a throaty chuckle.

'You see, folks: you have reacted in the worst possible way. For example, look at the young man over there.'

He was pointing straight at me. Within seconds, with the elegance of a matador, he wove his way round each intervening student and stood before me, with towering authority.

Aye, aye, I thought. I'm in for it.

And I was right. His eyes pierced me.

'Your name is Brian Blessed! Lovely name, lousy walker! And he's not on his own. All you boys are the same; you entered the room like muscular furniture removers. I half expected you to ask where you were to put the piano. Ghastly! Absolutely ghastly! You sway from the shoulders with your chest and bottoms sticking out. Anatomically it is totally incorrect and over the years you will develop problems with your spine. Stand up, Mr Blessed, I wish to borrow your body.'

He placed a hand at the base of my back and went on:

'This top muscle of the buttock controls the anus and is called the gluteus maximus. It is the key to good deportment.'

At this point he surprised us all by producing a lemon from his pocket.

'Now, Brian Blessed, I am going to place this lemon between your buttocks and I want you to squeeze them together and hold the lemon in place!'

Pandemonium broke loose as everybody screamed with laughter. The hilarity then increased as he asked me to bend my knees and hold the said object in place. Although I succeeded, I found the exercise terribly difficult. Had all my years of youthful study finally brought me to the gluteus maximus and hence to the anus? Did the sacred secret of correct posture reside in the sponge cake of the top muscle of the buttock and in that dark cave of eternal night, the rectum? If so, then the often-used modern-day term 'arsehole' is misunderstood and is, in fact, a compliment. Without doubt the experience had a profound effect on me and I have never been the same since. I am also pleased to inform you that other lads sampled the merits of that yellow citrus fruit and looked as big a nana as I did.

The young ladies who had all watched, helpless with mirth, were now themselves to receive the Shelley treatment.

What lovely young ladies they were too, with their smooth, vibrant skins and dashing eyes that shone brightly as they tossed back their long hair. We gazed at them with admiration and their every movement brought us pleasure.

'Aaah!' I moaned quietly as some poet's words hummed in my mind:

> An hundred years should go to praise
> Thine eyes, and on thy forehead gaze,
> Two hundred to adore each breast,
> But thirty thousand to the rest.

'Marvell, Brian, Marvell,' said Patrick, who had overheard me.

'I am marvelling,' I replied.

'No, Brian, you misunderstand. The words you've just recited are by Andrew Marvell.'

We both chuckled at this and then watched with fascination as Mr Shelley addressed the ladies. Their eyes had little effect on him as he gestured them aside.

'You girls, you are as bad as the boys. First of all, don't flirt with me. For example, don't swing your pelvic girdle – it's ghastly. Get it firmly fixed in your heads that your legs should be hanging legs that swing in the hip. But the actual hip region is radiantly quiet. You mistake sexiness for being charming. When you achieve this you will have attained grace and elegance. Elegance is hard to define, doubly hard to teach and can basically be described as good posture with economy of effort.'

The lesson ended on a musical note as we relaxed on the floor and listened to Samuel Barber's *Adagio for Strings*.

From that moment on it was rehearsals, costume fittings, lectures and make-up lessons. On my way to one of these lessons, Mr Shelley's booming voice stopped me in my tracks:

'Can you speak to music?'

I gulped, walked gingerly into his office and muttered:

'I'd love to try.'

'Right then,' continued the master. 'These words are spoken by God to people going to heaven. It is an extract from one of the York Mystery Cycle plays entitled *The Last Judgement*. When you are ready, speak.'

The words poured out as he turned on the inspiring last five minutes of Wagner's *Götterdämmerung*. This short audition was a gorgeous experience. There was Shelley's gaunt face framed against the large open window, the green hill beyond serving as a perfect backdrop.

'Not bad. Not bad at all,' he said. 'Thank you very much. The lemon has helped you. See you later, young man.'

For the umpteenth time my heart rejoiced, and I hurriedly tried on a costume for *Hiss the Villain*. The room was festooned with fabrics and ladies and had a happy feeling of organized chaos. In the midst of this turmoil stood a creature of calm and serenity, the lady of the haunting face, Ruth Wynn Owen. (At times this book must sound a little like George Gurdjieff's *Meetings with Remarkable Men*. Yet later Mr Shelley himself confided in me that Miss Wynn Owen was the most extraordinary person he'd ever met.) She smiled at me warmly, shook my hand, nodded to the dress designer that my costume was satisfactory and disappeared.

At that moment I realized I was the only male in the room. I instantly became self-conscious and uncertain of my self and edged towards the exit.

'You remind me a lot of James Mason and I think he's marvellous,' said a young woman behind me.

Keeping my nerve, I calmly turned round and faced the speaker. The room had gone completely quiet and you could have heard a pin drop. I was aware of the fresh, cold air from the moors wafting in through the window, and as I continued to look at the woman before me everything around her became misty and vague. Even the clocks lost their odd clicking sound and appeared to stop. All was motionless and for an infinitesimal moment the cosmos itself seemed to be playing statues.

'Who are you?' I asked.

'My name is Nancy Marshall.'

A further, effortless, silence took place as Miss Marshall smiled with kindness and a sensitive, enquiring gaze. Unexpectedly, a long ripple of laughter cascaded from her lips. It took on a tinkling quality, as if it came from far away, and when her breathing seemed unable to sustain it the ripple of laughter would start up again. I found myself laughing with her and making foolish comments about James Mason's films.

She sat gracefully on a table, her pretty, bare legs displaying tiny white ankle socks and small, flat-heeled black shoes. Her figure was slim and delightfully covered by a cheerful dress whose colours reminded me of barley-sugar and cream. Her elegant neck supported the loveliest face I had ever seen. Her hair had the blackness of Cathy's in *Wuthering Heights* and her eyes, which were identical in darkness, shone like prisms lit by unseen candles. Finally, her nose and mouth were delicate and fine and she was blessed with skin that was as white as snow.

Our eyes locked for what seemed an eternity, until I became aware of the grinning faces around me. I coughed nervously, made some lame excuse and vanished.

From that moment on the biblical story of Saul being enveloped by light and becoming Paul took on a new meaning for me. The immediate change in me was obvious to all. Patrick was vastly amused as I joined him and the rest of the cast for a rehearsal of a *commedia dell'arte* play called *Harlequin's Dumbstruck*. He was playing the lead and being his usual brilliant self, while I was at sixes and sevens. If there had been a part called Dumbstruck I would have filled the role perfectly, for I was totally dumbstruck by Nancy. D and A molecules collided and re-formed in me to further discombobulate my senses and to produce a new cellular component that was shaped like a heart and inscribed with the letter N. Nancy, Nancy, Nancy – the name raced up and down my spine like hot mercury. Rehearsals were great but when they involved her they were transcendent.

As luck and the gods would have it, we were in three plays together. Therefore we were at each other's side virtually every moment of the day. Only the nights intervened and I would jealously wish them away until dawn's welcome light heralded the vision of her face at breakfast.

The word 'love' was never mentioned; we simply adored being together. Locked arm in arm or hand in hand we feigned sadness if our daisy-chain of romance was broken by the demands of other productions. As soon as we had fulfilled these other obligations we would rush back to each other and resume our conversation as if nothing had happened. Not that we neglected our studies; quite the reverse, for the relationship stimulated our senses and heightened our appreciation of all we were being taught.

It goes without saying that spring had worked its magic in every corner of the school; there was not a heart that had not been kissed by its ethereal spell. Every Jack had his Jill, and the tutors nodded approval, while applying wise and tactful discipline when bedtime beckoned.

Sex did not belong here, for this was a haven of purity and delight. Yet one night, unable to sleep, accompanied by Patrick and Trevor Parks, I led the way through the gardens to the girls' dormitory. This was incredibly daring as beady-eyed matrons patrolled the vicinity. The traditional throwing of stones drew the all-clear signal from the girls, Nancy included, and I shinned up the drainpipe. After a tricky traverse I entered the forbidden kingdom.

Once inside, I gestured for the two lads to follow me, but much to my disgust, they declined. My sole objective was to hold Nancy's hand and to recite love poems to her, but my endeavours were scuppered by intermittent hoots of laughter from the other lasses. In an attempt to keep them quiet, my shushes became as loud as their whoops. A knock came at the door and the chief matron made her entrance.

After satisfying herself that the commotion was only attributable to the girls' high spirits, she sat on the bed next to Nancy's and began to talk about the 'facts of life'. As the girls were aware of me hiding under the next bed, their responses to the matron's

180

searching questions were understandably coy. Confused by their bursts of hysterical laughter, the matron decided that they were immature and changed the subject. At that moment I felt my foot being pushed further under the bed. For this I had Miss Ruth Wynn Owen to thank, who had silently entered the room.

The next day she poured me a coffee at breakfast and talked about the weather – a non-committal approach completely in keeping with her enigmatic personality. Sometimes I felt so sure that I had latched on to something that made her tick, only to realize I was way off target. This extraordinary woman confounded everyone. She possessed in abundance both mystery and a phenomenal grasp of human nature, the latter being allied to a profound love for all that was good in life.

We discovered that she had played leading parts with Gielgud and many other remarkable artists. Her humility drove us potty as we implored her to talk about herself. It was all to no avail, for the sands of Egypt simply deepened around the riddling sphinx.

Instead, she applied her energies to us. Golden wisdom poured from her lips as she explained the dramatic methods of Shakespeare and the other masters. In common with the rest of the tutors, she possessed a complete knowledge of every aspect of stagecraft, from lighting to design.

The plays took shape and on the evening before performance night a barn dance was held. This proved to be a wonderful evening of pandemonium, during which Nancy and I never left one another's side. Miss Wynn Owen smiled and cackled loudly at our possessiveness. Patrick, giggling like a demented Fu Manchu, displayed the love of his life, a delightful lass called Jane, and had the temerity to inform me that she was the prettiest girl in sight. He received a swift kick up the backside and a timely reminder that that honour belonged to the lass on my arm. Nancy laughed, fixed her prismatic eyes on me and kissed me for the first time, lightly on the cheek. My heart strained with happiness, beating to the rhythm of a French song: 'Boom, why does my heart go boom?'

The music in the hall increased in tempo as tireless legs shook the floor with zany glee. Hands clapped and voices roared in appreciation of the band and the good lady in charge.

181

Breathless and happy, we flopped down at the sides of the assembly hall and awaited the arrival of Mr Shelley, who was to give a solo performance. He glided across the room and gave one of the most stunning performances I have ever seen, conjuring up a world of fashion shows and rock 'n' roll that depicted male and female models of English, French, German and American extraction.

The assembly hall is large and yet he used the whole space with consummate ease. His mastery of movement and his stunning imagination filled us with awe. His ability to convey the twin masks of comedy and tragedy was particularly poignant. The end came all too quickly and we applauded this great performance with tearful gusto.

That evening we retired in a state of incredulity, singing our teacher's praises until exhaustion brought oblivion. As the chorus in *Henry V* says: 'Now all England is on fire'; and so indeed were we the following morning, for it was performance time!

It was interesting to observe my companions, many of whom had taken their O levels and were now embarking on A levels with a view to going on to college or university. Amusingly enough, they took it for granted that I could select any university I fancied; my seemingly sophisticated air and lively knowledge of the arts cunningly covered over the gaps in my education. They were genuinely impressed by my perceptive reasoning. My education in life was at that stage a little more developed than theirs. In any event, it would seem that my inadequacies were not evident. Then again, they may have perceived all and decided, lovingly, to refrain from prodding me.

In my heart I ached to be back at school with them and free from plastering. Still, I rejoiced in their academic revelations and felt a complete affinity with them; in our love of the muse we were fellow worshippers. On this final day Nancy, who was with several others, asked how many O levels I had acquired. Affecting an air of indifference, I muttered vaguely that I had gained eight.

'Clever boy,' said Nancy, as the rest gasped in admiration. I quickly changed the subject to the attributes of King Leonidas of Sparta in facing the Persian army of seventy-two thousand with only three hundred men of his own! Ruth Wynn Owen, with her owl eyes, had seen everything and to my intense relief led us away to begin the dress rehearsal.

After the rehearsal we had a couple of hours to spare in which the students entertained the tutors with soliloquies. Nancy delivered a speech from Shaw's *St Joan* and was very impressive. Walking in the gardens later, I urged her to take up acting professionally. She had grave doubts, she said, stressing the vital importance of education and how becoming a teacher appealed to her enormously. As we walked past a piano in the main hall she sat down and played a charming little piece entitled *Fleur-de-Lis*.

'Lovely in its simplicity, isn't it, Brian?' she smiled.

'Oh, yes,' I murmured. 'Very lovely indeed.'

That evening the public demonstration of dramatic work went marvellously, the only hitch being that the Archangel Gabriel came on wearing white socks. The culprit, of course, was me. Mr Shelley could have killed me, but when he questioned me about it later I offered no explanation. Little did he realize that I wore them out of consideration for Nancy, who, like several other girls, couldn't bring herself to kiss my bare feet.

Our parents had been among the audience and afterwards had tea and sandwiches with the tutors. After they had left a banquet was held, with speeches and tributes flowing like wine. Professor Heuger proved to be the star turn on this occasion as he comically highlighted the traumas and crises of the week. Hands beat rhythmically on the tables like African war drums as all the tutors and technical staff were cheered to the rafters.

This astonishing exuberance continued late into the evening, until Mr Tyler brought the celebrations to an end and bid us goodnight. Of course, for us students the fun was only just beginning, and half an hour later we found ourselves in semi-darkness in the gymnasium.

There, with our respective partners, we sat on cushions and mattresses and told ghost stories. These had the desired effect of making some of the ladies scream, which was greatly appreciated by the lads, for their broad shoulders could offer much solace and comfort. Generally though, the atmosphere was one of total hilarity. Nancy and I sat laughing at the antics of the couples in front.

'They're coming up for air,' whispered Nancy.

She interrupted my amused reaction to this by blowing gently on my forehead and demonstrating a butterfly kiss on my cheek. As her eyelashes danced delicately on my skin I felt for all the world that the fairy queen, Titania herself, could not have shown such extreme sensitivity. I felt that the ceiling above us was covered in soft white clouds, each one occupied by a chubby cupid raining intoxicating arrows down on us.

The room gradually became quieter as a suggestion of light appeared in the night sky. In that moment, between night and day, our youth became one with the certainty of spring. In that simple state our innocence was blessed. This experience continued as we left the gymnasium, Nancy and I walking hand in hand and glancing from time to time at the approaching dawn. Unexpectedly we came across Miss Wynn Owen, all alone, with her face pressed against a window, crying uncontrollably. She immediately reassured us that all was well.

'Oh my darlings,' she whispered, wiping her tears away. 'Forgive me. I'm so sorry you should see me like this but the week has been so miraculous and now that it's over I feel so terribly sad. This grief is sweet in its nature and I seem incapable of holding it in. You are both very dear to me.'

The tears started again when we held her close, but eventually her mysterious features lit up as she breathed out:

'Oh Nancy! Oh Brian! Life is so short. You barely have time to come out and have a look around before you disappear again. But you mustn't stay here, listening to my ramblings. You both need to be together. I'm perfectly all right, bless you! In the near future you will both come to my home in Hoyland.'

After a silent embrace we walked slowly to the top of the stairs that marked the crossroads between our dormitories. Gently we let our hands go and Nancy took several steps down. She then stopped and turned to look up at me. God! We were so young! In the cold light of dawn her pale features seemed like white marble. The breeze, fresh from its source, Top Withens, poured through the open windows, making us shiver. (This pristine purity of air I was to experience once again, nearly forty years later, on the north ridge of Everest.) Now, frozen in time, it was enough for us that we existed. We said nothing as we slowly receded from one another's sight.

Surprisingly, the following morning cheerful banter filled the air as each and everyone shook hands and promised undying friendship. Addresses were freely exchanged and future rendez-vous enthusiastically arranged. I was determined that we should meet again, in a few weeks' time, at the Brighouse Children's Garden Party. This cheered me enormously, as Nancy would be there too.

At this precise moment I was virtually on my knees with exhaustion: I had not slept or eaten for four days for the simple reason that I was, of course, out of my skull in love with Nancy. (Or, as Shaw's doctor might have said, 'he is suffering from overstimulation of the phagocytes'!) With every step I took I felt like an overactive sparking-plug!

Two young ladies who had become good friends, one dark-haired, Maureen Jenning, and the other blond, Pat Caldwood, were given the job of making sure I got on the bus. Then, happiness upon happiness, Nancy raced down the steps, hugged me passionately and announced that she could accompany me for most of the journey. Finally, all assembled together, we waved goodbye to our tutors on the balcony above us.

On the yellow-and-white bus Nancy revealed that her father was an undertaker. I stifled my smiles as I hid from her the fact that I had done the same work myself. After all, she thought I was still at school. Or did she?

After a couple of hours, with desperate sadness, I watched her leave me to embark on her journey home to Morley, or to be more precise a house called Lyngarth. What a lovely name, I thought: Lyngarth. In my delirious state I had failed to notice that the yellow-and-white bus I was in had become a red one and had reached Highgate Hill.

The Calder adventure was over, and after sleeping blissfully for fourteen hours I was back at work on the building site.

'What does it feel like to be back to reality?' asked my boss, Chris Riley.

I paused, smiled and replied:

'Is that what this is?'

A week later a Morris Minor drew up outside my home, and after a murmured greeting I climbed into the back to be taken to a small warehouse on the outskirts of Barnsley. The driver of the car was a man named Norris from the ABA (Amateur Boxing Association) and the other two men with us were trainers. I was dressed in a dark-red dressing-gown, black shorts and matching vest.

It had been arranged that I should fight a young boxer from Leeds called Al Dawes. This pugnacious individual had a string of victories to his name, mainly due to his strong body punching. Norris had seen me training with Chesty Oscroft in Thurnscoe and wanted to see how I would square up to someone who was already an experienced amateur. My mother and father were beside themselves with worry about this private contest and my father simply couldn't understand me allowing myself to be drawn into such madness. For me it was just another form of exercise. After all, we all boxed in those days.

It would take too long to go into the ins and outs of the fight, save to say that it was basically even-stevens, but halfway through I thought of Nancy and how shocked and horrified she would have been had she witnessed it.

When I was delivered home after the fight my mother was already out on the path and went as white as a sheet, for my boxing glove was pressed against my lower lip in an attempt to stop the blood and to hide a deep gash.

'You 'aven't got the brains you were born with!' she blasted at me as I ran upstairs.

Looking in the mirror, I was horrified at the state of my lip. It was the first time I had been injured and memories of Bruce Woodcock's beating by Joe Baksi came to mind. Eventually I came downstairs and quietly announced to Mr Norris and the two trainers that I had decided never to box again. They respected my decision and we all shook hands on it and they left. My father smiled and said:

I 'ave to tell you that they feel you 'ave the makings of a champion. Apparently, the 'arder young Dawes punched the 'arder you came back. In the end they said you were well on top. Norris said that you could go far and that you are very good.'

'Indeed, Dad,' I replied. 'But, as you have often said to me about boxing: "they are all good until they meet someone better". No Dad, it's all over. I want to be an actor with all my soul.'

This delighted him and he patted my back, adding:

'I thought it was only fair to tell you what Norris had said so that you could make your own decision.'

Five minutes later I received a long hug from my mother and much-needed attention to my lip.

For the next week the uppermost thought in my mind was whether or not my lip would heal in time to enable me to kiss Nancy. (It did heal up – just!) The Brighouse Children's Garden Party took place on a lovely July day and Patrick, Trevor and most of the students from the drama course were there. We lads were dreadfully shy as the young ladies appeared to have grouped away from us. And where the hell was Nancy?

Suddenly she appeared, showering me with her 'Tinkerbell' laugh and radiant in a new dress with a white background covered in roses. We both became dreadfully shy and the movement I made towards her required more courage than fighting young Dawes!

We embraced tenderly and our boldness served as a signal to prompt the other couples to get together. Patrick, grinning like a Cheshire cat, strutted around with his lady and Trevor Parks made us laugh with his bawdy jokes, at the same time impressing us with his deep observations on life.

The conversations were rich and original, and I reflected that since meeting such friends my loneliness had completely disappeared.

The arrangements for that weekend were quite simple. It was Saturday and I would stay at Trevor's for the night and so be able to see Nancy the next day. As the evening approached Patrick urged us to go to the local cinema:

'There's a marvellous film on called *Rough Company*, starring Barbara Stanwyck and Edward G. Robinson. The music is terrific.'

We followed his advice and he was proved right. At least I think so, for after the first twenty minutes Barbara Stanwyck's face disappeared, replaced by Nancy's.

The following day it was Nancy, Nancy, Nancy – no one else existed. Through woods and parks we strolled. It was, of course, Brighouse but it felt more like Arcadia.

From that day on letters flowed freely between us as the weeks passed by sublimely. In the autumn the Theatre Guild put on *The Brontës of Haworth Parsonage*, in which I played Branwell Brontë, and to this day I feel I have never equalled that performance. On came the winter, with a fierce December, until finally spring broke through again, heralding another drama course at the Calder High School. We gathered once more as fellow worshippers and stayed up burning the midnight oil and tying further knots of love and friendship.

In the late autumn of 1955 I found myself walking with Nancy in a quiet street on the outskirts of Leeds. Looking radiant and pensive, she spoke earnestly about her hopes for the future: her heart was set on teaching. What a marvellous ambition, I thought, for teaching is one of the most important jobs on God's earth. I was lost in admiration for her. Her grace and talent would one day enable numerous students to realize their full potential.

We stared at one another very hard until she broke the mood with a smile and said quietly:

'I completely believe in Jesus Christ. Dear Brian, you always seem to be acting. On the rare occasions when you stop I then find you the most appealing. I also sense that you will, ultimately, do something entirely different from acting.'

'Yes,' I replied. 'I agree, there is something else that I can't quite put my finger on.' (The clue was there, over a year earlier at Calder High School, in that cold breeze.)

For a while we said nothing, both staring into space. Then we turned and shook hands warmly, recalling together a relationship that had always been friendly and cheerful.

'Ah, Nancy,' I laughed. 'We all get there in the end.'

'Of course we do,' she replied.

A quiet ripple of laughter cascaded from her lips; the 'Tinkerbell' sound, as if coming from far, far away. We parted: she destined for college and I into the gathering storm clouds.

14

China

'You're a shower! You're a shower of shit. In all my life I have never seen such a dirty, manky, miserable heap of crap as you lot.'

These immortal words were spoken by Corporal Braithwaite on the evening of 10 January 1956 at R A F Bridgnorth in Shropshire.

The atmosphere of this place was gloomy and horrible, and thick snow lay everywhere. The long line of dark wooden sheds was lit outside by spotlights, whose harshness against the surrounding darkness reminded me of films of Auschwitz.

In company with several hundred other men I was about to embark on my ten-week Basic Training – the start of my two years of National Service.

Two years! I thought. Bloody hell!

Everything in my being objected to it – a feeling shared by a large percentage of my fellow conscripts, as well as the hundreds I'd already met at R A F Cardington the week before.

It was well known throughout England that the days of National Service were numbered, so we had fervently hoped that we wouldn't be called up. Make no mistake: there wasn't a lad with me who was not capable of fighting to defend his country. It was simply that anything to do with warfare was now out of tune with the way we felt about life.

The Second World War had ended in triumph for the Allies: after colossal courage and sacrifice Hitler's war machine had been defeated and the Rising Sun of Japan had finally been eclipsed.

As children, my generation had found the war marvellous and exciting, but at the same time we fully appreciated that it was a titanic struggle and that we owed our lives to many brave souls.

With the end of hostilities came a universal sigh of relief. Like the First World War, it had been known as the 'war to end all wars' and consequently the atmosphere of the years that followed was generally celebratory and peaceful, even though the USSR was now looming up as a prospective enemy. That mighty nation now had the hydrogen bomb and we had entered the Nuclear Age. It seemed such a shame when we recalled what glorious allies they had been. Our brave convoys had faced the fearsome wolf packs of German submarines to get much-needed supplies to the Soviet people and even the Americans had wholeheartedly embarked on the huge Lend-Lease programme in 1941, to assist the Russian Bear. Heroic stories of the battles of Stalingrad and Leningrad had moved the hearts of the entire Western world. Who can forget the final summer offensive of 1945, when Zhukov's tanks held their positions against the mighty Tiger tanks of the Wehrmacht before finally pushing them back to Berlin? And now these good people were our enemy. Oh, how awful! The words of the bastard in Shakespeare's *King John* came to mind: 'Mad world! mad kings! mad composition.'

But despite all this stupidity there was a feeling of hope in Britain: people wanted education, art, cinema, dance, music and the freedom to pursue their dreams. We wanted to benefit from the war effort and to realize the opportunities made possible by that great sacrifice.

God in heaven, the war had only just ended! Now wasn't the time to be putting on a uniform. If anyone wanted to be a professional soldier that was fine, but others, me included, wanted something else. We could all accept the argument that we should contribute to the defence of our country. But please! Not for a two-year period!

Basic Training, or 'square bashing' as it was affectionately known, involved learning how to march, fight and how to fire a 303 rifle and Bren gun. There were, of course, other things to learn but that was about it. Therefore we felt you could add a

191

further eight weeks, at most, to Basic Training if the powers that be wanted to introduce us to more sophisticated weaponry.

It was widely known that after this period the rest of the two years was a complete waste of time: you were inevitably stationed somewhere doing an inane job that you were totally unsuited to. If you're a farmer in Civvy Street then it's odds-on you'll end up as a nuclear physicist, was a common joke at the time.

Before receiving my call-up papers, along with scores of other lads I had attended the traditional medical examination in Sheffield. The antics that everyone got up to there in order to avoid National Service were unbelievable. One lad collapsed in front of me feigning a fit – a good act that had me secretly giggling. Another informed me that he had spent hours pouring tea leaves down his throat in the firm conviction that it would show on the X-ray machine as TB. And fifty per cent of the men claimed they suffered from migraine or other disorders. In fact, it was difficult to find anyone who was not suffering from something. Unfortunately, the doctors and accompanying experts remained unconvinced by all this: they were experienced and clever, employing subtle techniques to unmask deception. But this didn't stop the lads from trying.

Any physical idiosyncrasy was exaggerated to ludicrous proportions. One fellow started off slightly bow-legged, but looked like an old cowpoke who had been riding elephants in the OK Corral by the time he confronted the examiners!

Testicular pains, lumbago, asthma, partial blindness and an inability to understand a single question were all worth a try. All that was lacking was the raising of Lazarus. One lad deserved an Oscar for his performance: he arrived with his eyes pointing in opposite directions. The Medical Board stared at him for ages, totally nonplussed. They eventually shook him, and applied a strong light to his face, but his eyes resolutely stared east and west. When asked to walk around the room he collided with everything in sight, forcing the examiners to assist him. As a result of all this, after an hour or so he was considered unsuitable and released.

Later I spotted him in a café, his gaze perfectly normal, and received a crafty wink.

As for myself, I approached the Board quietly and with humility, resisting the temptation to cough unnaturally when the skinny doctor gripped my privates. My eyes, heart and general constitution were judged sound and it was only when they looked at my right foot that the examiners became concerned. Exactly what I was hoping for!

Let me make it clear: my foot is strong, and has served me well for years in football matches, but it is misshapen. It has no arch and the ankle bone is curved, sending the foot out sideways – not a pretty sight, but never has it given me any problems. In fact, years later when I took up judo it proved to be a useful weapon, its fossil-like structure giving hell to opponents when I applied an ankle sweep. Of course, this equanimity about my deformity I hid from the examiners. As they applied pressure here and gave a prod there I feigned a grimace, putting a brave face on it, before letting out a profound groan as they tightened their grip on my fallen arches.

My act was working perfectly, for I was convinced that there was no instrument that could detect pain. Finally the examiners patted me on the shoulder, expressed sympathy and retired.

In the meantime I was ushered into another room, where a bespectacled academic smiled and informed me that my written tests were appalling:

'The results for everybody that day are very low,' he continued, laughing heartily, 'but yours are the worst. It may interest you to know that we know a lot about you – your amateur theatre, for instance – and we cannot accept for a moment that you are as dense as you would have us believe.'

I smiled and replied:

'I'm sorry to hear that, as I have done my best.'

After a while the examiners returned announcing their decision: I had been given a Grade Three rating. I held my breath and refrained from showing any emotion. It was wonderful news! Good old foot! My con had worked perfectly! Now it was impossible to be accepted into the forces, for you had to be either Grade One or Two to be admitted.

I was on the point of leaving when one of the examiners added:

'Although you are rated Grade Three, Mr Blessed, we feel that we can still accommodate you. Your acting could be of use in the RAF and we all would like to congratulate you on your boxing performance against Al Dawes.'

I was devastated and nodded back at them like a sick parrot.

It was as a result of that decision that I now found myself facing Corporal Braithwaite at RAF Bridgnorth. Braithwaite looked like a cross between Boris Karloff and Desperate Dan. His voice was raw and guttural and he rasped out his commands like a malfunctioning steam engine, so that at times it was almost impossible to understand what he was saying. His steaming breath blew out into the freezing night air as he bellowed:

'You 'orrible heap of shit. I promise you, you will either leave this camp in ten weeks' time as airmen or never be seen again. You address me as Corporal, and don't speak till you are spoken to. God 'elp anybody who fails to obey the word of command. You can forget your mothers now; I'm your mother! Before I tuck you up into beddy-byes I am taking you for an hour's march.'

Then he approached the front line of men, including me, and slowly peered into each face. As he drew alongside me he addressed the man on my right: 'Are you in pain, airman?'

'No, Corporal,' replied the perplexed lad.

'You oughtta be,' continued Braithwaite. 'I'm standing on your hair. Get it cut.'

This forced me to smile and the corporal was on to me in a flash:

'You find it funny, do you, monkey?'

'No,' I replied.

'No, Corporal,' he roared back. 'What's your name, you 'orrible man?'

'Blessed, Corporal.'

'Oh?' he scowled. 'So you're Blessed, eh?'

This puzzled me, as he continued: 'Well, you scumbag, if I have any more trouble from you I'll put you on a charge so fast your feet won't touch the ground.'

He then stepped back a few paces and screamed out:

'Squad! Aaaa-ten-shun!'

As we came to attention he exploded:

'That was manky. You move like old women! Stand up straight, you bastards.'

He then began to shout repeatedly, in obvious frustration: 'Squad – 'shun! Stand at ease! Squad – 'shun! Stand at ease!'

This went on for a full ten minutes, until our heels felt numb with the effort, while he raced up and down the rank and file of bodies, giving hell to anybody who didn't measure up.

'Now, you shower, when I give you the word of command I want you to lead off marching by the left foot and to continue in a straight line for the next bloody mile. You won't talk, you won't look sideways, and you'll peg your ears back and listen to me! By the left – quick – march!'

The words were supposed to be: 'Left, right, left, right, left, right, left!' But Braithwaite's speech was so weird that it came out as: 'Yeft, yight, yeft, yight, yeft, yight, gawerrrrf!' (We never could work out what 'gawerrrrf' meant.)

After half an hour another corporal took over, by the name of Grout. He was thin, about five feet three inches tall and possessed a voice that sounded like a demented myna bird crossed with the robot of *Star Wars* fame, 3PCPO. It is almost impossible to write down what his commands sounded like as they seemed to combine the musicality of Bluebottle's song in the radio show *The Goons* – 'Ying-tong, ying-tong, ying-tong, ying-tong, ying-tong, yiddle-I-po' – with the clucking of a hen that has just laid an egg. The 'left, right, left, right, left' commands ended up sounding like 'puck, puck, purrrrk, puck, puck purrrrrrit!'

As his orders increased in frenzy, so we ended up colliding into each other in blind panic. Then, much to our relief, a third corporal appeared, by the name of Kramer. He was six feet tall and heavily built, and his lazy commands were slow, deep and soothing to the ear: 'Eff – high, eff – high, eff – high, urrrrf!'

All three corporals puzzled us, seeming incapable of pronouncing the words 'right' and 'left' correctly. In fact, the next day, as we marched up hill and down dale, we saw scores of corporals drilling their squads and all suffering from this ailment. Their peaked hats sat Germanically low, adding to their ferocious demeanour, as their cavernous mouths opened to bark out various versions of 'left' and 'right':

'Gurrrrf! Hight! Urrrrt! Yighter! Yiot! Burrrrf! Niurrrrf! Durrrrf! Gighter!' – and my personal favourite, 'Snighdet!'

God! I thought, this is a madhouse.

As the days and weeks passed, the gloomy evenings in the wooden billets remained deathly silent, for we all obeyed the command to keep our traps shut. Lying in bed in the darkness, I would become aware of the occasional individual weeping, and only when this had at last subsided would sleep finally overtake me. (I've heard many stories about sergeants and corporals which have given me a great deal of entertainment and pleasure. In fact, the whole history of the armed services is full of tales about marvellous personalities and brave individuals. But none of these were in evidence at RAF Bridgnorth!)

One evening our welcome sleep was violently interrupted by Corporal Braithwaite and fellow NCOs, who turned on the harsh overhead lights and raced the length of the billet, tearing the bedclothes off each bed and screaming blue murder. (It was two a.m. and apparently the point of this visit was to discipline us for the shoddy way we had made our beds.) All the while they beat their sticks on the metal bed frames and shouted obscenities in our faces. One lad was subjected to a frightful ordeal. It was obvious that he had been masturbating – the poor fellow was mortified. In desperation he had reached for his pyjamas to cover himself up but was instantly rooted to the spot by Braithwaite's stick under his chin:

'Stay where you are, you 'orrible little man,' hissed the corporal. 'We have a pervert in our midst, a scummy, disgusting little shit. I'll tell you what we do with filthy little tossers like you: we flush 'em down the shit-hole. Repeat after me: I am a manky little pervert.'

As Braithwaite said this he tightened the stick on the lad's throat.

'I can't, Corporal,' blurted out the terrified airman.

'You will say it,' growled Braithwaite, 'or I'll put you on a charge for perversion. Now, do as I say!'

God! We could take any amount of discipline but this was plain bullying. I couldn't stand bullying, and as thoughts raced through my head my gall started to rise. The distance between me and the NCOs was three yards. A wooden chair was near by and I inched towards it. With a few well-timed blows I could have levelled the lot of them, got the hell out of it and disappeared over the perimeter fence.

In all my life I have never had to exercise such control. I was positively shaking with emotion and one of the lads, sensing my intent, held my arm. Instantly the corporals turned around and moved towards me. There was one hell of a long pause before a mustachioed NCO addressed me:

'Where do you think you are, airman? In a nudist colony?'

Most of the lads were in pyjamas or underwear but several, like me, slept naked.

He then added with a grin:

'You're either shivering like a jelly, or are you just shit-scared? A big girl like you needs to keep warm. What's your name, airman?'

'Blessed,' I replied.

He then went berserk, shouting:

'When I ask you a question, you fucking 'orrible bastard, you address me as "Corporal" and give me your number, rank and name. Now, what's your name, airman?'

'2744376 AC2 Blessed, Corporal.'

There was another long pause as he looked me up and down before breaking into a false smile and whispering:

'So, you're Blessed.'

This was the second time I had been addressed in this manner, and it continued to perplex me.

'So, Blessed, were you about to assist the airman who plays with himself? Or are you both girls together, eh?'

On completing this he poked my shoulder with his stick and there was another lengthy pause as the whole bunch of corporals moved close and grinned at me. To their utter astonishment, I grinned back and said:

'It'll take a lot more than you lot to scare me. I suggest that you yellow-bellied bastards leave the lad alone. He's done nothing wrong. We all wank, including you lot, you great nancies!'

The moment I finished speaking I was put on a charge, ordered to get dressed and thrown in the cell for the night. There was no doubt that I was in serious trouble; after all, they were not about to let me off for such insubordinate behaviour. But I didn't give a monkey's.

The following morning I was sentenced to only seven days' jankers. The term 'jankers' means extra duties and fatigues — fatigues being hard work. It wasn't so bad; it was just that I had to complete these extra tasks on top of a full day's 'square bashing'. Therefore, in the evening, when I should have been cleaning my 303 rifle, webbing and boots, I was busy waxing floors, cleaning out the cooking vats in the kitchen or running, at double time, up and down the parade ground with a full pack on my back.

The physical side of this punishment caused me no difficulty. My main problem was in getting enough sleep. Arriving back at the billet at ten p.m. left me with only one hour to clean my kit and polish my boots before lights out. Preparing boots was an art in itself, requiring hours of spit and polish, and only after a certain amount of time would a layer of polish develop, solidifying into the much desired 'pate-warr', as it was affectionately called. The only way I could keep my boots in this condition was to polish them for hours after the lights were out.

If our boots weren't up to standard, or the numerous brass buttons on our uniform and overcoats didn't glisten like the sun, we would be put on a charge. If this happened to me again it would have added even more days to my sentence and thus put more and more pressure on me in my efforts to maintain the exacting standards. Also, there was the distinct possibility that if I was constantly on a charge I would be reflighted.

Our objective at the end of the ten-week course was to pass all the tests, including marching and parading at a high standard, proficiency with Bren gun and 303, general knowledge of tactical warfare, unarmed combat and fine use of the bayonet.

The camp comprised about ten thousand men, most of them

National Servicemen, and the rest regular airmen. The RAF formed these numbers into individual flights of about five hundred men. The flights were in alphabetical order and I was in A Flight.

At the completion of the course there was a passing-out parade. We were to be given ten days' leave before joining our next unit. Halfway through the Basic Training there was also a thirty-six-hour pass, or leave, which we were all looking forward to. If I was reflighted, it would mean joining a new bunch of recruits and beginning 'square bashing' all over again. This process could go on *ad infinitum*, and I was led to understand that if this happened more weeks could be added to my two-year National Service. That prospect filled me with horror, as I would have been further delayed in my quest to go to drama school.

Looking on the bright side, I was billeted with a fine bunch of lads. We all helped each other as best we could and were resolutely determined to win through and attend the passing-out parade. It was interesting to note the difference between airmen like ourselves, who had only been there for a few weeks, and the flights who were about to complete their passing-out parade: they marched with absolute precision and authority, leaving us gasping with admiration. Slowly but surely, however, we too began to improve.

Would you believe, we started to boast that our flight would be the best in the camp and win the coveted Drill Cup? In fact, our determination grew daily as we made concentrated efforts to streamline our marching. The corporals noticed it, turning a blind eye if we bollocked somebody for being out of step.

One lad had the extraordinary action of putting his left arm out at the same time as his left leg, and vice versa. Braithwaite went potty and bawled at him:

'What the fucking 'ell were you in Civvy Street – a fucking clerk? Reverse your arms, you pillock! Not that way – this way! No, no, no, you 'orrible turd. You march like one of the Flowerpot Men! Move out of line, you fucking pervert. Now 'shun! Stand at ease. 'Shun – stand at ease! Were you born with a brain? Don't answer that, you cretin! Were you ever born? Do you have a mother or were you knitted?'

The questions came fast and furious, giving the lad no time to reply. He was ordered to mark time on the spot, with his arms safely by his side, until he was completely knackered. He was then dismissed into the billet to wax the floor.

Several days later we found ourselves at attention in the main drill yard, being inspected for the first time by the CO. He reminded me of Jack Hawkins as General Allenby in *Lawrence of Arabia*. His manner was gentlemanly and he was highly perceptive. His blue uniform was absolutely immaculate. His handsome face never smiled and to add to his authority his peaked hat was covered in yellow braid, denoting high rank. This braid, by the way, was frequently described as scrambled egg.

We had been at attention for a long time before the CO's arrival and we were now feeling the strain of keeping perfectly still. The inevitable happened: several lads started to faint, among them the aforementioned airman with two left feet. He was close by me and as he was revived by Braithwaite he received unexpected kindness from him. Then, once the corporal had satisfied himself that the lad was OK, he said quietly:

'I'm glad you've come round, because you're now on a charge.'

I couldn't believe my ears and that evening I was joined by him, and the other unfortunate lads who had fainted, in the kitchen of the cookhouse. They were all intrigued to see me pouring a yellow liquid from a small bottle into the various jars containing food for the evening meal.

'What's that in aid of, Brian?' someone asked.

As I slowly stirred the concoction round and round I gave them a rendition of the Three Witches from *Macbeth*:

'Double, double toil and trouble;
Fire, burn; and, caldron, bubble.'

Then I added, in the voice of Braithwaite: 'This yellow stuff is to curb your evil, wanky ways, you 'orrible, manky perverts, for this is bromide.'

Much to my relief, a day later I completed my jankers. I could then, at last, concentrate on getting my kit up to scratch and, most importantly, catch up on my sleep.

One of the lads who had been kind to me during this period was Michael Tasker – a tall, handsome fellow with a cheerful disposition, and artistic to his fingertips. He was from Pontefract in Yorkshire, I think, and was a close friend of the great ballerina Alicia Markova. Michael and I became good friends. It was marvellous to have him around as we had a great deal in common and the time we spent together acted as a buffer against the rigours of the station.

In Civvy Street Michael had studied costume design, choreography and hairdressing. He frequently adjusted my hair, recommending that when I came out of the RAF, I should do away with my parting and become more bold! Having watched me work out in the gym, he would come to the canteen afterwards to express his admiration. He wasn't gay, but he had a splendidly natural manner and was very tactile. (I wouldn't have given a damn if he had been gay anyway.) The whole of our flight, including the corporals and sergeants, viewed our relationship with some detachment. If any upstart chanced his arm and uttered a disparaging remark about us I quickly and privately sorted the bastard out. The corporals always turned a blind eye to this because as long as an airman could fulfil his duties they didn't give a damn what else he did.

If this sounds like a happy period in my Basic Training, it was not. I was aware that the powers that be still had it in for me, but why was quite beyond my understanding. Why on earth were they being so vindictive? On the parade ground I was inspected ruthlessly. During drilling I was constantly hassled, even when I knew I was performing well. The CO himself, when inspecting us for a second time, viewed me with deep distrust:

'So you're Blessed, eh? Oh dear, oh dear.'

Much to his surprise, I stopped him in his tracks by saying:

'What is it about me, sir, that causes you and the NCOs to address me in this way? Am I bow-legged, barmy or some kind of secret agent, sir?'

The shocked CO immediately restrained the eager corporals from disciplining me, and nonchalantly replied:

'You are none of these things, Blessed. You are simply Blessed, and that is enough for the present. You may not realize it, but you are right on the edge. Jankers has obviously not done you any good whatsoever. I recommend you keep a civil tongue in your head and remain stum for the period of time you are with us.'

From that moment on it became clear that anyone found fraternizing with me was himself in deep shit. Therefore, out of consideration for my mates, I shunned their company, especially that of Michael. Of course, he wouldn't accept it and I had to be devastatingly rude to shake him off. Fortunately, the thirty-six-hour pass was upon us and I rubbed my hands with happiness at the thought of the longed-for freedom.

My mother and father had arranged to take me to Doncaster for dinner, my mother being beside herself with happiness at the prospect of it all. But, on the morning parade the day before the pass was due to start, I was once again put on a charge – this time for not shaving! In fact, I had shaved twice that morning and my appearance was immaculate.

Braithwaite looked at me coldly for signs of shock and disappointment. If his looks were inhuman then my answering gaze carried with it the ice of the Antarctic, calculated to freeze the balls off a snow-covered Siberian mammoth!

His stare lost its strength when he noticed me smile faintly at him. Then, with relish, he again announced in his limited, guttural way that he was placing me on a charge. The other corporals assumed reptilian smiles, informing me that they were going to break me:

'We are bastards, Blessed. We are the biggest bastards in the world. You are going to shit yourself so much in the next fortnight that when we've finished with you margarine won't melt between your crutch. Anything to say, Blessed?'

Nothing. I gave them nothing. My resolve was absolute: never in a million years would they break me. I would never bow down to aggression and intimidation. There wasn't a cell in me that was feeling fear; only a stubborn refusal to be beaten.

As I looked at them I was already formulating a plan to defeat them, but in the meantime I would box clever and obey their orders like a zombie. There was no way I was going to jeopardize my chances of going to drama school, despite my murderous thoughts.

My sentence this time was ten days' jankers. During this period I spent a great deal of time doubling-up around the camp with backpack and full gear on. Sometimes I ran around Bridgnorth town with various corporals running relays alongside me. They couldn't understand that my fitness was due to my work in Civvy Street and my obsession with exercise. At times I was thoroughly enjoying myself! On one occasion I was accompanied by a corporal who proved to be not quite as belligerent as the rest. The weather was atrocious, with snow everywhere, and he had a bad cold and was wheezing badly. I urged him to stop:

'Come on, Corp, slow up, or you're going to be ill. There's nobody here to see us, so just take it easy and rest.'

He was staggered that I should dare to speak to him. Later, when we were on the rifle range, I could sense that he wanted to talk but that he was under strict orders not to.

The rest of the lads had returned from their pass and were disturbed at seeing my chapped, red face and the fact that I had almost lost my voice. Then, with great subtlety, they contrived to help me. Again sleep was my main problem, and in the evenings I found myself dozing off in full gear on my bed. Helping hands would then remove my great coat and webbing and help me to polish my boots and buttons. Of course, Michael Tasker was among those chiefly to thank for this kindness. I was scarcely able to raise more than a murmur of gratitude through my chapped lips. When I think of these moments now they remind me of scenes from *Cool Hand Luke*!

Bayonet practice amused me enormously. It was fascinating to observe the way each lad attacked the large hanging target bag that represented the enemy. The sergeant's instructions were quite simple: run at the target as fast as possible and, with an intimidating roar, plunge the bayonet in up to the hilt, pull it out immediately and move on to the next imaginary foe.

Some carried out the task like born killers, roaring convincingly. Others shouted impressively but appeared to be in two minds about how to attack the bag, causing their sergeants to berate them:

'You'd have been killed five bloody times by the time you'd made up your minds, you stupid pillocks!'

One lad approached the target with trepidation and, after emitting a friendly squeal, had difficulty in skewering it. The bag, already pierced many times by previous combatants, now swayed tantalizingly from side to side, making it doubly difficult for him. He simply stood there like a great nana, stabbing away gently and completely missing the object.

'Why don't you hold it, hug it and kiss the bloody thing?' roared the sergeant. 'Just take the pissing bayonet out of the rifle and put it away before you do yourself an injury. You make me bloody weep. Have you all got girlfriends in Civvy Street?'

'Yes, Sergeant,' the poor lads replied.

This sent the sergeant into paroxysms of exasperation:

'Then how in heaven's name do you manage to hit the target and fuck 'em?'

It goes without saying that I welcomed using the bayonet and found it a useful practice to exorcise my murderous emotions.

'Who are you killing today, Blessed?' the sarge would enquire, with a faint smile.

All the while I remembered the CO's advice and remained stum. Through channelling my hatred into the Bren gun and the 303 rifle, I became the recipient of a Marksman's award and my Wings. Amusingly enough, one way or another I was becoming an airman. During one of the firing sessions I once again found myself in the company of the sympathetic corporal I mentioned earlier. This time he broke his silence and whispered:

'Blessed, you're your own worst enemy. You've got to stop being a communist.'

His words astonished me.

'What the hell are you talking about, Corp? I'm not a communist.'

'Your dad's a communist, isn't he? Well, they think it follows

204

that you're one too. Also, you've been seen talking to Wragg, and he's in the Communist Youth Organization.'

This made me laugh, and I replied emphatically:

'Get this straight, Corp, and you can tell the rest of the NCOs. I'm not a communist; in fact, I have no interest in politics whatsoever. My father was adamant that any communist who visited our house should never speak about their beliefs to me. He always wanted me to think for myself. Also, whenever I've spoken to Wragg I've advised him to shut his gob and keep his beliefs to himself.'

Later that evening, while mopping down the kitchen floor, I mused to myself: So, that's what it's all about. The fear that was rampant throughout the country was of the 'Red Peril'.

Surprisingly, this alarm had been perpetuated by a leading politician of the time, who had advised the nation to be aware of communists in everyday life. His outburst became famous and was nicknamed the 'Reds Under the Bed' speech.

The young communist, Wragg, who was in my billet, was a strange individual. Although he was physically very small he had the guts of a lion. By nature he was very passive: his thin face barely changed its expression and he had a tiny voice that droned on monotonously. There was no doubt that he was an intellectual, and suffered from verbal diarrhoea. It goes without saying that he was given hell by the NCOs.

It was obvious, though, that he had reached breaking point and we were all concerned for him. Coming back alone one afternoon from fatigues, while the rest of the flight were attending lectures, I entered the billet and was confronted by a dancing Wragg.

'Oh! Fruit! Fruit! Dangling from the gallows tree,' said the famous 'Hanging Judge', Judge Jeffreys, aeons ago! There was poor Wragg, making a complete mess of hanging himself! He was using his webbing, which was attached to the overhead beam. He had kicked the chair away and the webbing was tearing the skin off his neck and giving him terrible pain. His neck was in no danger of being broken at all and all he could think about was relieving the pain.

'Hold on, you bloody fool,' I shouted, and quickly put a table under his feet. After slapping his hands and telling him to let go I untied him.

'You can't even kill yourself, you silly sod. You make me sick, Wragg. Just think of all the people you'll upset. You'll be all right, because you'll be dead, but they'll have to live with it – much harder! Think how angry your communist friends would be. Jesus Christ, Wragg.'

Exploding with anger, I slapped him repeatedly across the face until he began to cry uncontrollably. As he simmered down a little he blurted out:

'They're always at me, Blessed – night and day. They're driving me mad.'

'Well, let it pass over you – water off a duck's back. Have the bloody sense to stop talking politics until you're out of the RAF. Also, try to remember how the people of Leningrad lived on sawdust and sugar in the war. How do your worries compare with that? I'll tell you this, Wragg: if you don't behave and shut up and concentrate on your passing-out parade, I'll break your bloody neck!'

After this I brought him a cup of tea, took him to the medical unit and told the doctor he'd slipped down the steps. From that day on Wragg was a political ignoramus!

That weekend I played football for the flight against B Flight, scoring two goals and making another in a 4–0 victory. It was a prestigious match for the Flight Sporting Cup. The CO himself was pleased, and throughout the game I saw him acknowledge my form. After the match I couldn't contain my delight. I loved playing football. Our flight toasted the whole team in the canteen afterwards, with mugs of hot tea laced with bromide! To top it all, my ten days' charge was over.

Later that evening I approached the unapproachable: Corporal Braithwaite's private room. I didn't knock, but just walked right in and shut the door behind me. He sat in his chair opposite, not moving, simply glaring in stony silence. It was the first time I'd seen him without a hat: his hair was close cropped and emphasized his fitness; his face was red and stocky, without any trace of fat, and he had deep-blue eyes.

'What do you want, footballer?' he growled.

I allowed myself a pause before saying:

'I'm here for more jankers.'

He immediately rose and stood in front of me.

'You want more, you stupid bastard? Where do you think you are, airman? I could charge you for entering here without permission. Box clever, airman, or you'll end your manky days cleaning rusty buckets.'

Straight away I shot back at him:

'Braithwaite, fuck knows what you are, but I'll kick yer teeth down your bloody throat if you don't leave Wragg alone. You and your cohorts almost had a ghost mascot for the flight the other day. Not to worry, Corporal: no names, no pack drill. But you leave him be.'

Braithwaite's pronounced jaw jutted out even further, in true Desperate Dan fashion, and the knuckles of his hand tightened, ready to punch. Surprisingly, he then turned his back on me and looked at the wall as I waited for the shout that would bring in the other NCOs. It never came. Instead, he just turned and looked at me for a long time. For a moment I could have sworn his eyes had lost a little of their animosity, even though his manner was stone cold.

'What do I get out of it, airman?' he said.

This question surprised me.

'What do you want out of it, Corporal?' I answered.

He paused again, looking at his feet, before finally saying:

'I want China.'

There was a long pause.

My days of cold, blizzards and jankers now enabled my brain to tune into his wavelength, and I answered:

'China it is.'

Just after dawn the following morning my drinking mug, full to the brim with sweet tea and Nestlé's milk, was placed on the cabinet alongside my bed by Braithwaite. Nothing was said and he pointed to his room. After leisurely finishing the hot drink, I meandered past the rest of the sleeping lads and joined the corporal.

My great coat hung on the door of his wardrobe, the buttons glistening marvellously. My boots, likewise impressively polished, stood below it – all the good work of Braithwaite.

The following days were a revelation. No longer was I hassled on the parade ground and, strangely enough, I was able at long last to enjoy myself and rid my mind of hateful thoughts.

Evenings in the billets took on an atmosphere that reminded me of the old BBC radio programme *Smoky Mountain Jamboree*. Every kind of physical competition took place, ranging from flat-hand boxing to Chinese wrestling. These activities even had the corporals participating, with Braithwaite, of course, excelling. Our childlike exuberance spilled over into the showers and our perspiring bodies catapulted into the air from the shock of the freezing water and wet towels painfully inflicted on exposed genitals and buttocks.

The fact of the matter was, our flight had now become a cohesive team and we were proud of it. Our marching and drill work was first-rate and we wanted, passionately, to defeat the other flights and to win the prized Drill Cup.

We could now move low on the ground with a heavy Bren gun; exchange the magazines when empty; reload and clear the barrel locking pin with our bayonet; and fire at will – all at speed. Once this exercise was over we could dismantle the gun in no time at all and then skedaddle. On manoeuvres no margin of error was allowed: if anyone didn't come up to scratch they got a terrible bollocking – and not from the corporals.

One day, marching back from one of these exercises, Braithwaite laughed as he ordered me to take his place, and then disappeared. There I was, for all to see, drilling the lads! Of course, I made their task impossible, as I imitated every corporal on the Base Camp, ending with my rendition of Braithwaite's 'Yeft, yight, gawerrrrf!'

By this time I had gathered an audience of NCOs, who watched the proceedings with amused tolerance. Milking the occasion for all it was worth, I brought the lads smartly to heel: 'Squad – 'shun! Stand at ease!' I then continued:

'Now, when I give you the word of command, I want you to

break, in orderly fashion, for lunch.' At this moment I, of course, introduced the traditional long pause: 'Squad – wait for it, you 'orrible little men – Squad . . . Dis – miss!!'

A week later the drill competition was held and we came second. The general consensus was that we had deserved to win but, because we had won the Sports Cup, it was considered slightly unethical to also award us the Drill Cup. We happily accepted this decision.

Finally, the most important event in our Basic Training arrived; the passing-out parade. At noon that momentous day we marched, in perfect unison, by what was called column of route, to the equivalent of the centre court at Wimbledon – the mighty Parade Ground. There we patiently awaited the other flights to arrive, and when they had done so we were all brought to attention.

The stillness was uncanny. At the word of command we stood at ease. Moments later a large blue open car arrived packed with officers with 'scrambled egg' all over their hats. Foremost among them was the CO himself: the Group Captain who had spoken to me harshly weeks before. A solitary trumpet sounded and the flag was raised triumphantly as we came to attention and presented arms. At the completion of the flag raising we resumed attention. It was now time for the final inspection. Eventually the CO arrived in front of me, and scrutinized my gun before playing searching attention to the minute details of my buttons.

At long last he seemed satisfied and stepped back to look at my face:

'Jankers seems to have done you good, Blessed.'

'Yes, sir,' I replied.

After a slight pause he smiled and added:

'Well done.'

It may seem odd but I must confess that at that moment I was flush with pride. I was also greatly relieved, because I was still on course for drama school. Braithwaite seemed particularly delighted and grinned his head off.

Twenty minutes later the CO completed his inspection and mounted a podium in front of us to pay tribute to the various achievements of the flights. At the conclusion of his speech we gave him three cheers – the cue for the military band to start up and play the famous signature tune of the RAF.

We marched smartly and happily past the CO, saluting him to our right as we did so, and at last completed the passing-out parade, which marked the conclusion of our Basic Training.

That evening we visited every pub in Bridgnorth: a famous town that features frequently in history books. Indeed, Harry Bolingbroke, better known as Henry IV, brought his armies there. How amusing to think that our flight, with its modern weapons, would have made short work of him and his large, much-feared army.

The friendly people of Bridgnorth had established a warm relationship with the RAF and they now welcomed our invasion of their fair town. After all, they had seen it all before.

Reasonably lubricated and standing on top of a bar, I responded to everyone's demands and gave my wild impersonations of the various NCOs.

'Only one bar,' I roared. To which the lads responded: 'Oh no!'

'A mile long,' I added.

Cheers came from the lads.

'Only one woman,' I continued in the same style, to groans from the lads. 'For every man,' I shouted, to thunderous cheers. The corporals and sergeants led the festivities with crazy zeal. Drink? God, they could knock it back! Braithwaite gleefully shouted across the room:

'Eh, do you know what? Blessed was going to kick my teeth down my throat. What do you make of that? He's the biggest bastard we've had.'

All the NCOs laughed hysterically as, pissed as farts, they rose as one and toasted me.

Eventually we were all crushed together like sardines as more and more lads poured in. As we each bellowed and screamed to be heard above the rest in the large pump room, the noise became an incomprehensible roar.

The following morning we crammed into the trucks that were to take us to the railway station for our desperately longed-for ten days' leave. Our dreadful hangovers took second place to our happy feelings as we viewed the station for the last time. The snow had started to melt and there was even a hint of spring in the air. As the water dripped down from the roofs of the billets the NCOs and the Military Police stepped forward to give the signal for the exit gate to be opened. Braithwaite, his stone face strangely troubled, pushed a letter into my hand and whispered:

'Don't forget, for the rest of life you have "China". God speed, Blessed, you crazy bastard.'

As he finished speaking he gave the signal. The gate opened and as we pulled away, Braithwaite and Bridgnorth gradually disappeared from view.

That evening, resplendent in my blue RAF uniform, I knocked on the back door of my home in Bolton-on-Dearne. As the door opened, revealing my dad's sweet face, I moved back into the shadows and asked in an old, squeaky voice:

'Have you got any scissors or knives to grind?'

He laughed out loud, instantly recognizing my voice, and shouted back into the house:

'It's our Brian! He's 'ome! Come and see for yourselves. It's our Brian and you'd 'ardly recognize 'im.'

I grabbed him in a great bear-hug and lifted him, as easy as pie, off his feet. Still holding him, I strode through the kitchen and into the living-room, with Alan dancing around us in ecstasy.

As I dropped Dad he was immediately replaced by Alan, who hugged me tight and buried his face in my stomach. All the while my unblinking eyes focused on my mother as she fought unsuccessfully to control her emotions. Backwards and forwards she rocked on the armchair, her face contorted with relief and joy. There is nothing on God's earth like a mother's love. Poor Mum! She was almost incapable of standing up.

'Thank God!' she whispered, kissing me. 'I thought I'd never see you again. I thought they'd imprisoned you for life. When you sent that telegram saying you'd been charged on your thirty-six-hour pass and that you wouldn't be coming 'ome I collapsed in yer dad's arms and was as sick as a dog for days. Oh, Brian lad, it's a miracle you're 'ere now! Just think: 'ome for ten days.'

211

Although there was so much going on, I hadn't failed to notice that my grandad was there too. He was a lovable old man of eighty now and his jet-black eyes were intensified by his snowy hair. In that quaint way of his he chortled:

'Tha's a right rum lad, and freetened us to death! Tha munt scare us again – your mum's and my heart couldn't take it. God bless thee, Brian lad, I'll be going nar.'

Ever the diplomat, he felt it was only right that I should be left alone with my parents and Alan, but I was having none of this:

'No you don't, Grandad. You'll stay for supper and never leave my side.'

Mum and Dad passionately echoed my sentiments and he happily made himself comfortable as I regaled them with stories of Bridgnorth, taking care to omit any sordid details for Mum's sake.

After a huge meal of meat and potato pie Mum and Alan went to bed, leaving Dad and Grandad to express anger at my general appearance. For, as much as I tried to laugh it off, I was noticeably thinner and my voice hadn't yet returned to its full strength. Also the skin on my face was cracked and my lips constantly bled when I enthused about anything.

After a while we looked into the embers of the fire and remained solemn for a long time. Eventually Dad broke the silence and said:

'You've all 'ad to suffer for my beliefs. We could 'ave 'ad anything; more money, everything our 'earts desired, if I'd agreed to join the bosses. Time and time again Mr Godfrey, the pit manager, offered me an olive branch and begged me to reconsider my position. "You're a fool, you know, Billy," 'e used to say. "Fighting on the side of the workers. They crucified Christ, yer know."

'Your mother could 'ave used the extra money, and when I look at you in this state, Brian lad, I sometimes wonder if I made the right decision.'

'Of course you did, Dad. We are all happy in this house and proud of you. Dear Dad, we wouldn't have you any different. Throughout your life you have remained constant in your beliefs.

Your faith in the limitless possibilities of the human spirit is unshakeable. I also deeply appreciate the fact that you've never pushed your beliefs down my throat but have allowed me to think for myself. As for the last few weeks, well, I've learned a lot. In fact, it's proved to be a rich experience.'

For the next two days I continued to relax and to enjoy life at home. Then, on the third day, I visited Harry Dobson and drank in his wisdom and news. His response to my tales of RAF life was typical: he laughed his socks off.

15

The Haunted House

The day after visiting Harry I found myself in the nearby village of Hoyland. My destination was the home of the lady with the haunting features, Miss Ruth Wynn Owen. Her house bore the evocative name Skiers Spring Lodge, but despite the good lady's detailed instructions, I simply couldn't find the place. Apparently it was situated in some fields, surrounded by a wood, a little distance from the village. The friendly locals I spoke to shook their heads and apologized profusely for never having heard of it. Over the meadows I traipsed, heading this way and that, crossing streams and climbing stiles, until I began to resemble the ouzel bird, which went round and round until it eventually disappeared up its own arse!

The mad March wind raced across the countryside, playing havoc with the low grey clouds, yet failing to make any impact on the higher black nimbus, which glowered down with a permanent frown. The oaks groaned with the impact of the gale, appearing to pull faces and reminding me of the poet's words: 'Do you believe they are trees? Oh, no! They are little old men, with twisted knees.'

Through their creaking trunks and frenzied, leafless branches I spied a smidgen of red on the hillside and went towards it. Fortunately, the phone box was working and I dialled the number, got through, put my penny in and pressed the button. After a short conversation Miss Wynn Owen told me to stay put and said that she would send the girls over.

214

After such a frustrating search I had almost begun to wonder whether the lodge and its strange occupant actually existed, or simply appeared once every hundred years like the legendary *Brigadoon*. However, Ruth's throaty cackle on the telephone had restored my equilibrium, and the prospect of a female rescue party cheered me enormously. Even so, I could have been excused for letting my imagination run riot: several months earlier Patrick Stewart had fascinated me with bizarre stories about the lodge, insisting that it was haunted. Observing my sceptical smile, he laughed and maintained that during one of his visits he had seen a pair of socks move across the kitchen of their own volition. He also told me that other visitors, entering the garden one evening, had encountered a young girl in medieval dress who had kindly directed them to the front door before disappearing. With these tales buzzing in my head, I found myself whistling and moving about to keep warm.

Before long I spotted three elegant female forms heading towards me down an unmade road. When they arrived it was obvious that, in their eagerness not to keep me waiting, they had become quite breathless. I introduced myself, jokingly berating them for exhausting themselves on my account. My comical outburst made them wheeze with laughter, prompting one lady to hold one of my arms while the second took the other. The third, laughing loudly, pushed me from behind and thus, under close scrutiny, I was marched up the lane.

I doubt if any prisoner in history has been apprehended by such enchanting captors. As we reached the top of the hill they unexpectedly disengaged themselves and, giggling, circled around me. So far they had tantalizing failed to tell me their names. But now they burst forth:

'I'm Meg.'

'I'm Sally.'

'I'm Anne.'

Then, in unison, they cooed:

'You're in the R A F, aren't you?'

Before I could reply they broke into song: 'You're in the army now.' Throughout this they marched sexily on the spot, saluting me, which made me laugh. My laughter wasn't returned, however, although their eyes did twinkle mischievously as they became as still as statues. They stared, unblinkingly and in total silence, for some time until I couldn't stand it any longer and attempted to break the mood by going bug-eyed. This didn't work, so I began to suggest other things with my eyes, which did have the desired effect, and they huddled close together as we continued walking.

As they homed in on me I felt rather like Pip in *Great Expectations*, surrounded by three Estelles. They were about seventeen years old and wore long, flowing skirts and light-coloured blouses. In many ways their personalities reminded me of my idea of the Brontë sisters. Instinctively I liked them immensely and, to be sure, they were marvellously attractive, each one beautiful in her own right. Meg had lovely, soft auburn hair framing a pale face, whereas Anne had light-brown hair and a thin, sensitive face that flushed and flared up with vivacity. The quietest was Sally, who had dense hair that was almost black, and who smiled broadly, flashing dark-brown eyes. Yes, indeed, three bewitching creatures who were, in a strange way, completely incongruous with the surroundings, for here we were, in the heart of Yorkshire, and they spoke without a trace of a northern accent. All of them could easily have got a job as an announcer on the BBC. Certainly their wit and style were getting the better of me and I shouted our 'Pax' and fluttered my white handkerchief.

'Sweet ladies, I can't fight you, have mercy. I give up.'

Their response was sweetness itself as they engulfed me with kindness and apologies, and propelled me along the path to Skiers Spring Lodge.

When I stopped a moment to take a look at Patrick's haunted kitchen, the bemused young ladies urged me on down a small passage leading to an oak door. This opened into a large sitting-room with Indian-style rugs scattered over a polished wooden floor.

The furniture was a comfortable mixture of ancient and modern, with a faded chintz sofa dominating the central area. In one corner there appeared to be a makeshift single bed and, except for the odd picture dotted here and there, the walls were completely covered in

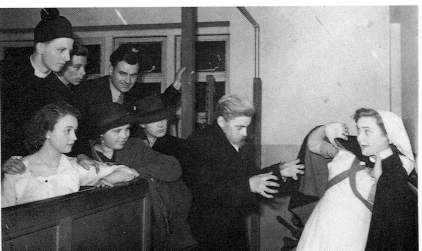

Top: Frank Cooper, my speech teacher, whose magical touch saved my sanity.
Bottom: X-certificate stuff! Me being very frightening in a Dearne Youth production of *The Second Visit*. Holding the post is Fred Lawson, who gave me my first acting break.

Above: Grandma and Grandad Blessed in 1953. She dragged her bulk up the hill to see me perform, while he kept pausing to cough up blood because of silicosis.
Right: Friends of my mother's — the Whispering Knights of Rollright, Oxfordshire.
Below left: Hoober Stand, the watch tower, 513 feet above sea-level. My dad pronounced it 'Uberstan'.
Below right: Aged seventeen.

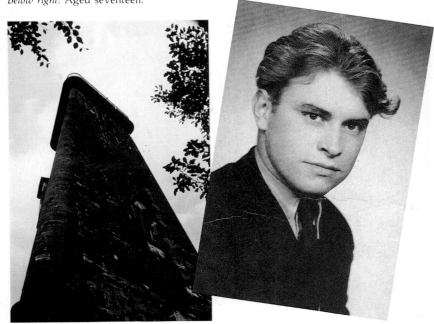

A favourite walk of the Brontës', and mine too. Top Withens is visible just below the skyline.

A Calder High School
production of *Hiss the Villain.* I'm on the far
left, with Nancy in the bonnet next to me, Ruth Wynn Owen in the centre and Patrick
Stewart — future Captain of the US Starship *Enterprise* — on the far right.

Harlequin's Dumbstruck at
Calder High School. I'm standing fourth from the right, with Patrick Stewart, as
Harlequin, seated left.

Top left: Calder High School. The top left window is where I climbed in to see Nancy — a tricky ascent!
Top right: The legendary movement teacher Rudi Shelley, here aged sixty-eight.
Above: The haunted house, Skiers Spring Lodge, Hoyland, Yorkshire.
Left: 'I've heard rumours that you are a white witch.' The haunting face of the mysterious Ruth Wynn Owen.

The brooding Brontë home in Haworth.

Top Withens, the core of the wind and the soul of *Wuthering Heights*.

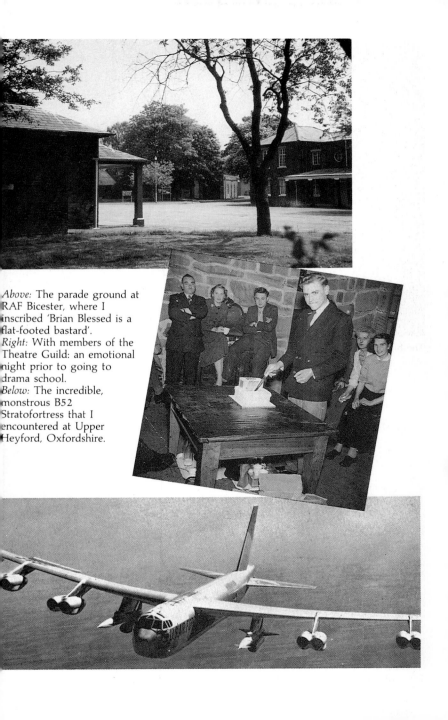

Above: The parade ground at RAF Bicester, where I inscribed 'Brian Blessed is a flat-footed bastard'.
Right: With members of the Theatre Guild: an emotional night prior to going to drama school.
Below: The incredible, monstrous B52 Stratofortress that I encountered at Upper Heyford, Oxfordshire.

Aged twenty, as Heathcliff in *Wuthering Heights.*

shelves, which seemed to contain every book that had ever been written in recorded history! I had never seen so many books! Several dozen or so were also lying about on various tables and chairs, left open, it would seem, by readers who had disappeared in a puff of smoke at my untimely appearance.

At the far end of the room large French windows looked out on to a deep-green lawn of Cumberland turf sprinkled with daffodils and crocuses. The afternoon sun had at last valiantly broken through and its rays poured into the room.

Suddenly a figure moved into view, silhouetted against the bright light. It was, of course, Miss Wynn Owen.

'Dear Brian. My darling boy! How lovely to see you.'

As she spoke I became aware of an animated bundle in her arms and, to my complete surprise, it turned out to be a baby. My puzzled look forced a chuckle from my hostess.

'She's lovely, Brian, isn't she? She was left abandoned at a local railway station and so I'm taking care of her. She's so innocent. Oh, Brian, there are so many uncared for children in this world today and one must do all one can to alleviate the suffering. She's just finished her bottle and I'm bringing her wind up. Would you care to take her and try?'

Without hesitation I held the baby firmly, in the right places, and calmly brought up the troublesome wind.

'Ah, you're experienced I see,' she said, smiling.

'Yes, it comes from looking after my younger brother.'

Seconds later the bairn was on her back, giggling away and mouthing 'raspberries', as Miss Wynn Owen expertly applied a fresh nappy.

'There,' she sighed with satisfaction, and then called out through the half-open door:

'Darlings?'

Instantly Anne popped her head round the door, like the genie of the lamp, and spirited the cherub away.

'Tell Sally and Meg to bring some sandwiches and tea,' the older lady continued in the same breath. 'I expect you're famished, Brian. You do look rather thin. Harry Dobson told me how upset your mother has been since you've been away. Oh dear, it's not easy for parents. My husband, Mr Danby, whom you'll meet at dinner, experienced, like so many soldiers, the hardship of the last World War. Now he has a wonderful dream of building a great big boat with the help of my young son, Charles. The project is doing him the world of good.'

Shortly afterwards tea arrived and Anne asked if all was hunky-dory. My simple thank you was received gracefully but caused the delightful lady to blush as she turned on her heels, creating music with her swishing skirt. Miss Wynn Owen missed nothing and her wide, owl eyes danced knowingly.

'Have the children been nice to you?'

'The children? Oh, you mean the three ladies. Oh yes, they are terrific. A real *tour de force*.'

My reply amused her greatly and after one of her marvellous cackling laughs the gorgeous lady asked me to call her Ruth.

'Darling Brian, they obviously like you and, from now on, will be your staunchest allies.'

After the rigours of Bridgnorth it was blissful to be having tea with such an accomplished lady. She was dressed in similar fashion to the girls and described how generally they all made their own clothes. These skills she had developed during her work with the famous Old Vic Company, for the artists were expected to muck in and help with the sets and to create and mend costumes. For the next hour I was enthralled as Ruth sat alongside me and took me on a ride to a land of artistic delights. Her voice ranged from a smoky, husky croak to the angelic clarity of Joan of Arc's bells. Images of Gielgud's Hamlet and Richard II still pulsated in my imagination as, in the flickering of an eye, she moved on to the world of ballet, giving electrifying descriptions of Fontaine, Ulanova, Ninette de Valois and Anton Dolin. Her abridged history of the theatre mesmerized me and ended with a mention of Inigo Jones.

'That's quite enough for the moment, darling,' said my haunting Scheherazade. 'Let's go for a long walk.'

While writing this chapter I was tempted to go and verify certain details about the lodge, and then to seek out Ruth, who now lives in Norfolk, for confirmation of certain facts. Finally, I

have decided against it, deciding it would destroy the impressions
I had as an eighteen-year-old; impressions which were, even at
the time, utterly confused. For instance: outside, at the beginning
of the walk, I couldn't work out which was the front of the
house and which was the back; it was all higgledy-piggledy.
Furthermore, Ruth's unfathomable personality and mysterious
companions continued to add to my bewilderment.

'Ruth, are you all ghosts? This strange house makes me think
of a daft poem I knew as a child:

> It was a bright September morning,
> In October, last July.
> The moon lay thick upon the ground,
> The mud shone in the sky,
> The flowers were sweetly singing,
> The birds were in full bloom,
> As I went up to the cellar,
> To sweep the downstairs room,
> I saw a thousand miles away
> A house, quite out of sight.
> The house it was a thatched one,
> The front was at the back
> And it was whitewashed black.'

Ruth cackled as she took me by the arm and led me round the
gardens, whispering conspiratorially:

'It's obvious that people have been filling your ears with stories
of things here that go bumpity-bump in the night.'

My nodding caused her to cackle again.

'Well Brian, they're quite right. They mainly belong to my
family and follow me wherever I go. The Wynn Owens have an
ancient line which is full of legend and mystery. I won't go into
that now. A little girl resides here and appears from time to time
and is very sweet and friendly. We do seem to have our share of
poltergeists and they can be naughty and a nuisance. They can
make a frightful mess of a room. One has to keep them in order.
They are particularly active when teenagers are around.'

Ruth laughed again and continued:

'Poor Brian, this must all sound double Dutch to you.'

Her laughter increased and I joined in, holding my sides and wiping the tears from my eyes.

'Miss Wynn Owen,' I gasped, 'I've heard rumours that you are a white witch. Is it true?'

On hearing this she kissed me on both cheeks and quietly replied:

'Yes, Brian. It's as good a definition as any. You must understand, you are asking questions that ultimately take years to understand. Remember Hamlet's lines:

> "There are more things in heaven and earth, Horatio,
> Than are dreamt of in your philosophy."

'From my earliest days I inherited these gifts. There is nothing hocus-pocus about them; they are simply natural and based on a love of the truth. Over the years we will discuss it often, as life will point you in that direction, believe you me. What is generally overlooked, for instance in religious study, is the importance of the female side, which brings balance alongside the male. Without it there would be chaos.'

As we walked towards the stables adjoining the house, I expressed my surprise at her candour.

'Oh, darling Brian,' she said quite loudly. 'You may think me an enigma but you will find I am a very simple person who is flat-footed and down to earth. Don't put me on a pedestal, please. I'm full of faults and have great difficulty in tolerating people who lie.'

For a while we stopped walking and gazed up at the trees.

'So, you're not an enigma. And yet months ago you wrote, directed and made all the props and instruments for your production of the ancient Egyptian tale *The Wanderings of Isis*. Egyptologists and professors from far and wide were dumbfounded by the authenticity of the instruments and haunting accuracy of the mystical dances. I believe BBC Radio Newsreel did a report on it. Ruth, where on earth did you acquire all that knowledge?'

There was a long silence as her usually wide, owl eyes narrowed into deep thought.

'In time, Brian, I'll explain all,' she said simply. And that was that.

'Look,' she began again, 'to convince you how simple and earthy we are, behold Sally with her horse.'

Sally was brushing away energetically and then, after a friendly pat, she stood back to admire her noble brown steed.

'Mummy says you're going to entertain us with some Shakespeare before dinner,' she said.

'Am I?' I answered, gulping nervously. With more cackles of laughter Ruth hurried me away out of the confines of the garden to the field beyond. Finding a shaded spot, we made ourselves comfortable and watched the sun set. I closed my eyes and experienced that same feeling I had first felt months before when looking down into the valley of Mytholmroyd: a sensation of knowing something original, something that was new yet familiar. I tried to hold on to it but it gradually left me, to become a memory. Yet it seemed to herald a beginning.

For a long while we both remained silent until Ruth finally said:

'When the children were very young I was very ill and for a while it was touch-and-go whether or not I would survive. When the crisis came I prayed to God to spare me in order that I could live long enough for them to have their mother until they reached their twenties. After they all reach that age I shall consider life from then on as a bonus. Meg, by the way, is not my daughter – her surname is Shuttleworth – although she intends to be an actress and wishes to adopt the name of Wynn Owen. It all sounds terribly complicated, Brian.' She laughed and added: 'I have always been known as Miss Wynn Owen but, of course, my married name is Danby.'

Before dinner that evening I duly gave my rendering of certain speeches from Shakespeare's plays and received enthusiastic applause.

Dinner was terrific fun. Mr Danby proved to be a tall, raw-boned man with a clear complexion and bright eyes. He was probably in

221

his late forties and gave the impression that his mind was elsewhere. When I suggested to him that it was possibly on his ship he nodded enthusiastically and broke into a broad grin. And as the voices of all present soared loudly he remained gracefully detached from the rumpus.

I touched on the subject of ghosts again and asked everybody about a student visitor from Rawmarsh who had screamed hysterically after seeing a galleon sail across their sitting-room ceiling.

'Hardly surprising, is it, Brian?' said Mr Danby, laughing out loud for the first time. 'She was probably picking up my thought-waves!'

Much merriment followed this remark and I suddenly found myself confronted by Ruth's resident friend, Stella. This formidable lady was in her late thirties and, as well as being absolutely charming, possessed a searing wit. She was very slim, with skin as tight as a drum on her thin, pale face. The lady also had short, red hair and her eyes flashed suspiciously as she curtly questioned the validity of some of my statements.

I nicknamed her the Ice Queen, which was unfair really, for she was kind and full of fun, but on this occasion she was loath to let me off the hook. I was buffeted from pillar to post by her brilliance and I foolishly resolved to stand my ground. For me it was an enervating experience, to say the least, but everybody seemed to enjoy the conflict enormously. At the end of it the gathering voted the contest a draw. You could have fooled me, for I felt that I was in need of smelling-salts throughout the entire debate! In fact, I mentioned that it was as daunting as facing the Yorkshire fast bowler Appleyard. This made Ruth enthuse like a ten-year-old:

'Oh, we saw Appleyard once, getting the hat trick in Sheffield.'

I must say Stella's goodnight kiss was infinitely preferable to her lightning tongue. Shortly before retiring, I again found myself alone with Ruth, who gazed serenely at me and said quietly:

Couldn't fault you this evening, Brian. But remember that the Finnish composer is not pronounced "Sibeelius" but "Sibaylius". Otherwise, darling Brian, you were a perfect poppet. Goodnight!'

At breakfast the following morning the 'poppet' received a severe dressing-down from Mr Danby for using his shaving kit. Ruth bit her lip, suppressed a smile and when her husband had stormed out proceeded to talk about the weather!

Half an hour later my hostess guided me to a remote bus stop and invited me to visit her again on my way back to the RAF in four days' time. I smiled and thanked her for all her kindness, and without further ado she kissed me on the cheek and sped away. Watching her disappear out of sight, I was more convinced than ever that she existed simultaneously on many levels.

On the last day of my leave I reassured my mother that there was nothing to worry about, gave my father a gentle one-two to the stomach and kissed and crushed Alan to smithereens. An hour or so later I made my way up the path to Skiers Spring Lodge, to encounter a troubled Miss Wynn Owen.

'Oh dear, Brian, it's not like me to get annoyed! But the wretched fox-hunt has created havoc here, riding roughshod through our grounds and devastating our lovely vegetable garden. I'm afraid I was so infuriated that I used an ancient sign, with my fingers above my forehead, and scattered the whole damn lot of them! Horses, dogs, riders – the lot! The animals won't come to any harm but I'm afraid the dogs have disappeared to the four corners and won't be seen or make any sense for days. Anyway, darling, don't mind me: I'm slowly recovering my good spirits and your timely appearance has cheered me up no end.'

Still chattering away about the fox-hunt, she led me into the kitchen and prepared afternoon tea. We then retired to her sitting-room to munch away happily on delicate sandwiches and gaze out of the large French windows.

'Do you want me to do the "dagger speech" from *Macbeth*, or any other piece?' I tentatively asked.

'No darling,' replied Ruth with a smile. 'I think I've given you enough notes about your speeches already. I think it better if you give it a rest and let them all sink in.'

It was clear now that Ruth was herself again and for the next hour richly entertained me with funny stories. She then introduced a more serious mood to the conversation by asking:

'How is your relationship with Nancy?'

I must confess I was surprised at the question.

'Oh,' I replied, 'Nancy and I are going in two entirely different directions. She has decided to go to college and train to be a schoolteacher. I told her that I thought it one of the most important jobs on God's earth.'

After a slight pause Ruth said:

'Darling Brian, you couldn't have spoken a truer word. Nancy is a rare spirit who will do wonders for education – I have no worries about her. But you, Brian, you trouble me.'

Again I was taken aback by Ruth's words.

'How so?' I asked.

Another long pause followed and then she said:

'Are you absolutely sure you wish to be an actor?'

Oddly enough, this question didn't surprise me.

'I sense, Brian, you love being part of the acting profession and it fulfils a deep yearning in you, and you certainly have the potential to make a success of it. Yet I frequently wake up at night concerned about you. There is something about your behaviour that is comically unreal. Being at ease with people is difficult for you. You appear marvellously colourful and easily able to entertain the largest of gatherings. We all admire you for it; but I feel we are instinctively loving someone who is remote and not activated.'

There was a further silence and we chuckled together quietly. This time I broke the mood and replied:

'What was it Stanislavsky said? – "There are two types of actor: the actor who loves the art in himself, and the actor who loves himself in Art."'

Ruth smiled and replied:

'Exactly, Brian. Don't you think you possibly fall into the latter category?'

'Oh yes, Ruth. I suppose I am guilty of that. But then I think most actors are, at some time in their lives, and this applies to anyone, whatever job they are doing. I simply feel, Ruth, that a permanent part of me holds on to the other category and therefore I can honestly say I am sincere in my quest.'

Ruth cackled at my reply and added:

'Then, darling Brian, I will join forces with Harry Dobson and back you up to the hilt!'

16

Big Bertha

That evening I stood in a large, brick-built billet in R A F Bicester, Oxfordshire, trying to work out which was mine among the fifty or so beds. Eventually, having found it, I suddenly became aware of a number of airmen coming towards me. Most of them were smoking and were jacketless, and as ties were not much in evidence and their shirt sleeves were rolled up, my impression was confirmed that discipline here was not quite of the order of Bridgnorth. You might say they were downright sloppy! In contrast, my appearance was immaculate, as was to be expected of someone who had only recently completed his Basic Training.

An unfriendly silence followed as I started calmly and methodically to unpack my kit and to place it tidily in my locker and bedside cabinet. Half a dozen of the men hovered closer and then, with nonchalant ease, rooted through all my belongings. I remained impassive, not moving an inch, as my *Complete Works of Shakespeare* was tossed from hand to hand and finally dumped on the floor. Various other personal items were then passed round and ridiculed, before likewise ending up on the deck.

All the while I said nothing and remained still. My cherished book of poetry, *Palgrave's Golden Treasury*, provided a short, stocky cockney lad with ample ammunition for extracting the Michael. He had a rare flair for the poet Laurence Binyon, and brought the house down with his foul rendering of 'The Burning of the Leaves'. His boundless talent then crucified Wordsworth as, continuing in this vein with a mouthful of an apple he had

226

stolen from my locker, he contrived to misinterpret and pour scorn on several fine love poems. Choking, and gleefully spitting out the apple, he vigorously demonstrated his much-admired art of simulating copulation. At every repulsive gesture the faces of the onlookers turned to me for the expected furious response. It was not forthcoming, however, as I smiled sweetly in appreciation of my tormentor's talents.

After a while he became bored with his own activities and retired into the background. Assuming this was the end of my trials, I set about cleaning up the mess. It was only then that I realized that the cockney orator was the warm-up man – the leading artist had still to make his appearance.

There was a hum of morbid anticipation from the swollen ranks as they parted to form a human corridor and reveal the star himself. Forward he danced, in the light fantastic, stopping a few feet away from me and completing the introduction with a girlish skip and a curtsy. I stared back at him with eyes that felt like dead fish; neither of us flickered an eyelid.

Immediately behind him his two jackals danced obscenely to the sound of Eddie Calvert's hit, 'Cherry Blossom Red and Apple Blossom White', coming over the Tannoy system. As these two arseholes completed their ritual with a pretentious kiss the room fell again into the same unfriendly silence.

Mr Gnashing-of-Teeth – the nickname I gave him because he ground his teeth constantly; I won't even bother to name him – had a foul face. His jet-black hair was thick with grease and was combed back severely, making the top of his head appear almost flat. A thin streak of white hair ran from just above his left ear to fade away into the nape of his neck. I would say he was in his late twenties, although he looked older: his skin bore all the signs of someone who had indulged in unhealthy pursuits and had aged prematurely. His pallor was so ghastly that he easily could have passed for someone hooked on opium. It contrasted dramatically with his dense, dark eyebrows and black eyes.

The basic fabric of my being chilled as I realized that, for the first time in my life, I was looking at someone who was utterly evil. So far I had held on to the conviction that all people were good at heart. But the man now in front of me totally contradicted that cherished belief. It was plain to see that his two cohorts were villains – a villain, in my book, is someone who will go on beating you when you are down and out and defenceless – but they were angels compared with him. He stood six feet tall, with wide, sloping shoulders and a narrow waist. He slouched deliberately, slightly to the right, as if ready to aim a right hook at any moment, and his rolled-up sleeves revealed big arms, covered in muscles, that seemed strangely misshapen. He was deadly dangerous and as hard as nails.

'Have you had any supper, Mr Actor?' he said in a small, asthmatic voice. 'Because, if you're hungry, you can have this sandwich here.'

The man's left hand had been hidden down his trousers and he now pushed it through his unbuttoned flies to reveal two slices of bread wrapped around his long penis. This subtle revelation produced the expected round of applause from his admirers.

My eyes never left his and, after what seemed like a lifetime, I produced a tiny, quiet voice that expressed high regard and gratitude for his offer. He was completely mystified by my reaction but, for the moment, decided to let me off the hook, obviously disappointed at my response. In military style he rasped out, 'Cock, about turn,' and marched off with his two sentinels and the stocky cockney.

As the door closed behind him a friendly man whispered:

'Keep clear of him, Blessed. He's a fucking dangerous shit and capable of doing anything.'

After lights out that night, I lay in my bed tired with sadness. I wanted peace, quiet and privacy but, by the look of things, I had a nasty little war on my hands. I thought of 'China' and then dismissed the idea: I could do without it.

The following morning, after breakfast, I had a short interview with a young officer who informed me that I need not start work until the following day as I was now part of TCPSU (Transport Command Parachute Servicing Unit). I hadn't a clue what he was talking about, but having the day off cheered me up enormously.

Strolling around, I discovered that RAF Bicester was cheerful and spacious. A public road leading into the town of Bicester split the station in half. In the half where I lived were scores of large, high, brick-built houses comprising the numerous billets for the airmen – there were a small number of airwomen too, officially known as WRAFs (Women's Royal Air Force) – and there were lawns and trees everywhere, blending attractively with the buildings.

There was a large NAAFI store where you could buy extra items of food, such as chocolate, tea and coffee. Above were several games rooms for table tennis and the like, as well as a good supply of reading rooms. All this was a welcome relief after the reception I'd received the night before.

Inevitably there was a parade ground too, but then, joy of joys, I discovered a cinema – things were really looking up! Also, near by was a gymnasium with a fine selection of apparatus, including a good heavy punchbag, which would help me sharpen my reflexes for any possible confrontation.

What really intrigued me was a letter on the notice-board asking anyone interested in fencing to contact Flight Lieutenant Foreman, who was offering lessons in foil, épée and sabre. The prospect of fencing delighted me, for it would help me considerably in my preparation for drama school; if I could arrive there as a competent swordsman it would be a great bonus. Ruth had emphasized how important it was to be a good all-round action man, saying that to be able to ride a horse, fence, fight and drive a car could prove advantageous when directors were considering you for a part.

Crossing the road that divided the camp, I was stopped by an airman on guard duty but, after identifying myself, was allowed through to the other side. This section was much more mechanized, with rows of small hangars occupied by regular airmen dressed in oil-stained denims, who were servicing and mending the vehicles.

Everyone gave me a friendly nod and one SAC (Senior Aircraftman) invited me in for a mug of tea. He then proudly demonstrated his expertise in radio and electronics; he had just finished a course on radar and was to be given an important post up north.

The surprises continued when I came across a marvellous education section in the form of a single-story building containing a fine library and reading room. There was also a more private room with a gramophone and a splendid selection of records. What more could an AC2 plonk like myself ask for? AC2, meaning Aircraftman 2, was the lowest rank in the Air Force and generally applied to National Servicemen, although some were L A C (Leading Aircraftman) and some rose to the dizzy heights of S A C. I received roughly two pounds fifteen shillings a week, which was rather good when you consider we were fed, housed and clothed for free.

At five p.m., back at my billet, the day shift of T C P S U arrived and I joined them for tea in the canteen. At the same time buses arrived to take the night shift off for work at the U S A F base at Upper Heyford. There were about four hundred men and fifty women in our section of T C P S U, which included a small sprinkling of thirty or so National Servicemen. The main bulk of the workforce consisted of regular airmen who had signed on for between three and forty-five years. Together with the other departments on the camp, I would guess that R A F Bicester had a force of four thousand.

For the moment I was placed on day shift, and at eight-thirty the following morning I climbed on to one of the buses for Upper Heyford.

My companions seemed a happy bunch and readily accepted me into their ranks. Fortunately, Mr Gnashing-of-Teeth and his followers were on the night shift, so the day promised to be free of strife. Indeed, the sun shone brightly as the bus ambled peacefully along the country lanes. Flat, rather like Lincolnshire, this kind of landscape suited flying bases perfectly and yet it did have a gentle beauty of its own. Stretching for miles in either direction, the fields were carpeted with bright-yellow flowers set against a powder-blue sky. All it lacked, I said, was Van Gogh to make it burn with life on the canvas. This vision caused the people in the bus to laugh and break into the popular song 'Earth Angel'. With their bodies rocking from side to side, the frolics continued as they switched to the haunting 'Unchained Melody', which poured out through the open windows of the bus, forcing a smile from a resting farmer.

After seven miles the singing stopped. We had arrived at USAF Upper Heyford. Situated inside this vast complex was our section of TCPSU and the bus trundled on deep into the interior until we were there.

I was flabbergasted by the sight and sounds that confronted me: the screaming of masses of jet planes filled the air, playing havoc with my senses. This gathering of monstrous mechanical silver birds formed a bizarre contrast with the peace and calm of the surrounding countryside.

Jets revved up their engines and took off with breathtaking power. Gigantic B52s, seeming for an infinitesimal moment to hover silently and miraculously in the sky, finally throttled down and thundered in, causing mayhem to the ears and incredulity to the eyes as their mammoth forms careered, apparently uncontrollably, along the runway. It was then that the mighty bird released the colossal, vibrating, bass sound of its vocal cords and with one final, earth-shattering bellow from its lungs, and with the help of a huge multicoloured parachute from behind, came to a stop.

As if that wasn't enough, titanic C47 (Globemaster) planes patiently allowed tanks and other vehicles to enter into the dark recesses of their cavernous jaws before finally gobbling them up. You couldn't help but be impressed by the sheer size and military might of the Americans.

'It's much quieter in here,' said a tall, thin airman with thick, wavy hair. 'You'll be working with me. My name is Sydney Schwarz.'

Syd and I immediately became good friends. He was cheerful and always saw the funny side of life, although when the occasion merited it he would reveal the deeper side of his nature. Above all, he was loyal and kind and had the courage of a lion. He was a cockney Jew from Stoke Newington in London and, like so many other National Servicemen, counted the days until he would be back again in Civvy Street. A little older than me, he had only eleven months to go. God! How I envied him!

Syd escorted me through a vast hall with dozens of tables

groaning under piles of used parachutes that needed packing for further use. The regular airmen were already pulling them out to full length, adjusting the long strings and folding the silk canopy for final packing. It was fascinating that so much material could eventually be condensed into such a small package so as to fit snugly on a man's back. The main 'chute' was called an X Type, but a smaller reserve one was fitted to the parachutist's chest in case the first failed to open.

Syd then led me into a massive adjoining room full of hundreds of hanging parachutes. The ceiling was about a hundred and fifty feet high and from this height the canopies of the chutes were hung, with long strings hanging down in their thousands and attached, at the bottom, to the QRB – the harness that fitted round the parachutist's body. The whole bloody place was nothing more than a giant drying room for wet and soiled chutes!

Looking around this surrealistic scene, I spotted half a dozen other National Servicemen, who waved to me gloomily and applied themselves to the job in hand. Our overseer was a Scottish corporal named Weir, a thin, medium-sized fellow in his late twenties who had signed on for life and who lived in the married quarters at Bicester with his wife and family. The man was pleasant and unassuming, although when people took advantage of his kindness he could prove to be tough.

The Scot greeted me with a warm handshake, shyly informing me that LAC Schwarz would teach me the ropes. That was it, then! Corporal Weir walked away.

Syd showed me how to hang a chute, which a blind, deaf and dumb chimpanzee could have done, and my training was complete.

'Is this it, Syd?' I asked. 'Have I left civilian life and friends and the hopes and aspirations of going to drama school and beyond for this? Syd! Am I to spend the next two years of my life unwrapping chutes and hanging them to dry in an airless hot room, devoid of sunlight and windows, with shaded neon lights beating down on my body and brain! Bloody hell! At least in Bridgnorth I was a soldier.'

Syd looked at me sadly and said with a resigned smile:

'You've got to accept it, Brian. There's nothing you can do but bear it patiently until you've completed your time. Anyway, to cheer you up, in an hour's time there'll be a break and the NAAFI van will be round with lots of tea and chocolate Wagon Wheels. Tonight there's a John Wayne film on in the cinema.'

Days passed; days and weeks of getting on and off the bus and hanging chutes!

Gradually I learned the art of skiving. Now, a skiver is someone who avoids work and yet, when observed by the powers that be, appears to be a model of endeavour and integrity. It would be fair to say that the regular airmen generally didn't fit this description.

At first I applied myself assiduously to my dull task, working as hard as I could and hanging as many chutes as possible. But soon I was advised to take it easy, even by regular airmen, and told that my efforts were considered foolish.

It was revealing, in the evenings, to hear the lads bragging about how they had conned their way through the day, avoiding anything that involved manual labour. To be a great skiver was considered by many to be a worthy occupation!

Quite a few Americans worked in our section and they were always flogging cartons of cigarettes and bottles of bourbon and rye. The sergeants and corporals accepted this with equanimity, considering it harmless fun and part and parcel of good relations with our allies.

It was interesting to compare our uniforms with the Americans'. Ours, though durable, were made of a material that frequently itched, whereas the Yanks had silk shirts and a smooth gaberdine outfit. They also had plenty of money, and the British airmen found it difficult to compete when it came to courting the WRAFs.

All in all, I liked the men from the New World: they were relaxed and generous and great fun. The real treat of the day was to go for lunch in the big American canteen. Boy, oh boy! What food! Huge chunks of prairie chicken, as much as you could eat, and steaks of ham and beef that made your mouth water. The vegetables were varied and plentiful, and vast urns contained a marvellous selection of pure fruit juices. The combination of this diet and the exercises I was doing in the gym in the evening made me bigger and fitter than ever: I was now about thirteen and a half stone.

During this time I often visited the library and also spent many evenings listening to classical music in the quiet room next door. Here I met a smashing bunch of artistic lads who were making the best of their National Service before going to university. One of them, Peter Comerford, became one of my boon companions and, later in life, became the prison chaplain at Wormwood Scrubs. Another was a tall, red-headed gentleman by the name of Anthony Smith, who was as clever as could be and wrote poetry from morn till eventide.

Anthony and Peter were marvellous for my education and introduced me to the delights of Oxford and its unique university. During a forty-eight-hour pass Anthony took me to his home, near Richmond in Surrey, where I was wined and dined and met his gifted friends.

The weeks passed by quickly as I settled into the routine of the camp. Bingo was very popular and this enjoyable ritual was held in the large NAAFI room, where light snacks and drinks of all kinds were available. Occasionally I had a go at calling out the numbers:

'She was Sweet Sixteen . . . Legs Eleven . . . forty-five – Pompey Ladies . . . Sign On – fifty-five . . . Clickety-click – sixty-six.'

Syd taught me the ins and outs of cleaning and ironing clothes, including the art of 'sponging', which guaranteed longer-lasting creases in a uniform. We charged three shillings and sixpence a uniform for this service and our business was so popular that we could hardly cope with the demand.

My behaviour at work became increasingly bizarre as I rebelled against the tedium of the job by indulging in crazy escapades. Most of the sergeants and officers cast a blind eye to my shenanigans, but others were determined to put me in a coffin and nail down the lid if at all possible. I ran a fine line between disaster and success in my endeavours to skive under their very noses. But, in my proud disguise as the Heyford Scarlet Pimpernel, I was astonished to find a rival.

This rival's name was Billy Baty, a champion cyclist from the North-East. He was a smashing chap with a fair complexion, short, blond hair and an adorable Geordie accent that captivated everyone. Every evening Bill would cycle off for a hundred miles or so to return, hours later, drenched in sweat, with his face the colour of a tomato. His reason for skiving was that work might interfere with the more serious business of training.

The section was a huge place full of nooks and crannies and I knew every one of them. Along with a sergeant, an irate Corporal Weir would search high and low in the hope of catching me and putting me on a charge. Therefore, it was an amusing sight, on one occasion, to find Bill sitting comfortably, with book in hand, in one of my favourite foxholes.

My favourite trick was to shin up a rope to the top of the drying room ceiling, to disappear into the folds of the canopy of a chute and to form a hammock. Swaying up there with the warm breeze I would then read Shakespeare. Imagine my surprise when one day I found Bill in the next chute!

There were times when I allowed myself to be caught for the simple reason that I enjoyed talking my way out of the charge. The CO was a fine man but was reluctant to ever pass sentence on anyone. Occasionally I would bump into him at the education section and we would listen to Sibelius together. (Despite my mundane job I used every opportunity to improve my education, setting myself the goal of reading all of Shakespeare's plays and milking Anthony and Peter for their knowledge of music and literature.)

During this period I contacted Flight Lieutenant Foreman and took fencing lessons twice a week. He was a wild, flamboyant character, with a florid face and mobile moustache that curled up at the edges, giving the impression that if you twisted it round and round it would set him off like an outboard motor! His style of fencing was reminiscent of a steam train that had been mated with a giant malfunctioning sparking-plug.

Up and down the room we went, knocking hell out of each other with our sabres, while a gramophone blasted out 'The Galloping Major'.

In all fairness, the RAF did everything in its power to help me, even sending me on the occasional weekend drama course in Manchester and Plymouth. Yet, despite this, I always felt imprisoned. When you're young and frustrated time can drag awfully. From the moment I arrived in that lifeless drying room I felt as if I was drowning, and so I was determined to work my ticket and to get out. The lads who were in my confidence said it simply couldn't be done, but I worked like hell at it.

The key to it all was, of course, my deformed right foot. I had been rated Grade Three but if I could lower it to Grade Four or Five I would be automatically discharged. Twice a week I visited the medical officer, complaining of pains in it, until he was fed up with the sight of me. All the while I put a brave face on, apologizing for being such a nuisance.

On Sports Day I valiantly tried to win the 880 yards race, only to collapse in agony near the finishing line. Syd and the lads, grinning from ear to ear, then helped carry me to the attendant medic. In football and tug of war the same thing happened, but confronted with my prized foot, the medics hadn't a clue how to treat it.

In desperation they sent me to RAF Collaton Cross, a hospital not far from Plymouth. I was there for three months having heat treatment and massage, but when offered surgery, I firmly refused. In the end they could do nothing for me and in September 1956 I returned to Bicester suntanned and hopeful.

I picked up where I had left off, and the doldrums of camp life continued to atrophy me. Syd and I were placed on night shift for a while, which meant working between five and eleven p.m. and being granted a seventy-two-hour pass once every fortnight.

This pass enabled me to get home frequently and to see my parents, as well as Harry Dobson and Ruth. During these visits my mum and dad clearly found it a slight strain to be with me. After playing a game of bowls with me, Dad reluctantly confessed that I had become a stranger. So after a while I stayed away from home and either went to Ruth's or travelled to London.

On one of my visits to London I met up with Patrick Stewart to see a production of *Julius Caesar* at the Old Vic. Afterwards,

on Westminster Bridge, Patrick recited Wordsworth's poem about that famous structure, which includes the line:
   Open unto the fields, and to the sky.
   With his arm around my shoulder, he concluded:

   'Dear God! The very houses seem asleep;
   And all that mighty heart is lying still!'

For a long while we took in the scenery until I said:
   'Patrick, have I changed?'
   My long-time chum smiled inscrutably and replied:
   'No Brian, you've always been as mad as a hatter!'
   From that day on, time dragged and I found myself going barmy once more. No amount of application to Shakespeare, fencing, music – the bloody lot – could relieve me of the excruciating boredom.
   With the passing of autumn I realized that my good friend Syd was about to be demobbed, having almost served his two-year sentence. Soon after Peter and Anthony would be going, and my isolation would then be complete. In desperation I increased my visits to the medical officer but my hopes of working my ticket appeared to be fading fast. Despite this I put an ambitious plan into motion: I decided to arrange to have an audition at the Bristol Old Vic School in the forthcoming spring and, if successful, to apply for a scholarship from the South Yorkshire Education Authority and arrive for the autumn term in September 1957. However, this was not taking into account the fact that I would still be in the RAF at that time. But then if I waited until I'd finished my National Service in January 1958, I would have to kick my heels before trying for the Old Vic School in September of that year. And that would have meant months of hanging chutes and then I would have had to have been a plasterer again for a year. I couldn't face that! I wanted to go to drama school!

Throughout my time at RAF Bicester Mr Gnashing-of-Teeth and his cohorts had continued, occasionally, to extract the Michael. Though nothing serious had happened, I had seen him physically

harass several new lads, in particular one regular airman, whom
he abused frightfully. One unfortunate chap was held down while
Mr Gnashing-of-Teeth peed all over his face and new suit.

Shortly after this little episode I was gathering my lunch in
the American canteen when the bully approached me with his
two jackals, and began to deride me and my acting for the
umpteenth time. As usual, I ignored him, and sat down next
to some Americans. Mr Gnashing-of-Teeth followed me and
let a slow gozzler, or long string of spit, fall on to my plate
of food.

'Brenda Blessed isn't hungry today. Now then, Brenda, how
about you finishing up your plate like a good little girl?'

I didn't smile at all and stood up slowly as if to leave. But
instead, I roared to the stocky cockney at the other end of the
canteen:

'You. The grand reciter of poetry. Yes, you! Bring your fat,
smelly arse over here to join your pissy boss!'

There must have been at least a thousand Americans in the
canteen and they were all stunned into silence. I wanted the
cockney lad in front of me, not behind my back. I then proceeded:

'Now, you four yeller-bellied bastards! Get this into your poxy
thick skulls. I'm not going to fight you, I'm going to kill you! But
I'll give you a chance – I'll tell you exactly how. You three I'll
crush with the fire extinguishers, and then you, bollock-brain [I
was, of course, referring to Mr Gnashing-of-Teeth] I will kill in
a different way inside ten seconds.'

For the next few moments, for the record, the US Air Force
witnessed four British airmen shit themselves with fear. It was no
idle threat: I was on the point of vaporizing the bastards! Then
Mr Gnashing-of-Teeth, whining like a hyena, muttered:

'No offence meant, Brian – it's just a joke. Look, just to show
there's no harm meant, I'll go and get you some more grub. It's
all a joke – just a joke.'

Without further ado he brought me a fresh lunch and I had no
further trouble.

Towards midnight, two days later, I was being driven by an

American captain and two of his friends to one of the massive hangars that housed the C47s. I'd had a few glasses of bourbon with them and was feeling relaxed, although intrigued by the detour we were taking.

On arriving, we passed through numerous doors and came at last to a quiet, secluded part of the hangar. The dark cloak of night seemed to penetrate the building, despite the presence of hundreds of green neon lights that cast hazy halos in every direction. In my slightly inebriated state the soft emerald bulbs seemed to dance like Sugarplum Fairies. The friendly officer poured me another drink and said:

'We're sure pleased you put that guy in his place the other day. Him and his partners have been a constant thorn in our sides on Friday nights in Bicester. To show our appreciation we thought we'd introduce you to Bertha.'

The name instantly put the fear of God in me. I thanked them for their kindness and explained that I had little experience in dealing with fast ladies.

'No, no,' they laughed. 'You misunderstand. Our intentions are strictly honourable. Trust us, young man.'

With that I was blindfolded and instructed to crouch down and walk on all fours. After a few yards they asked me to raise my back slowly and as I did so I felt a smooth, hard surface touch the base of my spine. As I moulded the rest of my back into it I was told to remove my blindfold.

It was difficult to define what it was in the gloom, but I appeared to be encased in sturdy metal scaffolding. Instantly, my friends pressed a button and a bluish light, like St Elmo's Fire, flashed eerily around the structure above me. Perplexed and fascinated, I examined the object more closely and ran my fingers along its shiny black exterior. It seemed, in shape, like a sinister septic tank. The whole thing hung over my body and its massive presence filled me with foreboding, for I knew instinctively what it was. My hosts confirmed my intuition:

'Yes, Brian! You've guessed! Bertha is a hydrogen bomb, and capable of eliminating a good-sized country from the face of the earth!'

After several minutes, to the astonishment of the Americans, I shouted out Mark Antony's words from *Julius Caesar*:

> 'With Ate by his side come hot from hell,
> Shall in these confines with a monarch's voice
> Cry "Havoc", and let slip the dogs of war;
> That this foul deed shall smell above the earth
> With carrion men, groaning for burial.'

The Christmas holidays were about to start when Syd and I were put on a charge. A corporal accused us of putting on an unnecessary light in our billet on returning from a forty-eight-hour pass. This was ridiculous, as we had only put it on for a few seconds to see what we were doing. The said corporal rubbed his hands with glee, saying:

'I'm going to make you two bastards go down this time.'

I reassured Syd that there was no problem. The officer on duty was well known to me and we often went out together – in fact, he was putty in my hands. Syd was very concerned because at Christmas he was to attend a special family ceremony.

Would you believe it? The officer sentenced us to seven days' jankers, which meant we would both miss Christmas! To the astonishment of the corporal, I raged at the officer:

'What's the matter with you? Have you lost your senses? Giving us seven days over Christmas for such a trivial act?'

In return, the officer sweated and coughed nervously, but was adamant about his decision. The corporal was ecstatic: he had finally got the Heyford Scarlet Pimpernel and his mate into deep shit. As we left the room Syd said:

'You see, what did I tell you? It's because I'm a Jew.'

His words absolutely stunned me.

'Well, if they're that sick, that's their problem. We're not beaten yet.'

Then the good Lord and his angels smiled on us. I discovered that my fencing teacher, Flight Lieutenant Foreman, was the officer in charge of guard duty over Christmas. Quick as a flash, I phoned him up.

'Hello, sir. Merry Christmas. Blessed here, sir. Sorry to bother you, but my companion and I have been put on a silly, trite charge, sir, which ultimately means that we lose Christmas. Could you get us off it, old boy?'

A tiny pause followed before my Galloping Major replied:

'Of course, Blessed. Goes without saying. Just sign yourself off in the guard room, and I'll do the rest. What's your friend's name, by the way?'

I choked for a second and replied:

'Oh, er, Sydney, sir. L A C Sydney.' I thought it prudent not to say Schwarz.

Weeks later Syd finally departed, having completed his two years. It was a body blow. I had depended on his friendship and wit to cheer me up and without him the place felt like a morgue.

Fortunately, my visits to Oxford, and in particular the new theatre there, were my salvation. Oxford was near by and I was blessed with the good fortune to see those two great actors, Paul Schofield and Michael Redgrave, perform there. Schofield was mesmerizing as Hamlet and Redgrave stunning as Hector in *Tiger at the Gates*. Having established a sweet relationship with Redgrave two years earlier, I was tempted to go backstage to see him, but I chickened out for the simple reason that his marvellous performance had overwhelmed me and made me feel shy. Also, I felt I was not the lad he had met in Sheffield. A further feeling took me completely by surprise: I somehow felt unclean.

At this time, I had the good fortune to see the great American artist Alfred Drake, in the musical *Kismet*. It was the only time I'd ever known an artist be on the front page of every newspaper in the land.

These performances spurred me on to beat the system and to work my ticket. Down to the sick bay I went every morning to confront the doctor with my famous foot. The pain, I emphasized, was unbearable and I even made out that the other lads considered me to be a leper. This was untrue, but they acted out the charade marvellously. I even hobbled heroically to the C O of the camp, expressing distress at my bogus victimization.

One of the stunts I pulled related to the parade ground. It had just been concreted, and in the dead of night, using my skill as a plasterer, I carved out in gigantic letters: 'Brian Blessed is a flat-footed bastard'. The following morning the CO and his NCOs were furious at the vandalism. I stood looking on, feigning shock and hurt at the writing, and pointing out, with a trembling voice, how humiliated I felt.

Suddenly I was judged by the doctors to be Grade Seven Invalid and discharged! I was asked to leave my uniform at the guardhouse and return to Civvy Street! After my tremendous efforts to be released, now that it had finally happened I simply couldn't take it in.

It is a tradition that if anyone beats the system he has to go through the ceremony of having his balls blackened with boot polish. The whole of TCPSU, four hundred men and auxiliaries, crammed into my billet and awaited my entry. Not to disappoint them, I put up a good scrap, which they much appreciated, before my fate was finally sealed. Afterwards we visited every pub in Bicester to celebrate.

The following morning they formed into a long line and whistled 'Colonel Bogey' and saluted me as I left by the main gate.

To this day I can't remember the journey home: delirious feelings of freedom and happiness eclipsed everything else. My family were flabbergasted and delighted to see me, although it was obvious that they still found me an enigma. Harry Dobson was over the moon and immediately cast me as Heathcliffe in the Theatre Guild's forthcoming production of *Wuthering Heights*.

It was now late July 1957 and in the nick of time I managed to arrange an audition for the Bristol Old Vic School. When I arrived in Bristol the principal of the school, Duncan Ross, put me through the hoop: after I'd completed the set pieces he made me do them all again at high speed and then with a variety of accents. As if that wasn't enough, he then bombarded me with questions and asked me to ad lib *ad infinitum*.

At the end of an hour and a half he shook my hand and told me I'd been accepted. Giggling like a maniac, I embraced him in a great bear-hug, tore out of the school and raced back home to tell everyone in sight that a Yorkshire lad had made it!

As quick as a flash, Harry Dobson took up the torch from my youth club mentor, Frank Lawson, and approached the Chief Education Officer, Mr Hyles, who then collared Gerald Tyler, the chief drama adviser of South Yorkshire, who chaired a committee in Wakefield Town Hall, to consider my case. After a friendly, in-depth interview, I was granted a scholarship on the spot and almost fainted! At last, drama school was a reality! My parents were stunned by the news.

Now I could relax and enjoy doing *Wuthering Heights*. In relaxed relief I walked over the Seven Fields and thanked my lucky stars.

Much to my surprise it transpired that rehearsals for the stage version of Emily Brontë's classic novel were disjointed and unhappy. At one point I even demanded that a certain actor jump on his cues. Harry Dobson observed all this, but bit his tongue and said nothing. That evening he ended rehearsals earlier than usual and asked me to walk with him to his house.

As we set off it started to rain heavily. Harry immediately put on his big, heavy trench coat, which was capable of protecting him from Noah's Flood, whereas my flimsy semi-waterproof mac quickly became drenched. For a long while Harry was strangely quiet and I was puzzled as he continued walking past his house and down into the valley. Now I was really getting soaked. Without warning, he stopped and turned round to face me, seething with anger:

'Who in God's name do you think you are? Eh? You march up and down the rehearsal room like God Almighty. Oh my! Oh my! How privileged we are to have such a big shot in our midst. In fact, Number One Big Shot! How fortunate we poor mortals are that you deign to grace us with your company. What in the name of heaven has happened to you that you have attained such God-like status? I've had to suffer your rudeness, unkindness and boring arrogance for days. How dare you behave like this? Have you forgotten how vulnerable and frightened you were two years ago when you first came to seek my help? Have you forgotten, you cheap bastard, how much people have helped you, and continue to do so, because they believe in you? You are betraying them all! You're unrecognizable. All the actors want to hide from you. Have you any idea how unpopular you are?

'And what's this bloody imitating you've cultivated? Oh, so bloody clever you are, my lad, at showing off how you can mimic any well-known personality. Have you any idea what harm it's doing you? It's worse than falling in love with your voice, and that's returned too. You are abusing and destroying your gifts! Never, never imitate! It doesn't belong to acting! It's shallow and cheap! It's acceptable to suggest how someone else speaks but one must not go further than that.

'I'll tell you, Brian: you have become a selfish, unfeeling bastard. I don't blame the RAF – they're innocent. I blame you! For months I've been hearing stories about you that have made my blood curdle. I hear, on good authority, that your mother cries herself to sleep every night! She's heartbroken! Yet when you passed your audition you couldn't even be bothered to go home to tell your parents but buggered off to Ruth Wynn Owen's to become a right show-off. If Ruth hadn't ordered you to go home and tell your mum and dad, they wouldn't have known for days!

'Also, it's come to my notice that you've been having a fine time with the ladies. People have been hurt, Brian, and you are responsible. Now, I hear you've been having an affair with a wonderful young lady who is a friend of mine. Well, that's natural enough, but what I object to is the way you have trampled all over her feelings. It may interest you to know that the woman almost had a nervous breakdown. She's all right now – no thanks to you. She was absolutely traumatized when you accused her of being a whore. I'm a school bobby, Brian, and I'll have you in bloody court if you dare to insult her again.'

At this point I blurted out:

'Ah, you can't trust any woman.'

Instantly Harry smashed me across the face with a powerful backhand. God! It didn't half sting! At the same time he roared:

'Your mother is a woman and she is the most trustworthy woman in the world.'

There was a horrible pause.

God! I thought. If only the earth would swallow me up!

Harry moved away a few yards and turned and shouted:

'I don't give a bugger if I ever see you again. There are plenty of other lads who can play Heathcliffe. Just bugger off out of my life.'

With that he left me.

That night I returned home like a zombie and rapidly ran up a fever. The doctor diagnosed bronchitis, but I eventually developed all the signs of pneumonia. My parents were beside themselves with worry.

In my dizzy state the room went round and round and I was unable to focus on anything. My bed at night became a sweat box of reverberating nightmares. It was impossible to free myself of kaleidoscopic images of my life, which throbbed uncontrollably, beating like African war drums in my head. All the while I shouted and protested against it all as my worried parents held me down and sponged my boiling temples. During a moment of lucidity I discovered my mother cooing and soothing and blowing gently on my face, all the while whispering softly:

'There, there, there. Don't take on so. You'll get yourself into a right paddy. Nothing to worry about, is there, Billy?'

My eyes followed her gaze to fall on the smiling face of Dad.

'Oh Dad, Mum. I'm so sorry to cause you all this trouble.'

'No trouble at all, lad,' Dad chuckled. 'All we want, lad, is for you to rest and take yer medicine, and you'll be on your feet in next to no time. And, in a few weeks, you'll be off to sunny Bristol.'

Several days later I was able to sit up and drink Mum's home-made soup. The worst was over and I improved daily. Jim Meek, the electrician who did the lighting for the Theatre Guild, came to see me and, after adjusting my pillows and pouring me a cup of tea, set about teasing me. In his dry Yorkshire accent he said:

'Tha's put the wind up everybody and freetened us to death. I've got better things to do, tha knows, than sit 'ere with a daft sod like thee. I'd 'ave though tha'd 'ave more sense than gerrin' thysen in a pickle like this. Tha's been a right monkey and we want to know when tha's coming back to the Guild.'

'Oh Jim, Jim,' I said. 'Harry doesn't want to see me any more because of the way I've behaved.'

Jim smiled at this and, ever the comedian, answered:

'I've told you before, the ladies dun't half fancy thee. Look, Brian lad, Harry loves yer like his only son and is riding round Mexborough as miserable as sin with a face like the back end of a bus. There's nowt wrong wi' thee, yer daft bugger, yer've just been a barmpot, that's all. Get some more grub darn yer belly and go and see the old man!'

A short time later, when I felt strong enough, I slowly cycled up to the Schofield Technical College in Mexborough and reached the rehearsal room a good hour before anyone else to await the arrival of Harry. Eventually, in he strode, undid his trench coat and became still. He stared boldly at me and after a pause I said:

'I'm going to be a good lad, Harry.'

There was another pause before he replied:

'Well then, in that case, you big ape, you can get me a cup of coffee.'

That was it, folks. As Laurence Olivier, as Richard III, in his film says to his horse, 'Richard is himself again'. So indeed I was myself again and the Theatre Guild welcomed me with open arms.

Rehearsals went smoothly and *Wuthering Heights* played to packed houses and was a great success. On the last night there was a party and, besides my parents, my speech teacher, Frank Cooper, was there to wish me all the best. Also, Keith Barron put in an appearance and was full of love and kindness. God only knows how I have missed mentioning Keith before. This marvellously talented actor had been with the Theatre Guild long before me and was immensely popular with audiences. His brilliant portrayals had been noticed by Sheffield Repertory Theatre and he was bypassing drama school to go straight into the professional theatre. Such was his ability, indeed, that he was a hard act to follow.

The evening ended with Harry and Jim Meek carrying in a cake with a stage on it and 'Good Luck Brian' written in pink icing. With great difficulty I controlled my emotions but fell apart when they sang, 'For he's a jolly good fellow'.

At home that evening Mum cried non-stop and Dad waxed lyrical until the early hours of the morning. All the while Alan, now twelve, held me close, wishing that I would never leave home.

The following morning I said farewell to my mother and kissed her on the forehead. My father mounted his Triumph Cub motor-bike and I sat behind him as we sped off for Bolton-on-Dearne railway station. Alan, on his bicycle, pedalled furiously after us.

It was wonderful to be at the quaint little station again, with the old posters of the *Bournemouth Belle*, the *Scarborough Flyer* and the *Flying Scotsman*'s cocktail bar still unfaded on the walls. The mature September sun shone brightly, heralding a new beginning and through the portals of the station and down the line, as it disappeared into the hazy morning mist, came voices from the past that melted my heart. More than ever before, I realized how I loved Yorkshire and its people.

Harry had arrived at the station before us and stood there silently watching me. Just then, my breathless brother arrived as the little steam train ground to a halt in the station with the embers of its fires revealing the sweaty, happy faces of its stokers.

My father shook my hand and told me to take care. Harry remained motionless and, with tears in his eyes, choked out 'God bless'. Alan almost joined me on the journey, remaining in the carriage until the last moment. Then, with a kiss and a push he was out, and the LNER train steamed out and the smoke hid them all from sight.

After a blissful journey of jicketi-can-diddly-dee-diddly-diddly-diddly-dee, I arrived at Temple Meads, Bristol. I then swayed with the bus's rhythm through the town centre to hilly Clifton to disembark at the top of Pembroke Road. I made my way to a large white building and paused at the gate as I encountered a charming young lady with a melodious voice, who asked:

'Oh hello, are you a student too?'

'Oh, yes,' I answered and introduced myself.

'Oh?' she continued. 'My name is Julia Paul Jones.'

With that she entered the school ahead of me. As much as I

247

wanted to race inside I held myself back and looked across the beautiful Downs towards the Avon Gorge and distant Somerset. Oh! How pure the air tasted. What bliss! What calm!

I lingered a little longer before slowly turning the handle to open the door, and then, like Tubby the Tuba, sighed with happiness. For inside this revered place was a legendary movement teacher by the name of Rudi Shelley!